MW01026825

For permissions requests, contact the publisher at:

Executive Excellence Publishing
1366 East 1120 South
Provo, UT 84606
phone: 1-801-375-4060
toll free: 1-800-304-9782
fax: 1-801-377-5960
www.eep.com

For Executive Excellence books, magazines and other products, contact Executive Excellence directly. Call 1-800-304-9782, fax 1-801-377-5960, or visit our Web site at www.eep.com.

Printed in the United States

10 9 8 7 6 5 4 3 2 100

ISBN 1-890009-74-1

Library of Congress Catalog Card Number: 99-75887

Cover design by Shannon Dunston

Printed by Publishers Press

Advance Praise for *7 Secrets of Marketing*

"Dr. G. Clotaire Rapaille is one of the most unique men I have encountered. He does market research in a most original, different, refreshing and, in the final analysis, effective manner."

—Kendall Brown, BM United States White Plains

"Today, with so many products at parity and often close to being commodities, Rapaille provides unique and critical insights and a spring-board for separating our products from those of the competition."

—David Tree, Creative Director, DMB&B, New York

"This book will do for you what Dr. Rapaille's work did for us. We gained a much better understanding of the U.S. consumer's value set relative to our products."

—Tom Leonard, President, Samsonite USA

"We are indebted to Dr. G. C. Rapaille, who has added a new dimension to our lives and the lives of many others. He gave us a new set of tools to discover the American archetype of quality. He enabled us to make a major breakthrough in our understanding of the way Americans function and brought to light the critical elements previously missing from the human side of quality."

—Marilyn Zuckerman, manager, AT&T

"The model we have developed for the emotional content of quality complements the engineering approaches and the discipline necessary for quality improvement that already existed. We believe that American industry faces a critical imperative—it must improve quality to survive. But it must structure and support this improvement in ways that align with the collective unconscious of America's employees and citizens."

—Ray Peterson, quality director,
AT&T Network Systems, Morristown, New Jersey

"Dr. Rapaille provided a unique, powerful way for us to understand our market challenges at a much deeper level, and to develop effective strategies whereby we can thrive rather than just survive."

—William Dennison, President,
California Forestry Association, Sacramento

"Dr. Rapaille and his work represent a fundamentally different way of looking at a product or concept within a culture. It is like using a sub-particle physics process to find out what the fundamental building blocks of the subject are—be it a product or an idea. The process works."

—J. Paul Everett, Manager
Operations Improvement, Simpson (Seattle)

"Dr. Rapaille helped us achieve profound results. Using the insights from the archetype study, AT&T developed a transformation process, which is an emerging American model for continuous improvement."

—Joshua Hammond, President,
American Quality Foundation

"Clotaire Rapaille is taking marketing where it has never gone before."

—Jack Hitt
New York Times Magazine

"The applications of cultural archetypal research are far-reaching. Like the act of learning to read, the whole world suddenly opens up with this singular key. Archetype studies are a new way of reading culture, of looking beneath the bewildering multitude of surface detail to see the framework underneath."

—Jeremy Tarcher, Publisher, Los Angeles

"The Archetype Study results are very precise, different from any other studies, and very responsive to the question: If we produce this product, how would the consumer react?"

—Mr. Scherrer, President, Gringoire-Pillsbury, France

"I believe in this approach very much. It is a very interesting approach not comparable to any other approach."

—Mr. Jean Drieu, Vice President,
Baufour Laboratories, Hong Kong

"The depth of insight and the detail and precision are far greater than those from traditional studies."

—Mr. Soucaret, President, Pfizer, France

"Archetype studies give us a good picture of prevailing attitudes, are very useful to help us understand the environment, prevent us from making big mistakes, and help us avoid positioning our products incorrectly."

—Mr. Jean Claude Gaul, General Manager,
Rhone Poulenc, Japan

"A breakthrough in the understanding of what motivates workers to achieve quality. Rapaille has discovered a unique logical and cultural structure."

—James I. Lader, The Quality Review, New York

"I have always preferred mythology to history because history is made of truths which after a while become lies, whereas mythology is made of lies which after a while become truths."

—Jean Cocteau

Contents

FOREWORD

BREAKING THE CODE

Looking at the world through a new set of glasses.

When people ask me, "What do you do?," I reply: "I decode cultures." Cultures, like individuals, have an unconscious. This unconscious is active in each of us, making us do things we might not be aware of. This book is about breaking the code of this collective cultural unconscious. It is about what makes us tick, what makes us behave the way we do, and what the hidden forces are that make us buy certain products, vote for a candidate, or choose a hotel.

This book gives you a new set of glasses to look at the way you—and the rest of the world—buy and sell, live and function. Just as using the microscope to see microbes changed the way we practice medicine, and breaking the code of the hieroglyphics suddenly gave us access to an incredible amount of information hidden for centuries, archetypology—the new science of decoding cultures—is changing the way we look at ourselves, at others, and at organizations.

The globalization of the world—by threatening the very existence of cultures, ethnicity, and diversity—is creating a resurgence of local search for deeper identity. We have a mission of crucial importance: to avoid a cultural World War III.

I have a personal mission, too. To grow, I need to be able to use the unconscious cultural forces that shape my mind. To be a better person, I need to decode my culture. To gain freedom from my own genetic birth in 1941, I need to understand how these unconscious forces—power, control, happiness, creativity, challenge, and change—affect my thoughts, emotions, behaviors, and habits.

Every culture has, in effect, a secret code. In this book, I demonstrate not only what the secret codes are in various cultures for such things as quality, food, improvement, door, team, timber, and cars, but also how to break these codes. Once we start decoding cultures, we can start improving them. I have a vision of a new world, one in which cultures have rights and engage in positive, creative, and synergistic relationships with other cultures.

My First Imprint of America

I was born in 1941 in German-occupied France at the outset of World War II. The Nazis had overrun France shortly before my birth. My father and grandfather had been taken away for slave labor in Germany. My perception of the world was that the Germans were running the show, and the French people were merely trying to survive.

For the first four years of my life, the Nazis were the stuff of a little boy's nightmares: swaggering, barking orders, and beating the defeated French citizenry into passive submission. Although I was a small child, I was conscious of their displays of authority—the saluting rituals, the raucous, commanding tone of voice of the non-commissioned officers, the unquestioning obedience of their disciplined rank and file, the shining black leather belts and boots, and their ferocious motorcycle riders, as dark and sinister as angels of death. Most of all, I was aware of their capacity to inspire fear, of the local French deference to them, and of the hushed whispers at the dinner table whenever the war, the occupation, or the "master race" was being discussed. This is the reality into which I was born: the world was run by tough guys with boots and uniforms who spoke a harsh language I didn't understand.

For me, the world consisted of one set of people who spoke French and another set—the people in charge—who spoke German. That was it. Very simple. I didn't ask questions. France was bilingual at the time, and I thought that was the way it was supposed to be.

Perhaps I sensed that my mother and grandmother were very sad, especially when they spoke about my imprisoned father, or when I started questioning why my grandfather, who had escaped from a camp, had to hide all the time. But mostly I accepted the situation as reality.

Then one day in the summer of 1944, when I was about four years old, everything changed. The Germans started running away in trucks, on stolen bicycles, or on foot, leaving behind in their panic their guns and uniforms. They were no longer barking orders at us; in fact, they ignored us completely. My reaction was: Why is the world different today? Why are the Germans running away? Who are they afraid of? I was vaguely pondering these questions as my grandmother and I walked along a small road to the nearby farm where we bought milk.

This was my first experience with the notion that reality is relative, or as a friend of mine told me one day, "Reality is subject to change without previous notice."

That day, the German soldiers were tossing their guns and helmets on the side of the road, stealing bicycles, and pedaling away quickly. I thought to myself, "The world is different today."

Suddenly, I saw a huge green beast come out of the forest; it was an American tank. I thought, "Now I know why the Germans are running away; they're afraid of the big monster."

The huge creaking monster emerged from the forest, crawling on giant caterpillar tracks along one of the dirt paths that led to the farm. Even now, I can remember the emotion evoked by that ghostly apparition, the strange smell of its fuel, the ear-splitting noise of its engine.

Somehow I knew that the monster was my friend and that it would not harm me. My grandmother was less convinced, but before she could stop me, I ran toward the massive machine.

The tank stopped near me, the top of the turret opened, and out jumped a friendly American soldier. He was a big man with a helmet and a strange accent. He didn't seem at all threatening.

Perhaps it was his uniform's leafy camouflage that made him look like a creature from one of my storybooks. Or maybe it was because he was smiling. He spoke to me from the top of the tank turret in a nasal, low key, sing-song language, and had a voice that was very different from the German ones that I identified with superiority and military power. Today, having lived many years in America, I might say that he was from the South, perhaps Texas, but at the time I didn't know a single word of English and had never heard country music.

He said something to another huge man wearing the same disguise who was walking along behind the tank. Then, before my worried grandmother could intercede, he had lifted me up to the man in the turret who gave me chocolates, chewing gum, and an unforgettable ride in the monster's belly.

Soon I saw American Army units careening along provincial roads in pursuit of fleeing German troops, the GIs waving to cheering French villagers and handing out chocolate and gum to the kids swarming over their Jeeps.

After the ride and the chocolates, the big man handed me down to my grandmother. The soldiers had other important business to take care of that day. As I stood waving and watching the tank fade in the distance, I told myself, "One day I'll go with them; one day I want to be one of them."

I didn't know it, but a mental highway had just been paved in my mind. This childhood experience, my first American experience, had a definitive influence on the course of my entire life.

Emotional Imprints

The strong imprint left from that early experience changed my life; it was my first imprint of America. I thought, "Wow, I want to be an American." After the war, my fellow Frenchmen tried to tell me that de Gaulle liberated France. At school, they showed me movies of the general walking down the Champs Elysées liberating France, but there were no Americans there. No one ever succeeded in making me believe in de Gaulle's triumph because my experience, my first post-war imprint, was that of being lifted into an

American tank. That experience, I believe, is why I am an American today. The emotions generated during that occurrence were among the strongest imprints of my entire life, and they have never left me. To this day, when I recall that experience, I not only feel the emotions, but I can actually sense the sounds, smells, colors, and even the taste of the soldiers' chocolate.

I did not realize the enormous impact this experience had on me until many years later when I came to America and immediately fell in love with its people and culture. I had an instant sense of belonging that I had never felt in France. In fact, the feeling that this was the place I had been searching for all my life was so strong and unambiguous that I realized that somewhere inside me a choice had been made long ago. I have always been an American, at least from the day of that tank ride—I was just not aware of it. I often jokingly say that the experience turned me into a late 20th century founding father because I chose to become American, crossed the Atlantic as an almost penniless immigrant in the wake of the French economic plunge led by a socialist-communist government, learned a new language, fought the savages in Manhattan for two years, went west to pursue the American dream, and became a citizen—all because of a ride in a tank more than a half-century ago.

Certainly, the next generation of French people didn't inherit my outlook, and they have a hard time relating emotionally to my tank story; to be politically correct in France today means associating Americans with big money and imperialism. I, however, am imprinted forever. No new or recent emotion can have the power of that first imprint, and the more I ponder it, the more it reinforces my mental highways. It's rather like the little Colorado River patiently wearing away the rocks in order to carve the Grand Canyon, itself growing into a vast river in the process; no new storm or flood can change its course.

Emotional Experiences

In every mind, we can find similar powerful imprints. They are early emotional experiences that have molded our minds and our lives into what we are today. These imprints vary from one culture to another, and they are powerful constituents of our minds. Together, they make up our cultural unconscious—the part of our being that makes us feel and react as American, Japanese, or French. Cultures, too, possess a collective unconscious that can be decoded.

Archetypology is the science that unveils the hidden beauty of these unconscious codes that shape and direct our lives. Understanding a culture can be thought of as breaking a code—a way of reading people, places, art, commerce, symbols, events, and history. The meanings of such basic elements as time, space, family, work, money, and death vary immensely from culture to culture.

For example, American culture stresses individual ambition and achievement, while the Japanese value interpersonal life and group activity. In American culture, time is a commodity like any other, to be saved, spent, bartered, sold, or shared. In other cultures, such as those of Brazil or Spain, time is more like an open-ended environment, a free atmosphere in which everything just happens. In one culture, old people are treasured; in another, they are held in low regard. What is food and what isn't food, what is beautiful and what is ugly, is all culturally determined. We are products of our culture, the children of largely invisible forces that shape our thoughts and behaviors from birth to death. And we barely understand any of it.

I am exploring the deep, underlying elements of culture—archetypes—that provide the clues to decoding people's basic values, the unconscious forces behind each of our lives. I apply this archetypal research to behaviors, social issues, and marketing challenges.

Archetypal psychology, anthropological structuralism, learning theory, and marketing research are merged to decode deep patterns of thought in different cultures. Working on an unconscious level, these thought patterns determine the actions and feelings of an entire culture at large as well as the individual's vision of reality, security, conflict, love, relationships, work roles, education, success, failure, aesthetics—in short, all of the attitudes that make us who we are. Ideals, values, and, ultimately, political trends, social policy, and consumer choices are determined by cultural archetypes.

Marketing Roots

Cultural archetype discoveries often receive their initial impetus from corporate marketing research. For the past 25 years, I have conducted hundreds of product and values archetype discoveries. Many companies have consulted me in an attempt to understand the unconscious desires of their customers, employees, and stakeholders; to design fresh marketing strategies, advertising campaigns, and new products; and to create programs that enhance innovation, creativity, productivity, and quality.

All of my clients have at their disposal the most sophisticated advertising, organizational development, and marketing techniques and experts in the world. What they seek from me that they can't find elsewhere is the archetypal discovery process that reveals the unconscious forces at work in their customer or employee base.

When my clients hire an advertising agency, political research organization, or marketing consultant, they receive surface information about whether people like or dislike a particular product. However, they don't get a real understanding of the unconscious forces that underlie the surface information. They learn *what* people are saying, but they don't learn *why* people are saying it. Understanding the "why" is the most crucial element for business decisions because it predicts what people will do.

Answers to the Wrong Questions

Large corporations have surveys, statistics, and other traditional research material. They have scientific answers, but frequently to the wrong questions. Through archetypal discoveries, companies can learn the correct questions to ask to discover the answers they truly need. With this information, companies can pinpoint the unconscious scales on which their products or services are weighed in the marketplace.

Ultimately, the cultural archetype discovery helps a corporation understand what business it is truly in, and what is going to be successful—either as a product, a communication, a program, or a strategy. This type of analysis provides a new, more in-depth method for connecting with the customer.

With the understanding of the customers' unconscious associations with a product or service, market preferences and trends suddenly begin to make sense. We can understand why customers do or do not buy a product, and what turns them on or off in communication, advertising, promotion, or public relations. We can comprehend why rational and scientific explanations alone do not convince buyers.

Advertising should appeal to emotion, but what few advertisers understand is that this sentimental dimension of advertising has a logic of its own. It is a cultural logic, and it is an unconscious logic. To be fully accessed, it must be unearthed through archetypal discoveries. What we come to understand through these discoveries is the "logic of emotion" as it relates to the product. Many corporations call this approach a "marketing revolution" and now train their people to use it as part of a systematic approach to marketing.

Preface

Welcome to the Multi-cultural World

The more we become global, the more we become local again.

We have entered the multi-cultural century. Everywhere we look, nationalistic, ethnic, and racial issues are affecting business, political, economic, and social trends. How quickly we learn to accept—and even value—our cultural differences, as these may make the difference between life and death for brands, organizations, and nations.

The end of the Cold War may have brought a temporary end to the threat of global nuclear devastation, but new ethnically based political factions have brought the threat of worldwide local struggles and conflicts to even greater prominence.

We live in a new world where two forces are in conflict. First, we are witnessing the rapid development of a unified "global culture" brought about by both political and ecological necessity, as well as by the internationalization of media and finance. Thus, the world is going global. This process can be seen through the evolution of technology, the creation of a global network of telecommunication, and a stock market that never sleeps.

However, we are also seeing the resurgence of "local cultures," such as those in eastern Europe, and the subsequent intensification of the politics of independence. So, from another point of view, the world is going local. We are witnessing an incredible resurgence of recognition of cultural and ethnic identities, as well as a recognition of different religions.

These movements have nurtured conflict on the macroscopic level in world trade issues and, on the microcosmic level, manifested in wars that are not merely nation against nation, but ethnic group against ethnic group and tribe against tribe within the same culture.

This clash of cultural energies, simultaneously working against and moving toward one another, creates a great demand for a new level of multi-cultural understanding and tolerance that will encourage the attitudes and behaviors that allow the varied world cultures to live in peace rather than in a new world disorder. Through a new understanding of the roots and the mechanisms of cultures, we may obtain this more enlightened and necessary perspective. America, both the product of diverse cultures and the dominant culture in the world today, must first learn to understand itself in order to then gain a perspective of other cultures.

Throughout the world, people are generally unaware of the effects that cultural conditioning has on events as major as national policy or as minor as how we brush our teeth. We are individually and collectively the children of our culture, and yet we live in a cultural trance that makes it very difficult for us to see who we really are and why we do what we do.

My goal is to provide new insight into the unconscious forces that make us who we are. Through the exploration of popular cultural archetypes, political and social values, and everyday products, we come to understand the actions of our organizations and nations in both the past and the present and also gain greater control over those actions in the future.

Fortunately, we live in a time when the study of how cultures work to make nations what they are and people who they are is becoming a significant field of endeavor. Academicians in a variety of disciplines are addressing such questions as: What commonalities must a multi-cultural society have to be a unified society? How can we be unified yet still allow for cultural diversity? Should a society require cultural adherence? "Multi-culturalism" has also become the watchword of business and marketing.

Why Archetypes Are So Important

Cultural archetypes are the laws of the culture in which we are born that pertain to human relationships and human organizations. They are part of a culture's condition, conscious and unconscious, and represent the degree to which people recognize and live in harmony with such basic concepts as freedom and prohibition, equal opportunity and unequal wealth, individualism and uniformity, fairness and violence. The members of a culture move either toward survival, stability, and growth on the one hand, or disintegration and destruction on the other.

The basic structures of the cultural psyche and the formal patterns of its relational modes are archetypal patterns. Cultural archetypes are not invented by us; they pre-date us. They are somewhat modified by historical and geographic factors. These patterns appear in the arts, religions, dreams, and social customs of cultures.

Archetypes are not only anthropological and cultural, but also spiritual. They transcend the empirical world of time and place. Biological schemata are universal, common to all members, but the forces adopted by a given culture for survival are cultural archetypes. They organize myth, religion, art, architecture, epic, and drama, but also basic rituals such as cleanliness and eating habits. The archetypal image is cultural because its effect amplifies and depersonalizes, and because it resonates with the collective unconscious.

Cultural archetypes are self-evident, self-validating forces. They don't change or shift. They provide a "true north" for our lives as we navigate the "streams" or "flows" of our environments. They constantly point the way, and if we know how to read them, we won't get lost, confused, or fooled by conflicting voices, opinion polls, trends, or surveys. They apply at all times and in all places. They surface in the form of myths, heroes, rituals, sports, business, politics, products, services, values, or ideas, and eventually crystallize into language and law.

Cultural archetypes are the "eyeglasses" through which we look at the world. We evaluate, assign priorities, judge, and behave based on how we see life through these eyeglasses. When people align their personal values with their cultural archetypes, they live in harmony with their culture. One great lesson of history is that people's prosperity corresponds to the degree to which they operate in harmony with their cultural archetypes.

The study of cultural archetypes has proven to be an effective way of approaching marketing practices worldwide. Individuals are more effective, and organizations more empowered, when they are guided and governed by a respect for cultural archetypes.

Unlike values, which are subjective and internal, archetypes are objective and external, operating in obedience to cultural forces regardless of conditions. In other words, values are like maps. Maps themselves are not the actual territory, but only subjective attempts to describe or represent territories. The more closely our values, or maps, correspond to our cultural archetypes—the actual territories—the more useful they will be.

In this book, I explore the nature of culture to understand cultural differences as they are expressed by cultural archetypes—the deep-seated collective attitudes and values formed by a culture—with particular emphasis on business and marketing. I'm trying to understand group behavior in relation to political choices, social values, marketing decisions, and consumer preferences.

I hope that by reading this book you will understand the way cultures work, and that you will appreciate the strengths and weaknesses of your own culture, acknowledge its limitations, and gain a sympathetic perspective toward other cultures and what they have to offer. By understanding your own and other cultures, you will have the tools for greater success in both your business and personal life.

Introduction

A New Era for Marketing and Communication

This is the start of the 21st century. Just watching the news confirms the feeling; the world has made a historic transition from one grand epoch to the next. The old era was defined by the warfare of ideologies of different nations.

The new age needs new concepts and new intellectual tools. The new tool for understanding this era is the cultural archetype—a way to break the code of a culture and identify the forces that influence the choices people make. This tool can be used in marketing, politics, and business to increase awareness of how these forces govern many of our actions. In so doing, this tool can help us to free ourselves from these forces.

Traditional research qualifies what people do. Archetypologists are not satisfied with this approach. They want to understand why people do what they do. What are the cultural forces in action that led to Germanic rule in Europe or Japanese rule in the Pacific? These forces do not disappear; they are simply repressed for a while, becoming shadows of the cultural persona. Then, when the circumstances are appropriate, they resurface.

We need to understand the resurgence of cultural archetypes worldwide. From a political point of view, we need to know if we are going to see tribal warfare taking over Europe and North America in the name of multi-culturalism. In the marketing world, we wonder if we should assist the hyper-segmentation of markets when the world is going global. Without this archetypal tool, people worldwide might move into cultural or ethnic warfare that promises to be as painful and as dangerous as the warfare of ideologies. By becoming aware of the archetypal forces within our cultures, we become aware of these shadows of the cultural persona and reach a higher level of global consciousness.

This book is a guide for global managers, a bible for leaders, and a path to improvement for those who want to become citizens of the 21st century. By assisting readers in understanding cultural archetypes, this book will help them become cultural partners in a global world.

Why This Book Is Necessary: Answers to Tough Questions

We need to understand how cultures function. We need to be rid of cultural neurosis or psychosis and be cured of the destructive forces of the past. The world needs to understand the American mind. We need to rediscover America and return to the nation's roots in a time when becoming global is a necessity. Let us be sure we know who we are and secure our base in order to be able to explore new frontiers. Let us use the science in anthropology and marketing to study the way people of different cultures think.

In this new era of multi-cultural marketing, we have no choice but to examine our local, unconscious, cultural forces and their effects on the world at large. This new epoch will then be born from the dynamics of global and local forces. Only by understanding both local and global forces can we begin to realize the opportunities that await us and escape the prisons of marketing ineffectiveness, ethnic violence, and the destruction of endangered cultures. Recognizing cultural differences frees us from the burden of individual pathology. We need to decode cultures other than our own if we want to become partners with their citizens.

The 20th century has been very much about nationalism, individualism, uniformity, and borders. All of these notions are now obsolete, and have been replaced with more universal concepts:

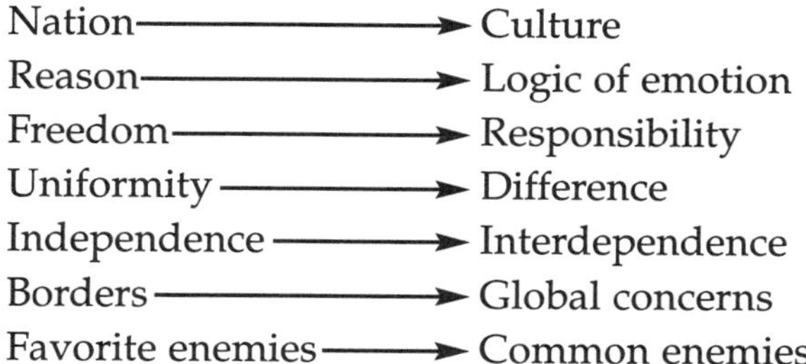

We need new decision-making processes with which to approach this new century. In order to develop these new processes, we must first undergo several steps.

Step 1: Break the code. For centuries, great thinkers have tried to explain different aspects of the world (from military power to economic laws, from wealth to knowledge, from technology to politics) through the use of logic and rational analysis. Without denying the immediate influence of the economy, politics or technology, I submit that these aspects of life are pre-organized and predetermined by the cultural collective unconscious. We must break the code of these forces in order to better understand each other as individuals, as well as the world in general.

Step 2: Conduct archetypal studies of culture. We must acknowledge cultural forces, not in a demagoguery or political manner, but in a truly anthropological one. We need to become aware of these forces to avoid repeating the mistakes of the past.

Step 3: Look at culture in a different way. Cultures are obviously different; each donates its own unique contributions to the world's treasure chest of creative solutions. Each also has its own rights, just like individuals. But along with having rights, cultures have duties and responsibilities.

Step 4: Vaccinate the culture. How can we vaccinate an American against the quick fix and a Frenchman against arrogance? Rather than let these traits take their course, we might help people become aware of the forces contributing to their behavior so that they can then become free to make better, or more educated, choices. We need not be manipulated by cultural forces; we can choose to submit to those we deem appropriate.

This book will answer several questions: What role can the American culture play in shaping world culture in general? What forces will shape American culture in the future? How do American cultural archetypes bind this ethnically diverse nation? Why do "impossible dreams" have such a strong appeal in America? Why do Americans become desperate when they think other cultures are ahead of them in technology? Why is an ATM not a bank? Why should doors in American ads never be depicted from the inside and closed? Why is Hollywood so successful at exporting American archetypes, while Detroit is not? Why do American movies and music appeal to young people worldwide? Why do foreigners hate Americans and yet want to become one?

Do Americans have a chance to play the leading role in shaping the world in the 21st century? Will we see an end to the cultural war between men and women in America? Can the Soviets succeed in a free market economy? Will the Japanese ever understand Americans? Why does the sun carry a different meaning for a German, a Frenchman, and a Norwegian, and how does that difference change the way sun-related products should be sold in each country?

Why is the Japanese definition of quality unintelligible for Americans? What is it in the Japanese and German cultures that has caused those two countries to become successful again? Are we witnessing the birth of a new single world culture? What is the meaning of the resurgence of ethnic violence? Is cultural diversity an advantage or a handicap? What is the biological dimension of culture? Do cultures age and become senile? Are some nations obsolete? How can we create a global force to fight common enemies such as AIDS, pollution, and terrorism?

Today's high-speed changes are not as chaotic or as random as we are led to believe. There are not only distinct patterns to be found in culturally specific behaviors and attitudes, but also identifiable forces that shape members of these societies. Once we understand these forces and the way they are organized, we can deal with them strategically.

SECRET 1:

THE STRUCTURE IS THE MESSAGE: People don't buy products and services— they buy relationships.

Notes, simply a bunch of notes, do not make a melody. Likewise, a group of people does not make a family, a company, or an army. A batch of words does not make a book. So what does? The relationship between the elements: the "grammar," not the vocabulary. The placement of structure, then, ultimately determines the meaning.

We are trained the wrong way. We ask the wrong questions—questions like "Who are you?" "What do you know?" "What is this?" Instead, we should ask: "Who are you related to?" "How do you use your knowledge?" "How is *this* influenced by *that*?"

We look at life as if it were made of stone. If the structure is the message, we should look at the space between the notes, the tensions and forces in action between people, and how the elements are connected.

Connection is the magic word. Structures constitute a system of connection. A family, a company, an army are systems of connections. Life in its biological dimension is connection. Death is to be disconnected.

Creativity is the art of connecting elements for the first time, of discovering relationships unknown until today.

Leadership. When people do not see why they are supposed to do something, they feel no motivation to do it. A true leader shows people the connection with the goal, thus making what they do more meaningful. A leader also connects with people through images and emotion and says to them, "Follow me; stay connected with me."

Internet. The most advanced technology will always go toward higher connections (faster, broader, larger, etc.). *Branché* in French means to be cool, to be connected. Cellular phones, pagers, Internet, and email, are all manifestations of the incredible need we have to be permanently connected.

Quality means quality of the relationship. We see that people do not buy a product or a service. They buy a relationship, a connection.

Loyalty is a permanent connection, and permanent reinvestment into the relationship to keep it forever. You don't buy loyalty.

Team. The structure of the team is what matters. When we say: "a team is more than the sum of its elements," we mean exactly that. The connection, the synergy is what makes a team. The same elements, without this dynamic, do not make a team.

Reward and recognition. The best reward is not to give money but to show a new connection toward the future. "You have been so good that I'm going to give you this new tool, which connects you with this new future and new potential identities." That's reward.

Cultures. If we look at cultures as systems of connections, as dynamic structures that create a human grammar to survive and perpetuate our genes (maintain life), we see that different historical and geographical conditions create different solutions, different structures, different systems of survival.

New technology. Some cultures are open to new technologies; others are not. Some culture are open structures; others are closed structures. Some cultures provide reference systems, cognitive systems that integrate newness; others do not. Looking at culture through structural glasses, we can see which ones will survive.

So it becomes crucial to explore more and understand better what we mean by *structure*, if the "structure is the message."

Chapter 1

The Quality of the Relationship

This is the key to success in management and marketing.

When we start looking for structure, we begin to see patterns. Most managers focus on developing products and services, improving their processes, and optimizing their employees to deliver the best products and services. But focusing solely on content (product and process) and not on the structure or relationships (people) is short-sighted.

Companies have become very analytical and mechanistic in their approach to product and service quality. They continually refine their processes and products in an effort to achieve zero defects, but perfecting the product and achieving zero defects are not enough. Customers want more from companies. A perfect product is not perceived as an added value by customers for two reasons: They don't believe that anything is perfect, and they wonder if they could get a better price for the product somewhere else.

The quality of the relationship between a company and its customers is what counts. Customers want, even need, quality relationships that are synergistic, systemic, symbolic, and symbiotic.

Through several studies done for major companies worldwide, I have discovered two significant trends: first, traditional methods of achieving quality tend to make commodities of products and services; second, there is an increasing demand for loyalty. Today, employers, employees, and customers are more concerned with what is really important to them: loyalty, or the quality of their professional relationships. The quality revolution has entered a new phase. I call it PQRS.

P: Product, Process, People

The "P" in the PQRS formula stands for product, process, and people.

Product. We once thought, "Customers buy products." We thought that what they wanted was zero defects, so that's what we provided. However, this is often not enough. For example, a restaurant might have "zero defects" in the sense that no one ever dies there, but that fact isn't an incentive to dine there. Lack of defects is not enough to attract and keep customers.

Customers expect good products, but we all know that perfection does not exist. All products are ultimately designed by humans, and humans make mistakes. As long as we can learn from those mistakes, however, they can end up working to our advantage. For example, General Motors did a survey and learned that customers who had bought a car that had no defects were less satisfied than ones who had bought a car and had a problem that had been fixed by the dealer. The message was clear: the people who had a problem with their cars had a chance to experience how much the GM people cared. The ones who had no problems never experienced personal interaction with the company.

The first two laws of quality in America are: 1) quality is perception; and 2) the problem is not the problem; the problem is how you deal with the problem. In the American mind, a problem is a fantastic opportunity to demonstrate your integrity and concern.

Of course, we need good products that do not break. We can't afford to have products of poor quality because we must match or beat the competition. But this is not enough. Many customers now assume that all the products are about the same. They shop around, and price becomes the primary issue. Many generic products score quite well on "quality," so why bother paying more money for a brand name? The contradiction becomes very apparent. By increasing the quality—achieving zero defects—of products, we only accelerate the transformation of those products into commodities, losing customer loyalty in the process.

Companies should not purposefully make products with problems so that they can show customers they care, but companies need to consider another attribute in addition to the quality of the product or service: the quality of the relationship between the product and the customer.

Many managers think of products and services in terms of objects, without considering how customers relate to them. Dumb products are designed to perform without breaking. Smart products are designed to relate to customers. What makes a relationship with a good friend so special? This person is easy to talk with; this person enhances your life; and this person fulfills your need for belonging. We can apply these same three criteria to products.

• ***Does the product or service effectively communicate with customers in a language they understand?*** Products have to speak to customers in a language they understand. This does not mean providing instruction in Spanish to Spanish-speaking customers, providing "customer friendly" instruction that explain everything in simplistic terms, or making products that literally speak to customers. What this does mean is illustrated in the following examples.

Renault planned to have one of its car models speak to its customers. Renault hired me to find out how the car was supposed to speak to the driver. Should the car say, "You better put gas in the car soon" in a feminine voice or in a masculine voice? Should a matter-of-fact tone or a cautionary tone be used? The answer was unexpected: Drivers didn't want the car to speak to them. They didn't want to be "outsmarted" by a car; the driver was supposed to be the intelligent one, the one in control. Rather than having the car tell them when the fuel tank was low, the drivers wanted direct, simple access to the information whenever they needed it. A digital gauge did not meet this need because drivers found the information hard to read and process quickly. The drivers preferred having a simple, visual representation of how much gas they had left in the tank.

This finding was confirmed in research conducted by ***Volvo***. According to Volvo, "The instruments on the interior of a Volvo are designed ergonomically. They appeal to the eye; they also have analog dials, not digital displays. Research has convinced us that drivers feel more comfortable with familiar analog dials than with digital readouts." Both Volvo and Renault have discovered the correct way to communicate fuel status to customers: through a visual gauge.

Another example concerns ***Seiko***, the watch manufacturer. Many years ago, Seiko was contemplating going full force into manufacturing digital watches. At that time, all of the marketing statistics and customer surveys indicated that the market was ready for digital watches, with the rationale being that they were more precise and more accurate than traditional face watches. But before it took this giant leap, Seiko hired me to confirm what the marketing statistics and customers were indicating. What I found was that for a watch to be intelligent, it had to match what was in the customer's mind or match the customer's code for time. In people's minds, time and space are one. People are imprinted by the sun. The position of the sun tells them when it is time to get up (sunrise), when it is lunch time (high noon), and when it is time for bed (nighttime). Since I found that people felt uncomfortable when they had a relationship with time without any relationship with space, I told Seiko that there was a smaller market for digital watches. Today, most watches sold are face watches. Even though digital watches might be more accurate, they are not intelligent in that they do not communicate the time and space relationship to customers in a way that makes them feel comfortable.

• ***Does the product enhance or change the way the customers function or live?*** The relationship between the product and the customer is the most important dimension, not the product itself. Customers don't care about the perfection of the product as much as they care about the relationship that they have with the products they buy. In other words, they care about how the products enhance their lives.

But most companies have an isolated, mechanistic, simplistic way of looking at products without understanding the product's influence on the customers' lives. A few companies, however, are heading in the right direction. One of these is ***Volvo***, whose motto is "Building a Reputation for Safety." The Volvo 900 is a highly intelligent product. If you look at one that has been in an accident, the front end and back end might by completely destroyed, but the passenger's compartment will likely be intact. This car is intelligent because the company designed it so that the car body—not just the passenger's body—receives the shock. As the company states: "The Volvo has been designed to spread and transfer the energy of an impact throughout the frame and around the passenger compartment. Through a unique structure of interlocking body elements, crash forces are deflected." In other words, Volvo didn't try to make a car that doesn't break but rather a car that breaks at the right places. The real purpose of the car is to protect the passengers.

Velcro is an intelligent product in the sense that it helps people perform tasks that they otherwise could not. For example, when my son was four years old, he couldn't tie his shoelaces. But when he received shoes with a velcro tab, he could easily put on and take off his shoes. So, a product doesn't have to be highly technological to be intelligent. In fact, high-tech products can be quite dumb. Many have features that most people never use. If customers have to pay for a product that has features they won't use, something is wrong. Engineers need to determine how often people are going to use the bells and whistles that they want to add. Dumb products might have a lot of engineering intelligence, but they have poor people intelligence because these features don't enhance the users' lives.

• ***Does the product meet the unspoken needs of the customers?*** A product has to meet the customers' unspoken and perhaps unconscious needs. Most companies will try to determine customers' needs through surveys and focus groups. Although helpful, the results can be misleading. What people say in surveys and interviews can be very superficial. Often they tell you what they think you want to hear or what they just saw on the television or read in the newspaper. So companies need to go beyond what the customers say they need.

For example, boats, unlike most apartments, are very space intelligent. In a small space, the boat must have accommodations for people to sit and sleep, prepare food and eat, work and navigate, shower and go to the bathroom. As a result, everything must have several uses. A bench might serve as a place to sit and its cushions as flotation devices or mattress for a bed. If builders used this same approach in apartments, tenants could fit more into them and live better.

An otherwise intelligent community of engineers can still produce dumb products by failing to consider the needs of customers. The new Denver International Airport is the "dumbest" in the world because it was not designed with customers' needs in mind. It takes at least an hour to get to your rental car, and you still have a 15-mile drive to Denver. Baggage delays are common, thanks to the "new and improved" baggage handling system. Confusing signs prompt the need for an army of assistants to rescue those passengers lost in the maze. Companies head in the wrong direction when they think only in terms of the product or service. What customers really care about is whether the product or service effectively communicates with them, whether it changes the way they function, and whether it meets their needs. Companies need to be more concerned about how customers relate to their products and service.

Process. In most quality programs, we do no better with our employees than we do with our customers. Insistence on *doing it right the first time* is a clear mistake; Americans don't want to do it right the first time. They need the experience of learning from their mistakes. People do not live in America to produce zero-defect products. We live here to have the opportunity to discover how good we are and how far we can go when given the chance, or often a second chance. We live in America because we want to create a new world, not to produce zero-defect products.

So, the quality process should focus on how employees will be transformed, how they will become better people, and how they can discover their identities while maximizing their potential.

Employees should be provided with new tools to help them achieve both of these objectives.

The purpose of an improvement process is not only to improve an output or outcome, but also to improve the person performing the process. Most people are continually working to achieve a new identity, position, or promotion. Life is movement, and people want to progress and improve themselves. People are more interested in growing personally than in achieving zero-defect processes.

People who have a bias for action make mistakes. By making mistakes, they become upset, a strong emotion that causes them to correct the mistake and improve. By making this mistake, people learn faster than if they performed the task right the first time. Not only do people learn to do it right, but they change and grow. This is the real added value in the process. If people are not allowed to make mistakes, they won't grow very much.

Any improvement process has to fit the cultural archetype. In North America, that means learning by doing, making mistakes, and trying to fix them. To facilitate this process, companies could have a program where people meet briefly every morning to share with others the mistakes they made, what they learned from them, and how others might benefit from what they've learned. This would be much more effective than a quality circle.

Many companies have processes and procedures that are rigid and fixed. If a customer says "I want this" but the request does not fit into the company's processes and procedures, the company replies "Sorry, it is not allowed." Companies should have flexible processes and procedures that allow employees to be creative and say, "Let me see what I can do," rather than "Sorry, I can't do that."

For example, at the Ritz-Carlton Hotel Company, employees are trained never to say "no" to guests and to try to find a way to fulfill their guests' requests. The hotel's processes and procedures enable employees to adapt to the situation. Once my wife, son, and I were staying at the Ritz-Carlton in Palm Beach, Florida. We had a reservation for dinner at the hotel restaurant. When we arrived, the restaurant was full, and we were told there would be a half-hour wait. The host suggested that we have drink at the bar. I politely declined, indicating that we would rather eat and reminding him that we had made reservations. The host then said, "Give me a minute, and I'll see what we can do to seat you." When he returned, he asked us if we would mind being served in an adjacent salon where they served afternoon tea. I agreed. When we reached this room, people were already busy setting up our table. We literally had our own private dining room. Although this was an inconvenience for employees, they fulfilled their goal of providing us with a "memorable visit." Flexible processes enable creativity, innovation, and adaptability. They allow companies the opportunity to create a synergistic relationship with customers.

People. Americans discovered long ago that customers were important. We often hear phrases such as, "The customer is number one" and "The customer is always right." The immediate translation of these axioms in an employee's mind is, "So, I'm number two? You, my employer, don't care about me? I have to accept anything from customers, just to make you more money?" The hidden message behind the priority of customer satisfaction is that no one cares about the employees.

Focusing on customers exclusively, then, is a mistake. Employees have experiences all the time that demonstrate that the customer can be wrong. What is important is not who is right or wrong, who is number one or number two. What is important is the quality of the employer-employee and employee-customer relationships. We all agree that customers are important—indeed, vital to our businesses. But if we acknowledge customers as being number one, we make the employees feel like number two.

Employees begin to think: "The company doesn't care about me. It only cares about the customers because they bring in the money." Perhaps such thoughts are justified. Once a company executive said to me, "I don't care about employee loyalty anymore." When I asked why he felt this way, he replied, "Times have changed. There is no way we can keep our employees happy. We are not responsible for the quality of their lives."

Business practices that view people as objects and numbers don't work because they go against the quality of the relationship.

Employees want to feel and experience loyalty in their jobs. People are not disposable commodities.

To build the quality relationship, we need both to care and demand. We can't be demanding if we are not caring. By showing that we are a caring and demanding company, we induce the same behavior in our customers. If we show that we value reciprocal quality of relationship, we make a higher-quality relationship, a win-win synergy that is more profitable for both sides.

Tough love is often the expression used to explain this relationship. When the Ritz-Carlton speaks about "ladies and gentlemen serving ladies and gentlemen," it speaks first to its employees, inducing in them a sense of self-respect and pride. And, when customers are treated like ladies and gentlemen, they are induced to behave that way.

Quality relationships are both caring and demanding. The concept of being both caring and demanding can be seen within the family unit. Parents are usually demanding of their children because they care deeply about them. Most parents demand that their children go to bed at a certain time to get the rest they need. The more you care, the more demanding you have to be and vice versa. Most parents seek the proper balance between caring and demanding so family members benefit and grow as the result of the relationship. Smart business managers also seek the right balance between being caring and demanding. If they are demanding without being caring, employees and customers will leave. If they are caring without being demanding, employees and customers will like take advantage of the situation. If customers have a win-lose attitude, they will create one problem after another. Horst Schulze, president of Ritz-Carlton, is the only one in the company who can say to a customer, "We don't want your business anymore." He does not do it very often, but he does it if he has to.

To entice customers, some companies go overboard in what they promise and deliver to customers. Once a company starts treating their customers like spoiled kids, customers become spoiled kids. And then what do they do? They start treating employees badly because, as spoiled kids, they expect the employees to do anything customers want. For example, one retail chain had a no-questions-asked return policy. Most customers didn't abuse this policy, but some became spoiled kids, returning items that were obviously worn or used. The notion that the customer is king can be detrimental to employees, customers, and the company.

Caring and *demanding* represent two sides of the same coin. The more you care, the more demanding you have to be. The whole notion of "the customer is always right" has created a bunch of spoiled consumer brats who don't appreciate the efforts of employees. Employees, therefore, feel undervalued and don't care much about customer service.

QR: Quality of the Relationship

The "Q" and "R" in my formula stand for "quality of the relationship." I find that the quality of a business relationship is most important to most people. Horst Schulze once told me that he is not selling rooms or meals; he is selling "memorable experiences." To do that, he redefines the relationship between customers and employees. He does not have "staff" who look after customers, but rather "ladies and gentlemen serving ladies and gentlemen." His message is this: "No one is number one or number two; no one is right or wrong. We are all in this together, and we should all care for each other."

Empowerment must go both ways. We have to empower our employees as well as our customers. If we don't, we will experience disempowerment. One example of disempowerment is the way some airlines treat their customers. Customers know they are going to have a terrible experience no matter what, so they figure they should at least try to get the cheapest fare. So, airlines embark on "fare wars," not "quality of service wars," because they don't understand that the problem they perceive is not the actual problem. Few airlines tap into the fantastic emotional energy that their customers possess. Instead, they just give out frequent flyer miles, which mean more harrowing experiences.

The quality of a relationship should focus on *the emotional value* added. This is what customers care most about—not the best or the cheapest product, but the one that brings the added emotional value they're looking for.

Each time you get on board a plane, you are treated like a child that needs to be instructed again and again on how to buckle his seatbelt. You are parked like cattle for hours, without explanation as to why your flight has been cancelled. Airlines are in the business of disempowerment. They are demanding without caring. They don't understand the basic quality law that the problem is not the problem itself, but how you deal with the problem.

When products and services becomes commodities, people switch from one supplier to another, caring only about the cost. And in price wars, there is no loyalty.

The purpose of business should not be solely profit—the purpose should also be life. "Bio-logic" means the logic of life. In a mechanistic world, decisions about process, procedures, products, and services are based on facts, statistics, and other information. But companies are discovering that quality is largely perception, meaning a product or service has quality only if the customer perceives it. Customers care about the quality of the relationship as well as the quality of the product or service. By building the quality of the relationship, companies build loyalty. Many companies stray away from the purpose of life, and that's why many eventually go out of business.

How can companies avoid this fate? Since life is based on biology, they need to practice biological principles. For example, here are three such principles:

1. Customers and employees are pressured to take care of their physical and emotional needs first. You don't argue with your body when it indicates that you are hungry or you have to go to the bathroom. When you have to rest, you must rest; and when you need to eat, you must eat. These physical hot buttons can benefit companies. When companies help customers and employees understand and deal with their physical needs and emotional hot buttons, they will be loyal to them. Why? Even if people can take care of their physical needs, they still need someone to take care of their needs on the emotional level. Adults still need tender loving care.

2. Emotions are stronger than the intellect. One day, a student of mine told me that he wanted to get married. I said that was great and asked him about his plans. This student, who was an engineer, produced a long list of criteria that he wanted his future wife to have. This list contained such criteria as the color of her hair and eyes, her education, her age, her size, and so forth. Several months later, this student announced that he was going to get married. I asked, "So you found someone who met all of your criteria?" "No", he replied, "she doesn't meet any of the criteria on the list, but I love her." The cortex can dictate a lot of criteria, but the limbic system often overrides rational reasons. Companies should take note.

3. The rational mind does not act alone. Many companies believe that they must give customers a lot of reasons why they should buy their products and services. But the customers don't decide to buy a product or service at the rational level; they decide at the emotional level.

For example, why might you want to buy a Mercedes? You might say that they have dual air bags and that they are built like tanks to protect your family. Although you might list good reasons for buying a Mercedes, the reality is that you don't know why. Emotionally, you might want to buy this car because of the prestige of owning one or because it represents the success you have achieved in life. *What customers need are intellectual alibis* so they can feel good about their emotional buying decisions. Intellectual alibis help customers feel good about their logic of emotion. Today, companies need to understand and satisfy their customers' hot buttons (biological needs), provide the right logic of emotion (satisfy their emotional needs) and then give customers the right intellectual alibis (satisfy their intellectual needs).

S: Synergistic, Systemic, Symbolic, Symbiotic

The "S" in my formula stands for four dimensions of this new quality relationship: synergistic, systemic, symbolic, and symbiotic.

Synergistic. *Synergy* comes from the Greek *synergia* and describes the capacity of two people or systems to optimize one another, achieving mutual enhancement. The correct attitude is this: "We are in this together; we need each other; we can achieve more together than we can alone; we can get more out of the relationship than we put into it in the beginning."

The whole can be more than the sum of the parts. One plus one can equal three or more. In biology, life is synergy. For example, the basic biological scheme is woman + man = woman, man, and baby. This is 1 + 1 = 3. This is life. Biology gives us the basic scheme, and if a company is strong, it's because it has managed to translate biological schemata into cultural forces, or archetypes.

As sellers, buyers, employees, and customers, we seek more from a relationship than we put into it in the beginning. For example, if I buy a book for $20 and this book helps me to increase my profit by $200,000, I obviously get more than just my money back. Also, from now on I will speak very highly of this book; I will be its advocate and promote it. The publisher, author, and bookseller will also receive more than just the $20 I gave them for the book. Companies need to rethink the way they do business. Business is not warfare; it's not a match where the one who scores the most points wins. Business is about real life, about growing together, about caring for each other, and about being demanding on both sides of a relationship. It is about empowering customers, as well as employees. When there is a problem, ask customers for ideas and solutions. Link promotion and customer satisfaction, and make this linkage well known. Give the power to evaluate every employee to every customer, and publish the results.

In a synergistic relationship, those involved are transformed so that they get more out of the relationship than they originally put into it. In the quality movement, companies were encouraged to have an ongoing relationship with suppliers and think of them as an extension of the company. Most companies now do this, and yet few think of their customers as suppliers. In a synergistic relationship, however, customers become suppliers, because both parties are transformed by the relationship. Which store would you rather deal with? One that sells you the latest computer that will become obsolete in six months or one that manages your informational needs for the next 10 years, giving you the computer that best meets your current needs at the best price? I would take the later, even if it charges a bit more.

Synergistic relationships distinguish Saturn Corporation. Saturn's slogan, "A Different Kind of Company, A Different Kind of Car," represents a key competitive strategy that has been built in from the company's beginnings in 1985. Saturn knew that it was entering a saturated market, so it tried to differentiate itself in two respects: Selling the company rather than the car; and developing a relationship with customers. Rather than focus on mind-numbing facts, Saturn opted for another approach: treating its customers and employees with respect.

To create a relationship with customers, Saturn has reinvented the car-buying experience. Salespeople are trained in how to approach and treat customers. First, they provide competitors' prices on similar cars. They know that people shop around, so they save their customers time by doing it for them. Second, there is no price-haggling policy. The car's price is uniform across Saturn retailers; Third, there is a low-pressure sales environment. Rather than pressure customers, salespeople invite them to events where they can meet and talk with Saturn owners.

After a sale is made, the relationship continues at both the retailer and corporate level. For example, retailers organize social events and offer service clinics to teach owners more about their cars and how to perform minor maintenance tasks. The corporate office provides the *Visions* newsletter as well *The Saturn Magazine* on Internet and also sponsors events. The real test of whether Saturn has created a quality relationships with its customers comes when current Saturn owners buy a new car. Only then Saturn will know if they have achieved the ultimate: customer loyalty.

Systemic. A second characteristic of a quality relationship is that it is systemic, meaning that all parts of the system are interrelated. Changing one element changes the whole system and reorganizes the energy throughout all parts of the system. For example, if the Lincoln Tunnel is closed, traffic is affected everywhere in and around Manhattan, New York.

We don't just sell a product—we sell a new element that will have consequences in the whole system. Doctors have learned that a symptom is also part of a system. They can't simply treat the symptom; they must take into account the whole system, including what is going to happen when the symptom is no longer there. If a child has a headache and doesn't want to go to school, curing the headache won't necessarily resolve the problem with school.

Understanding the systemic approach might be as simple as providing a rental car to customers who need their car repaired, or a daycare center for employees with small children. If you change the way you look at the people you interact with, many new ideas will surface about how to improve the quality of relationships, and these will multiply in value far beyond your expectations.

Products and services don't exist in isolation; they are a part of people's *systems*. Just as doctors realize that they have to address the patient's lifestyle not just their illness, companies must address *all* elements in the customer's personal, family, and business life. By selling a customer a product or service, the company is possibly changing other elements in that person's life.

For example, once you have your driver's license and access to a car, your life is completely different. With this new independence, you can go where you want, when you want, and with whom you want. Although driving is only one element in your life, if affects your whole life. Changing one element can change the whole system. Companies need to start thinking of their products and services in the context of the customer's system. Companies that simply sell products and services that meet customers' immediate needs are in a *need relationship*. To have a quality relationship with customers, companies need to facilitate a *desire relationship*. In a desire relationship you feel safe, and so you choose to come together.

Most relationships in business today are need relationships. Employees need an income to live, so they work for a company that offers them the highest wage and benefits. Customers need a certain product or service, so they buy it from the company that offers them cheapest price and least inconvenience. But when a company knows how to be caring and demanding and cultivate a desire relationship, customers and employees *choose* to interact with that company because they know they will benefit and grow from their relationship with it over time. The desire relationship results in loyalty.

Sometimes establishing a desire relationship means *not* selling the customer a product or service right away. For example, when my family and I moved to Florida, I was approached by a real estate agent who said, "I would like to sell you a house." When I told this person that I had to sell my house in California first to avoid having two mortgages, I never heard from him again.

Then I found a real estate agent who was not looking to sell a house right away, but was looking to establish a relationship with us. She told us, "I know you need to sell your house in California before you can buy one here, but let me help you." She took care of our immediate needs by finding an apartment for us to rent, even though she didn't make any commission by doing so. A week later, when I was away on business, my wife became very ill and had to go to the hospital. This real estate agent took my wife to the hospital and back home again. Obviously, this real estate agent was establishing a relationship with us. And we would not buy a house without her. Even if I found a house on my own, I would buy through her so she would get the commission. She is selling a relationship, not a product, because she understands that the relationship is a long-term investment that pays dividends over time.

To enter into the realm of quality relationships, companies need to change more than just their attitude about customers. They also need to change the way they train employees and reward performance. Employees must be trained to sell the relationships, not just the product or service. Asking customers, "How much money do you want to spend?" without knowing their needs sends the message that the sales agent will take as much money as possible from them.

The best sales agents build a relationship. Customers then realize that the agents care more about them than their money; the agents understand their real needs and priorities; and the agents will be there when their needs and priorities match what the company is selling.

In addition to training employees how to sell the relationship, companies need to make sure its performance and reward systems are appropriate. The way a company measures and rewards performance tells employees how they should behave. Thus, results should be measured in terms of how many long-term relationships are established, not how many products are sold. If companies establish a system in which the capital is the relationship with customers, then employees will strive for that. A company's products and services don't exist in isolation, but rather are a part of people's systems.

Companies need to be concerned about employees' whole systems, not just the element that relates to their employment. For example, knowing that its employees have a life outside of work, Maryland Bank, NA (MBNA) has: 1) created an on-site day-care center for employees with small children; 2) invited a dry cleaner to open up a shop in the bank so employees can drop off or pick up their dry cleaning during lunch; 3) has a hair dresser come in twice a week; and 4) asked a local drug store to open a rent-free shop in the bank. When the owner said he couldn't have a full time employee attend the store, MBNA asked retired employees to volunteer—and many jumped at the chance because they could see their old friends. Although it doesn't cost much money to offer these various services, the added value for the employees is incredible. The symbolic dimension for the employees is that the company really cares about them. The company is not just a place where they go to work to earn money; it is a place where they can take care of other elements in their lives.

Another bank makes its retirees part of an advisory board. The retirees get a business card (a symbolic dimension) indicating this new status, and they help train new employees. These retirees receive a little money, a new title, and the chance to meet new people and remain active in the business. The bank benefits from having experienced employees train new employees. Once again, this program costs little, but adds a lot of value for everyone involved.

Another benefit of using the systemic approach comes in the form of new business opportunities. With the systemic approach, companies can also venture into new industries. Consider a car manufacturer. Does a car manufacturer sell cars? No, it sells the driving experience. As a result, many business opportunities become apparent. Since most customers can't pay cash for a new car, they need financing. Since customers want to protect their investment, they need auto insurance. Since customers don't want their new cars stolen, they need alarm or security devices. Since customers want to conduct personal or professional business on the road, they need car phones. Since customers want their cars to run, they need gas. Since customers want music in their cars, they need sound systems, cassette tapes, and compact disks.

Many car manufacturers are already taking advantage of these systemic opportunities. GM, for example, has its own financing company, the General Motors Acceptance Corporation. The more a company understand the customers' systems, the more possibilities there are.

Taking a systemic approach can also bolster a company's odds of surviving. For example, an organization called PLM in France operated trains between the cities of Paris, Lyon, and Marseille. At first, PLM considered itself a train company. But then it realized that providing customers the opportunity to travel by train was only one element in the customers' system. Other elements included handling luggage, taking taxis to and from the train station, and staying in hotels. So PLM started adding products and services. First, it opened a chain of hotels in the three cities. Then it started selling luggage and renting cars. One day, the French government nationalized the train service, so PLM could no longer operate its trains. Still, PLM not only survived, today it is one of the most profitable companies in France and Europe.

Symbolic. Relationships reach their apex when they achieve a symbolic dimension. A symbol is what unifies diverse parts and is an element of a culture that is loaded with the cultural codes and logic of emotion. For example, if you buy a red piece of material for 50 cents, and then buy a blue piece for the same price, and then a white one, you have $1.50 worth of material. No one wants to get killed for $1.50. However, if you arrange those pieces of material to create an American flag, you suddenly add a symbolic dimension to this simple material, and that dimension changes the owner's attitude. Some people might now be willing to die for this material; others might want to make it illegal to burn. Obviously, this is now more than just three pieces of material of three different colors. Somehow, sewn into a tri-colored rectangle of cloth (a flag), this material represents the collective memory of a nation and its common ideals and dreams. This is what we tap into when we add a symbolic dimension to the quality of a relationship.

For a decade, people were buying personal computers not to use them or because they really needed them, but because they were symbols of the future. They were buying the future for their children in these machines. A symbol is a way to open a logic of emotion to reach a deeply imprinted cultural archetype. When Russians or Hungarians buy a Coke, Levis, or Marlboros, they buy more than just a soft drink, pants, or cigarettes. They buy American ideas, ideals, and attitudes. They buy symbols.

Two companies have succeeded in bringing a symbolic aspect to their customer and employee relations by emphasizing the quality of their relationships:

- ***Club Med.*** At Club Med, they do not speak of hotels or resorts, but of "villages." These don't have managers or directors, but "chiefs." Employees are GOs (gentle organizers), and clients are GMs (gentle members). Employees not only do their jobs at the kitchen or the pool, but at night they have to be on stage, singing, dancing, and performing. Customers, too, are part of the show, and all talents are welcome. Everyone is active and contributes to forming a quality relationship. Club Med is successful not because it provides better service (there is no room service) or because its employees are better paid, but because it takes the time to form a systemic, synergistic, and highly symbolic relationship with its customers and employees.
- ***Walt Disney.*** When you join Disney, you take a course called Walt Disney Tradition 101. From the beginning, you realize that

this is a unique company. You are not an employee, but a "cast member." You will not work, but will be "on stage." You are not selling anything, you just want your guests to have "the best time of their life." Suddenly you are part of something bigger than you, and you are getting more out of it than what you are putting in. It's not just a job anymore, it's your life, a mission, and a new way of looking at the world.

Most companies make the mistake of assuming that customers purchase products and services for rational reasons, and so they give them several rationale reasons to buy. These reasons emphasize price, features, benefits, quality, or guarantees. Some companies, however, know that the real reasons people buy a product or service aren't scientific or rationale. They know that emotion plays a big role in making purchasing decisions, and they tap into this emotion through symbols.

A *symbol* is something that unifies and creates a high density of meaning and emotion. The opposite of a symbol is a *diabol*. In French, *diabolic* means devil. The devil is the one who divides. Symbolic and diabolic are opposite forces. A symbol is the unconscious expression of a cultural archetype. Members of a culture all relate to the same symbols without knowing why. If a symbol is wrong, it just doesn't ring a bell. If it is right, it taps into their emotions.

In addition to unifying a culture, symbols bring meaning. People want to know that what they are doing today has meaning; otherwise, they wonder why they are doing it. What is a life without meaning? People would rather die than lose the meaning in life. All people share the need to understand the symbolic aspects of their lives and deaths.

People need symbols, but they can't create them; the culture creates them over time. Symbols can be: An object (flag), place (Ellis Island), person (George Washington), animal (bald eagle), concept (equality). The concept of symbol creation can be thought of as the difference between normal light and laser light. The particles of normal light go into all directions and do not create much energy and power. The particles of laser light, however, are in sync and create enough energy and power that they can go through steel. A symbol is the creation of laser light by the members of a culture.

Every culture creates it own symbols. Companies must be aware that different cultures will have different symbolic value-added dimensions. For example, once I worked with a business unit within AT&T that produced cables. One of its clients was Nippon Telegraph and Telephone (NTT) in Japan. NTT gave AT&T a list of specifications for the cable. Before AT&T shipped the cables to NTT, it made sure that all of the specifications were met. NTT received the cables and immediately sent them back to AT&T. The Americans were perplexed because the cables met all of the specifications. When they asked why the cables were returned, NTT replied, "Because they were ugly." The Americans were dumfounded for two reasons: First, an aesthetics specification was not included on the list; and, second, no one would even see the cable once it was in use. But in the Japanese culture, if something is ugly, it cannot be good. That is the symbolic dimension of aesthetic in Japan. Aesthetics is the final proof of the value of the item being sold.

Subcultures can also have their own symbols. For example, several age subcultures exist in the United States. When Americans are young, they usually have one set of values (speed, productivity, quantity, or performance), but when they get older, they adopt another set (time, quality, music, and beauty). Since these subcultures have different values, they also have unique symbols. Companies need to be aware of such subcultures because if they use the wrong symbols, they could lose their customers.

People want more meaning in their lives. Customers want more symbolic value. One advantage of adding symbolic value to a product or services is that it doesn't cost much money, but it adds a lot of value to the customer or employee. So companies can add value without adding expenditures. But companies can't create symbols overnight. They must discover what symbols already exist and match them with their products or services. Matching symbols with products and services can be challenging, but many companies have tapped into the incredible potential of symbolism.

• The International Food Information Council (IFIC) asked me to study how Americans perceive genetically engineered food. I discovered that people want to know everything about these products, so when the issue of ***labels*** came up, I recommended that all of the information be included on the labels. At first, the IFIC resisted this advice, indicating that the type would be so small that no one would read it. I replied that it didn't matter if people ever read the label—the information had to be there because it is symbolic of total disclosure. If there is symbolic proof that the customers have access to all information, they trust the company and don't need to read the information. But if the company is hiding something and customers find out about it, they won't trust the company or its products anymore.

• When visitors tour the Maryland Bank, NA (MBNA) in Newark, DE, they are first taken to a special ***mural***. The mural features the hand print and signature of every employee who helped build the bank. The employee who gave me my tour proudly pointed out her hand print and told me an extraordinary story. When the mural was created, all employees talked about it. Soon, the bank received a call from a person representing the bank's retirees. The retirees were upset because they weren't included in the mural. They felt that this was unfair since they, too, had worked hard to help make the bank successful. So, in a special ceremony, the retirees were invited to include their symbolic mark on the mural. Now, this mural was not done by a famous artist, but its symbolic power for the employees makes the mural priceless.

• Another bank discovered the symbolic value of giving customers the ***home phone numbers*** of bank officials. When a customer calls this bank with a problem, the employee who handles the call tells the customer: "From now on, I will be in charge of your account. Don't hesitate to call me directly at work. If you have a problem after business hours or on the weekend, call me at home." Giving customers your home phone number is highly unusual, but the symbolism is powerful. Survey results reveal that although less that 1 percent of the customers use the home phone numbers, 97 percent of those given the numbers rate the bank highly. The symbol shows that the bank cares about its customers.

• U.S. automakers know the value of symbols. A ***car*** is the symbol of independence. Although people can use subways, buses, or taxis to get around, they don't receive the same feeling as when they own and drive their own cars. Different vehicles have their own unique symbols. For example, in a study for Chrysler, I found that a ***Jeep*** is a symbol for a horse. You can go anywhere because you don't need roads—suddenly "the West" is yours for the taking. So, Chrysler is not really selling a vehicle; it is selling the freedom to go anywhere. If the Jeep dealer says, "Buy a Jeep because it doesn't use much gas, and it has good suspension," people will say "That's nice." But if the dealer says, "Buy a Jeep so you can go anywhere," suddenly the pitch is a lot more powerful. People buy jeeps largely for the symbolic value.

Similarly, why buy ***sport cars*** that can go 150 miles an hour when the speed limit is 65? Sport car enthusiasts might say they need such speed for passing cars, but the real reason isn't rational, it's emotional. The sports car symbolizes power.

People buy ***sport utility vehicles*** and ***vans*** because they are buying the freedom to pack up their bags, load their dogs, gather their children, and go. Even the features in a van can be symbolic. For example, when one van manufacturer decided to put a console in the space between the two front seats, the van stopped selling well. Why? That space enabled van owners to move to the back of the van. With the console between the seats, people had to stop the van, get out, walk to the back, and open the rear door. When pioneers traversed the wild west in their wagons, they did not have to stop the horses to go to the back of the wagons. The console stopped the freedom to move about, breaking with the symbol.

By using the power of symbols, Chrysler, MBNA, IFIC, and others have provided products and services that communicate effectively with customers and employees, enhance their lives, and meet their needs, including those at the unconscious level. Again, people buy products based on emotions. Sometimes these emotions are so deep that people are unaware of them. Products or services should be thought of as vehicles for selling the symbol. The symbol is what is important. This is difficult for most engineers, analysts, and scientists to accept, because they are driven by hard data. Companies should use the symbol's unconscious, unifying power. Its value-added dimension can't be duplicated. If companies bring the symbolic dimension into their relationships with employees, customers, suppliers, and shareholders, these relationships will have a lot more value, and people will do their best to be loyal to the relationship and the company.

Symbiotic. Several companies have brought the symbolic dimension of quality to their relationships with customers, employees, and other stakeholders to improve the quality of these relationships. The climax of this improvement is symbiosis. This principle of dynamic relationships exists not only among plants and animals in nature, but also applies to animals and humans, humans and humans, companies and companies, and companies and the environment.

Symbiosis, then, is the next step in quality. It suggests that a quality relationship is all about the spirit of mutual benefit—of treating people (especially customers and employees) as partners, as people who live and work in the center of a web of interactions. A symbiotic relationship brings harmony and enhancement to all partners. When you reach this level of quality in your relationships, loyalty is the number one payoff.

Although symbiotic relationships are common in nature, they are rare in the business world. By selling products and services, companies are selling a medium. The medium is not the goal, but rather a way to organize their relationships with customers. Only then they will understand their real goal: selling the relationship.

To see how selling the relationship can create loyalty (whereas selling just the product or service cannot), consider this example: Rather than turn down the request of 17-year-old Judy for a credit card, a representative of The Neighborly Bank takes the time to find out why Judy wants a credit card and to learn her plans for the future. He tells Judy: "If I give you a credit card now, it might destroy your life by getting you into debt. Let me help you get to the point where I feel good about giving you this credit card." He gives Judy literature on how to properly use credit cards. So instead of saying "no" to Judy's initial request, The Neighborly Bank said "not yet" because it wanted to establish a quality relationship that would benefit both. The bank was demanding yet caring. Saying "no" to a potential customer likely negates any future interactions, but by saying "not yet" in a caring way, you establish a bond of loyalty with this person.

One way to have symbiotic relationships with customers is to develop symbiotic relationships with other companies. Since no one company can possibly provide everything to everybody, companies need to think in terms of combining services. For example, in the travel industry, airlines, hotels, car rental agencies, and restaurants all need each other. For the customer, it is one business, and so these businesses should be promoting each other. Another example is the possible symbiotic relationship among car manufacturers, gasoline companies, and insurance companies. In the driving experience, customers need insurance to protect themselves and their new cars, and they need gasoline to drive their cars. There should be a symbiotic relationship among these companies.

When you have a symbiotic relationship, the parties are part of the same system. In symbiosis, each party in the relationship is a respected, independent entity. These two parties, however, form a mutually beneficial relationship.

If our emphasis is only on product quality, or zero defects, because customers seek the best value for their money, they will change suppliers without any qualms if they find a better deal next door. Does that mean loyalty is dead? No, the code for loyalty is the "quality of the relationship." Customers are not satisfied with the endless search for the best deal or the cheapest price. They want real partnership.

What happened at Saturn is a good example of how priority given to relationships can turn business around. When you arrive at a Saturn dealer, they first provide you with all of the competitors' prices. They know you are going to want this information, so they gather it for you. Second, their prices are fixed. Their message is: "We're not trying to 'get you.' We want to form a high-trust relationship." This is not easy in America, as car dealers often have poor credibility. Third, customers at Saturn form a "club." The dealer invites you to an event where you can meet other Saturn owners, ask questions, get some advice on how to maintain your car, and make friends. Of course, Saturns are good cars, but the success of Saturn comes from concentrating on the quality of their relationships, a move that everyone in management and marketing must make to succeed.

People want mutually beneficial relationships with companies they can trust. Quality of the relationship transforms the 3 Ps into the 4 Ss, and loyalty is the payoff. In effect, customers are saying "Give me what I'm looking for—the symbolic, systemic, and synergistic dimensions of a symbiotic relationship—and I will help you survive." In this relationship, a company can make a mistake, be rude on occasion, or provide a not-so-perfect product or service as long as it deals with the problem quickly and correctly.

Companies have to stop treating customers like spoiled kids. They are not children; they are adults who understand their responsibilities in the relationship. They want caring and demanding on both sides of the relationship. They want the added value of a quality relationship with the people behind the product or service. This is not brand loyalty, product loyalty, or service loyalty; it is loyalty with the employees and the symbol behind the product or service. Most companies believe that customers are loyal to a brand or product, but people don't buy just products. They buy relationships because there are people behind the product.

Characteristics of Quality Relationships

In a quality relationship, there are four things: someone who is always there for you in a crisis, face-to-face communication, freedom of expression, and direct involvement.

Always there for you. A quality relationship is one in which the company will be there for its customers and employees, here and now. A quality relationship speaks to the logic of emotion of the customers or employees, not to the intellect. This is why loyalty is not money, numbers, deals, extra miles, or coupons. Loyalty is a deep feeling that you are in a symbiotic relationship in the same system. It is the feeling that you are both going to grow together in a systemic, synergistic, and symbolic relationship.

Face-to-face communication. What type of communication do you have in your company? Are you a memo company, electronic company, or face-to-face company. If an employee of the memo company finds a fire in the building, he will write a memo in triplicate: one for his reference, one for his boss, and one for the organization. By the time the memo is distributed, the building burns to the ground. But the employee is safe because he did his job and distributed the memo—and he has a copy of the memo in his file for proof. If an employee of the electronic company finds a fire in the building, he makes a phone call to his boss. Since he gets the boss's answering machine, he leaves a message. The boss didn't return in time, and the building burns to the ground. But he is safe because he made the phone call and left a message. If an employee of the face-to-face company finds a fire in the building, he does something about the fire immediately. He quickly tells his coworkers and boss about the fire and instructs them in what to do. The building is saved from destruction.

Companies deal with "fires," such as customer complaints, daily. Once I worked with a company that was concerned about customer complaints, so it followed a process to deal with them. Letters containing complaints were given to the person in charge of dealing with them. Every six months, the president received a memo on the number of complaints received. When I asked the president how he felt about the process, he replied, "Good, because the numbers are going down." I then asked him to meet his dissatisfied customers face to face to get some insight into their problems. He told me, "You don't understand. I'm the president. I don't have time for that." So I proposed that he talk with dissatisfied customers who called the company. He agreed to do this for 30 minutes. The first customer the president talked to was very upset with the product he purchased. The president was in shock. Two minutes later, he received another call from a customer with the same problem. Five minutes later, he called an emergency board meeting, demanding to know what was going on. "But, Mr. President," replied one board member, "you had all of this information in the memos."

Freedom of expression. We constantly experience pressure. How we deal with pressure—through expression or repression—is greatly influenced by the environment. The business world, for example, is mainly into repression. You're not supposed to say what you want; you are supposed to control yourself and behave in a professional manner. But people who don't express themselves can become depressed, or they might express themselves through violence. So the more repression that an environment imposes, the more depression and violence it induces. In a quality relationship, there is more room for people to express themselves. The more companies repress freedom of expression, the more customers and employees will become depressed or violent. It is better for dissatisfied customers or employees to express their dissatisfaction, because their negative energy is released. This negative energy can possibly be transformed into positive energy and, ultimately, loyalty.

There is nothing wrong with expressing negative feelings. When they are expressed, they can be addressed. The real problem is when people don't express negative feelings. This repression can destroy people or make them turn to violence. When companies get negative energy from their employees or customers, they shouldn't be afraid. How companies react to or handle that energy will determine whether it becomes destructive or productive.

Direct involvement. Involvement means risk as well as the opportunity to be creative. When two people get together, there is as risk. The risk could be that they will fight and someone could get killed. But there is also the chance to procreate—to be creative. So there is life and death; that is the major risk in biology. The notion of the quality relationship is that, of course, there will be more risks, but there will also be more productivity and creativity. By adding time and space, there is less risk, but there is also less productivity and creativity. For example, many companies have a reward system that gives employees rewards every six months or every year. But how can employees learn appropriate behaviors if feedback is given to them six months later? The only way you can influence behavior is by giving immediate feedback. By moving into the "here and now" dimension, a company can improve its performance in incredible ways and improve the quality of the relationship between the company, employees, shareholders, and customers.

Companies need to move from emphasizing the elements—the products, processes, and people—to emphasizing the relationships between those elements. Companies must realize that establishing relationships with their customers and employees is more important than improving products, services, and processes. If they care about these relationships, they can create loyalty.

Chapter 2

Technology Does Not Change the Structure

Mother banks, father banks, and ATMs.

One fear many organizations face is how the introduction of a new technology will affect their relationships with their customers.

In this chapter, I explore this issue using a study I conducted for Security Pacific Bank when the Automatic Teller Machine, or ATM, was being introduced. The bank wanted to know how their business would be changed by these new machines—would customers accept them, or would they turn to a competitor who still did things the old way?

One group of managers predicted that ATMs would replace the company's branches, and that in the future everything would be done by machines; people simply would not go to the bank anymore. For them, the ATM was the new definition of a branch. Since the bank had grown by putting a branch at every block and telling customers (through advertisement) that convenience was key when choosing a bank, they believed Security Pacific should do the same with ATMs—put machines on every block. Of course, this group of managers wanted the machines to be owned by their bank, to be accessible only to their clients, and to bear the name, colors, and logo of Security Pacific Bank very visibly.

Another group of managers, however, was concerned that the human factor would be lost and that people, especially elderly citizens who often have a lot of money, would not trust machines. These manager thought clients wanted to be called by their names, see friendly faces, and have human interaction.

Some of the questions the bank was facing were: What is a bank in America? What is the archetype of a bank? What is the future of branches? How will ATMs be accepted?

The field study was fascinating. Taking participants back to their first experiences with a bank brought back powerful memories. A 45-year-old woman in San Diego told us: "I remember, I was three years old, and Mummy took me with her to the bank. I remember the smell of the marble floor, the columns, the high ceiling, the silence. It was like going to church. At the time, I thought this was another kind of church."

A 40-year-old man in Los Angeles said: "I was proud that the teller knew the name of my mother and spoke nicely to her, even if I could not see her face because I was too small."

A 60-year-old San Francisco man recalled: "One day, my mother told me to take the money out of my piggy bank and to go with her to the bank because we were going to open an account for me. When we arrived, she introduced me to the president (actually he was the branch manager). That was a very small branch, but for me at the time it was like the White House. I told him that I had saved $2, and that I wanted to open an account. We went to a teller. They gave me a little book. For the first time in my life, I had to sign my name on an official document. I was so proud, and I felt so grown up. I wished I could have put in more money. I took the little book and put it under my pillow and kept touching it all night. Something had happened to me, and I did not know what it was; but I knew I was different now!"

The analysis of these and many other stories quickly revealed to us the logic of emotion strongly imprinted at a very early age: *the bank was a temple of identity*. For many Americans, money serves as a sort of proof of their social identity, and the bank is thus a place with which they retain very strong ties. For many, to some degree, the amount of money they possess lets them know how well they are doing at life in general. Bankers traditionally supply the means to evaluating these social identities. To much of the world, you are your credit history. You do not exist if the bank says you do not exist; you cannot rent a car, stay in a hotel, or buy an airline ticket without credit. This type of proof that you exist is unavailable if the bank does not supply it for you.

If the American dream is to have a car and to own a house, a very important stage of one's identity quest involves a bank. So if the mission of a bank is to contribute to the development of our identities, could the ATM perform that function? Is banking becoming simply a commodity, along with everything else done by machines? Following a biological scheme, what I discovered was that, just as we need two parents to exist, we also need two different types of banks to achieve our desired social identity—the "mother bank" and the "father bank."

The Mother Bank. A mother is supposed to feed a child, despite its behavior. A mother is always supposed to be there for her child. She is the home base from which one leaves to explore the world, and the security one returns to when scared or lost. One aspect of a bank is that maternal aspect: a loving, caring, non-judgmental entity, a place where one can always have basic needs fulfilled. This description perfectly fits the ATM; it is always there, it always has some cash for you.

The Father Bank. Fathers, on the other hand, are judgmental. They want to know if you did your homework, why you were late getting in, and when you're going to pay them back that $20 they loaned you for gas. Fathers sometimes say no. That's why kids always go to Mom when they need a few dollars; they only go to Dad if they need more than Mom is good for. Going to the bank for your first car loan or your first mortgage is like going to your father for money. It is an initiation, a turning point in your permanent search for a special identity. This is a ritual that requires a ceremony, sacred documents, and an audience. At the conclusion of the "ceremony" or the ritual of receiving your first mortgage, you are so proud to sign your name on that document. You are a new person. In a way, you have a new life.

Various parts of this banking story were repeated by several participants. When the bank respects the ritual, it creates loyalty for life, a strong emotional imprint that can last forever. No other American institution provides so much social identity.

ATMs. There is crucial difference between the role played by the "mother bank" and the "father bank." A bank's design should always reflect both elements, with a clear distinction between the marble floor and the young teller behind the counter, and the fancier carpeted office with the older manager behind the desk. Not understanding this code has led some banks to try to deliver all of their services in an old fatherly atmosphere, intimidating for many customers. Or, on the other end of the scale, some have tried granting first loans by mail, without the ritual, the audience, or the ceremony. That approach, however, doesn't create loyalty or a feeling of belonging. Neither of these approaches creates return customers. Clearly, then, the ATM could not replace the "father bank," but it could play the role of the "mother bank," providing 24-hour, easy access.

A few months after the conclusion of my study, a service company began the option of ATMs to customers of several banks along the East Coast. These banks found that, due to the fact that they had properly divided the "motherly" and "fatherly" aspects of their organizations between the ATM and the branch, even when customers moved, they did not leave their banks. Thus, most banks have now successfully assigned their "motherly" aspect to ATMs.

High Tech/High Touch

This is a great example of how technology does not replace human interaction, but rather reorients it to that which is really important. At its best, "high-tech" means deeper, stronger, more meaningful personal service. The financial supermarket approach is a mistake; banks' selling everything, everywhere, all the time causes them to lose their symbolic appeal to the American process of gaining social identity. Instead, they become commodities that are no longer trusted.

With the right approach, however, banks can play a very important role in American culture. According to archetypal studies, banks should concentrate on their overall mission, centered around identity and initiation. In particular, a strong emphasis on first experience is important, especially with children and young adults.

Each bank should have one "temple." Each branch need not be a "temple," but all the members and employees of the bank should be familiar with the "temple," as well as with their common ancestors (i.e., the bank's founder). The Rothschild Bank, for which I did work in France, understood this ritualistic need very well; an oil painting of the founder of their bank's dynasty was hung in the hall of every branch.

The major conclusion of my study was this: ATMs should not replace the "father bank," but should play the role of "mother bank," being as easily accessible as a telephone. Banks should not own the machines (in the sense of serving only their own customers), and ATMs should be everywhere. As a result of my study, branches have been designed according to the bank archetype existent in American culture. "Father bank" branches are now more impressive, with a leather-wood-carpet environment. I designed the training programs of bank employees accordingly, with special "father bank" training concerning loans and customer relationships.

Yet another valuable lesson was learned from exploring how banks deal with mistakes: when a mistake is made on a statement, the customer is usually upset. He calls the bank, has to go from one source to another, is kept on hold, sometimes disconnected, and has to call again. We have seen customers close six-figure accounts, sometimes even those containing millions of dollars, and switch banks due to a mistake involving less than $50, simply because of the treatment they received.

In response to this type of problem, I designed a special training program for bank employees who deal with these kinds of problems. The first element of the training is to help employees realize that a complaint is not a problem, but rather it is a great opportunity to gain that customer's loyalty for life, if they recognize the customer's emotional logic.

The logic of emotion here is that when customers complain, they are experiencing a negative emotion, which, instead of being suppressed, needs to be transformed into a positive one. In other words, through taking positive measures, the customer's emotional energy can be turned to the company's favor.

When tested, the impact of this approach was impressive on both employees and customers. Employees felt empowered; they had the feeling that they were in charge of their relationship with the customer. An employee survey showed a very high satisfaction score from these employees. Also, in a survey taken after this program was initiated, 95 percent of customers who called the bank from home said this was the best banking experience they had ever had.

A similar program and survey created for General Motors produced comparable results. Customers who did not have any complaint gave a medium score to the company, but those who had had a problem that had been fixed gave a higher score of satisfaction.

So, we learn that technology does not change the structure and that the structure is the message. Again, people don't buy products and services, they invest in relationships. Technology does not replace human interaction. At its best, new technology results in more meaningful personal service.

Every organization needs to know how the introduction of new technology will affect relationships with customers. I suggest that the same principle discovered in my study of banks has widespread application: Following a biological scheme, we see that just as children need both a father and a mother to meet their needs, customers may require both a judgmental "father" who sometimes says "no" or "not yet," and a loving, caring, nurturing "mother" who is always there for them. The wise use of technology can help achieve this marketing objective.

CHAPTER 3

THE 12 LAWS OF RELATIONAL COMMUNICATION

Survival is based on creative communication.

I would like to submit that modern communication is not real communication. Real communication is based on biology: 1 + 1 = 3. This occurs when two human beings of opposite gender decide to combine their genetic codes through a communication, resulting in a third person. So, real communication is a product of person-to-person interaction.

A medium is a filter, and thus mediated, communication is incomplete or partial. Telephone, fax, TV, and email create reduced, impoverished communication with possible negative consequences such as frustration, violence, and depression.

The normal purpose of mediated communication should be as a conduit to a real relationship and creative communication—not as a substitute for real communication. Mediated or broadcast communication is, in reality, an impoverished communication. Humanity is the message, not the medium. Marshal MacLuhan was wrong; the proliferation of electronic media will not turn the planet into a global village, but into a global psychiatric hospital. The preference of mediated communication to real relational communication has become a pathological tendency of modern electronic culture.

Mediated communication reinforces isolation and schizophrenic tendencies within society. Purely cybernetic feedback allows adjustments within a system, forming a sort of endless circle. Relational communication, (short-term feedbacks + real communication), on the other hand, is the source of creative communication. This type of communication doesn't form a circle, but a spiral, allowing escape from the system.

Real life is here and now; between people is where creative communication can happen. Relational and creative communication are necessary to the advent of a communicative society. A new species of professionals must be created: The social, relational, and creative communication specialists. Creative communication will be possible when media returns to its originally intended role as a means, not an end—that is, an intermediary that allows real human encounters.

The 12 Laws

The following 12 laws of relational communication are my attempt to create a checklist that will allow us to diagnose our styles of communication. The less we respect these laws, the more impoverished our marketing communication will be, and the more hostility and violence we will generate as a result.

The emphasis on the content of our marketing communications is a distraction (from the Latin *dis-traer,* to pull aside, to take to another track). What matters most is form—the structure or system of communication.

The following 12 laws are designed to create awareness of our unconscious communication systems and the steps needed to transform our impoverished communication into real, creative communication. Today's marketers, advertisers, publicists, sales managers, and journalists have a responsibility to redefine their professions. There is more at stake than simply selling products or entertaining people.

The world of mediated communication is experiencing a crisis, as people no longer believe the media; television is perceived as a major inducement of violence. The more advanced communication technology becomes, the more backward our education system becomes. The "TV parent" does a poor job of teaching duties and responsibilities to our children.

All those who must communicate professionally are particularly concerned. Creative communication is crucial for business; absence of creative communication could have catastrophic consequences for our children as well as for ourselves. What is going wrong with the way we approach media and communication, values and education, growth and ambition, information and entertainment?

These 12 laws explain and organize the concept of communication between partners—between individuals and groups, organizations, or even nations.

Three Laws of Preparation

The first three laws of relational communication deal with the preparation necessary for meaningful two-way communication.

1. The desire to communicate must be manifest by at least one partner. I can choose to send information to someone who never asked me for anything; usually, I would get a very poor response rate. However, if I first communicate my desire to communicate, I introduce the possibility for the other party to say yes, no, or maybe. In any case, he or she is thus already communicating with me. This expression of initial desire is what is required to connect. Once the connection is established, further messages and information can be sent. Many people send information without first having established this type of connection, thinking the content of their communication is sufficient. This what I call "aggressive communication," and it rarely works very successfully.

2. You don't know if communication has been established until you receive feedback. The content of this feedback is irrelevant as long as it is there, since refusal is still a form of communication. Thus, once a connection has been established, further communication can occur, even if it is nothing more than an attempt to get the other person to change his or her mind. Establishing any connection is the main priority.

3. The relational communication requires the recognition of the other as an integral (equal) partner who is given the right to refuse

the communication. After a day of hard work, I'm finally back home having dinner with my family, and the telephone rings. It's another call from a telephone company trying to get me to switch long-distance carriers. The conversation usually goes like this:

"Hello, this is Mary calling from AT&T. Are you Dr. *Ratallo*, or *Rapallo*? I don't know if you are aware that you can save 25 percent on your telephone bill. Are you aware of that?"

First, Mary doesn't really know my name, so I don't feel like my identity has been acknowledged. Second, who is Mary from AT&T? The CEO's wife, or the cleaning lady? Third, she goes directly into the message that she wants to deliver without first finding out if I want to communicate with her. Of course, she tries to get my attention by asking me a question about something that is supposed to sound good to me, similar to a door-to-door salesman sticking his foot in my door; I just hate it. I usually give this kind of answer: "My name is not *Rapallo*, and this is not the right time to call me. Why don't you try tomorrow morning during office hours. Thank you!"

I want to be acknowledged as an active subject, not just a receptor or target of information. Being a "target" implies that I am no longer a partner in a relational, creative communication, but more like a passive prey. Two partners who really communicate know each other and acknowledge each others' identity. This opens the door to personal involvement and commitment.

One of the first goals of communication is therefore not to transmit information, but rather to verify and prove identity, then expressing the desire to communicate and giving the other person the opportunity to accept or reject communication.

Three Laws of Implication

The next three laws of relational communication deal with the implications and commitments that must be manifest by the participants.

4. Relational communication requires that each partner use the language of implication and commitment while excluding abstractions and generalities. When AT&T calls me, the caller inevitably uses language full of abstractions and generalities. Mary could be anybody; she doesn't tell me who she actually is. When I read the dialogue between the press and the government, or the war between men and women, I realize that we are falling into the trap of using dehumanizing language. The danger is not only one of generalization, but is also one of indirect involvement.

5. Creative communication is, in itself, an unpredictable event. The outcome of creative, relational communication is unforeseeable because two separate people come together in this unique moment to create as they communicate. This creation is only possible in the present. Any effort to locate the action yesterday, today, or tomorrow is an effort to transform a person into an object, to create a distance, to destroy the involvement and the commitment necessary to the relationship. Think of the difference in impact between watching the Super Bowl live and watching a replay the next day. When we already know the outcome, we are less involved, and we experience less excitement.

6. Creative communication represents a high-risk situation for each partner. Standing up as an individual carries more risk than belonging to a group; likewise, the present is more risky than the past or the future. Individual involvement and commitment are proportional to the risk taken by each partner in a relationship.

Three Laws of Identity

The next three laws deal with identity and honesty—full disclosure.

7. The identity of each partner has to be specified before the beginning of the relationship and explored more in depth during the relationship. If I'm sick, I might want to see a doctor. When I arrive, I declare my identity. When I speak to the doctor, I tell him where it hurts. Also, I want to be sure that I'm speaking to the right kind of doctor. If I'm telling a urologist about my a heart problem, I might just be in the wrong place. So, before a relationship can form, we have to be sure of each other's identities—what kind of patient am I, what kind of doctor is he, and is this the right match?

8. Each partner's goal must be clear and openly disclosed to the other. The goal of a doctor is to make a living by curing people. The goal of a company is to make a profit. When goals are not clear, things get confusing and sometimes destructive. People are not always aware of what they are after, or what other people are after. To clarify goals is a crucial part of any creative relationship. Because relationships are creative, it is also important to acknowledge that goals might change along the way.

9. Each partner must be informed by the other of all changes or transformations of identity or goals that occur during a relationship—especially if the change is a consequence of the creative relationship itself. If I'm sick and it hurts, I want that to change. If my back is hurting and the doctor manipulates it so that it doesn't hurt anymore, I have to tell him. My identity has changed; I'm okay now. Most of the time, however, the only feedback the doctor gets is that I'm not showing up anymore. He doesn't know if this is because I'm cured, dead, or went to see another doctor.

Three Laws Related to the Environment

The final three laws of relational communication deal with environmental factors.

10. The creative relationship cannot be separated from the whole communication environment. It is impossible to isolate a communication from its environment. We are a structure inside a structure inside another structure. Speaking to an actor after a play is not the same as speaking to her while she is on stage performing. Although this is an obvious example, most of the time we are not aware of the more subtle changes in environment around us. For example, speaking about divorce statistics to someone who just got out of a bad marriage might bring back painful memories.

11. Creative communication can be amplified by a supportive field, minimized by a contrary field, or simply received in a neutral field. If a tourist is murdered in Florida, the impact of that event depends on the field. If it happens to be the 20th murder of a vacationer in just six months, the impact on tourism in that area will be dramatic. If it is an isolated case, the impact will be different. If we are in the middle of a fire and I tell you where the fire exit is, you'll pay attention. However, if there is no fire and you are watching the news on TV, I have very little chance of catching your attention. In creative communication, timing is everything. In other words, a positive field is necessary for successful communication; a neutral field will not do, and a negative field might even be dangerous. So, recognizing the nature of a field is crucial.

12. A field can be complete or incomplete. An incomplete field asks for communication that will complete its structure. The situation is similar to a biological imbalance. Some element is missing—for example, sugar in our blood—and we feel the need to eat. Likewise, a partial field demands completion; unfinished business can haunt us forever.

Mediated Communication

When we use a medium to communicate with other people, we have to know the nature of the medium and how it transforms the communication. All mediums have archetypes. In addition to discovering the archetypes for various products, services, and concepts, I have also uncovered archetypes for several media.

Each medium is like a color. What we get at the end of a communication is the color of the message plus the color of the medium. Suppose the color for TV is red, and the color for radio is blue. If we broadcast the same yellow message on TV and on the radio, we obviously cannot expect to see the same outcome. At the end we will have orange on TV (yellow + red) and green on the radio (yellow + blue). If a message is blue and communication is done via radio (yellow), the result is green. If the message is sent out on TV instead (red), the result is purple. The implications are clear. Your "blue" messages to your potential customer has now become green or purple. The two messages, both different from the intended "blue" message, can also be confusing or contradictory. As a result, people don't buy the product. Those who believe they can deliver the same message through various media don't understand the basic identity of the media they are using.

Through archetypal discoveries, we have found that the imprinting moment of each medium is very different, thereby creating a different logic of emotion for each medium. Media are message conveyors, and different media are most appropriate for different messages.

Radio was the first medium to be imprinted. As children, many listened to the radio in the kitchen, while their mothers were preparing food or feeding them. Thus, radio is the most dramatic of all the media studied. Radio is most often live and therefore very immediate, helping explain why several people committed suicide when Orson Wells announced on radio that the Martians were coming. Radio is associated with drama (current events) and satisfies a short attention span. It is generally a secondary activity, listened to while doing something else.

Television is often a family thing, where parents and children gather to watch a show. If radio stimulates imagination and inner visualization, television is image. People will keep watching even if the sound goes off, but will not keep listening if the image disappears. The television imprint is associated with excitement, drama, and sensuality, but also with the enjoyment of a collective experience: a child experiencing something in the company of parents. As with radio, TV's credibility factor is far lower than a newspaper's. Advertising agencies have consciously used these findings to orient their campaigns most effectively.

Newspaper means exclusion, as opposed to TV's association with circular integration. Father is reading and wants peace. Since he represents authority, the child has to wait. The imprint of newspapers is very different, and it comes later in a child's life. Understandably, the newspaper's credibility factor is high compared to radio and television.

Magazines. The imprint of magazines comes still later in life. It is linked to privacy, to the need to be alone and savor its contents. Magazines are also associated with refinement and narcissism. Magazines enable one to experience such sensations again and again, for they are kept around the house, to be read in one's spare time, and thus have a relatively long shelf life.

Billboards. Knowing this archetype explains the success of the Marlboro man. Billboards can have an immediate, emotional impact.

Movies. Nowhere else but in Hollywood, California, have American cultural archetypes assumed such importance. Here we see archetypes such as the underdog, the preacher, the lonesome cowboy, the frontiersman, the person who goes from rags to riches, and the mistress. American films are full of these constantly repeated, recognizable cultural archetypes. They exemplify American behavior and American "mental highways" so vividly that it is difficult to assess which came first—the films or the myths. Hollywood also illustrates the quintessentially American delight in creating heroes only to destroy them. In America in general, as in Hollywood, the "rituals of success" cannot escape from the "rituals of humiliation." In films, tycoons go from extreme power and wealth to precarious obscurity. Similarly, in America at large, the sagas of Jimmy Swaggart and Jim Bakker, along with the ups and downs of Donald Trump, correspond to an overwhelmingly strong imprint related to money: it is not for enjoyment, but for accumulation. It is more praiseworthy to have made and lost a fortune several times than to have attempted nothing—a very American view reflected in countless movies. Knowing the movie archetype explains the success of the movie "Titanic."

Internet. To break the code of the Internet, we first need to understand the essence of what we are saying just by using the Internet. The Internet discovery process uncovers how the Internet is imprinted, what its code and logic of emotion are, and how the code and logic of emotion should be applied when using it to communicate messages. Is your product, service, or concept compatible with the Internet archetype? What are your chances of success using this medium? How should your communication be adapted to fit the Internet archetype?

The challenge is to understand the underlying structure that would create the platform needed to be successful at marketing on the Internet. To succeed, we need to understand the relevant reference system already imprinted in people's minds.

Over the past five years, the Internet has emerged as an important medium for businesses and consumers. During this time, it has grown to reach 30 percent of all homes, making it the fastest growing medium in history. Rapid growth will continue, as countless numbers of businesses take advantage of the millions of customers already online. This past year alone, there were $100 billion of transactions conducted via the Internet, ranging from computer hardware and software to books and CDs. Until recently, consumers were wary of exchanging sensitive information on the net. This slowed the growth of e-commerce, but the success of Amazon.com, Dell Computers, CISCO, and Barnes and Noble indicates that attitudes are changing. These companies, already doing millions of dollars of business daily, provide clear evidence that the consumer views the Internet as a platform for commerce.

As a result, many business will add e-commerce capabilities to their Web sites over the coming years. Today, most Fortune 500 companies have Internet sites, but only 15 percent offer transnational capabilities. Most will try to employ what they know about their customers from traditional sources even though the Internet has its own culture and distinct characteristics; once again, learning what sort of archetypes are associated with the net will be the only successful way of approaching online advertising.

Electronic communication tools may change the way people communicate with each other, but they *will not* change the nature of people's communication. When there is a filter in the communication (such as a telephone or computer), the communication is never complete. If you don't see or hear the person, you miss voice inflections and facial expression. Although there is less risk in mediated communication, the communication is poorer and there is also less fun, less productivity, less creativity, and less quality in the relationship.

Mediated communication with customers and employees will lead to frustration, dissatisfaction, and possibly aggression. Face-to-face communication relieves frustration and fulfills the human need to interact with each other. Many managers have told me, "Now that we have teleconferencing and e-mail, we don't need to travel to meet clients." These people don't understand the purpose of mediated communication: to help establish the quality of the relationship. It is not a substitute for face-to-face communication. A lot of work can be done over the phone or on the computer before two people meet in person—and thus increase the quality of the relationship when they meet. Distance is no longer a problem. People can contact each other across the country or across the world.

Instead of new technology replacing quality relationships, new technology frees us to pursue them. We can be more selective in our relationships. We don't have anymore alibis or excuses not to have quality relationships. We can use technology to enhance our relationships. For example, Ritz-Carlton hotels use computers to store information about customers, such as when they request wake-up calls and what newspapers they read. Employees use this information to have direct, personal relationship with their customer right away. Technology changes daily, but loyalty has existed for centuries. Building a company around technology is difficult. Building a company on loyalty and using technology to help achieve this value is the right way to go.

Again, the more we observe these 12 laws of relational communication, the more effective our communication with our stakeholders will be, especially our marketing communication with our customers.

Chapter 4

Archetypology: the Study of Relationships

"I do not believe in things, I believe in relationships." —George Braque

Although you may think that archetypology—the study of relationships—has little to do with sales and marketing, I would argue that it is the essence of marketing. Archetypology studies the relationships among the forces of a culture and the system or structure that organizes these forces into the field of tensions necessary for the culture to survive. Archetypology does not study the musical notes, but the space between the notes; it does not study the vocabulary, but the grammar and the syntax that organize the words.

Men and women are "language animals." Our dealings with the world are characterized by the structuring and differentiating operations that are most clearly manifest in language. We organize things into systems by which meaning can be transmitted. Archetypology looks for an underlying system rather than individual causes, thus making possible a fuller understanding of human experience. Objects, then, are defined by their relationships with one another.

If language is a system of signs and conventions, the union between a form and an idea, we could say that the object of cultural archetypology is the development of a relationship between the biological need and the cultural forces that address this need. I am interested in the forms taken by these forces and the tensions they create. These forms are what we call cultural archetypes.

The biological need for survival is the central element of culture. If cultures do not successfully address this biological need, they will disappear.

Each culture not only perceives the world differently, but also articulates and organizes the world differently. Cultures and their languages do not simply name existing categories, they articulate their own in a system of relationships. This system gives meaning to the categories; each category can only be understood through its relationship with others.

We can't understand what "woman" means in a culture without understanding the relationships of women with other cultural categories, such as "men," "children," "work," "home," "violence," and "minority," to name a few. Any of these categories can only be understood within a system that includes all the others. Work cannot be understood without studying its relationship to money, personal achievement, family, home, and taxes. We cannot treat the sign as an autonomous entity, but must see it as part of a system.

In linguistics, for example, we can't understand what the French word "fleuve" means without understanding its distinction from and relation to the term "rivière." We might want to translate them respectively as "stream" and "river." However, a different concept is involved in English than in French. The signified "stream" differs from "river" solely in terms of size, whereas a "fleuve" differs from a "rivière" not because it is necessarily smaller, but because it flows into the sea, while a "rivière" does not. The relation between "fleuve" and "rivière" in French represents a different concept than the relation between "stream" and "river" in English. Thus, we cannot explain the French concept of "rivière" without reference to a "fleuve."

A system of forces is also made up of units whose value depends on their relationships with one another. Each unit's most precise characteristic is that it is what the others are not. For example, in the game of chess, the basic units are king, queen, rook, knight, bishop, and pawn. The shape of the pieces and their material form are of no importance. The king may be of any size and shape, as long as we can distinguish it from other pieces. Moreover, the two rooks need not be of identical size and shape, so long as they can be distinguished from the other pieces. If a piece is lost from a chess set, we can replace it with any other object, provided that that object will not be confused with those representing pieces of a different value.

Likewise, in a cultural system, there are only differences and relationships between elements or units. This is why a culture is independent of the individuals who are part of it.

Every element can only be defined by its position in the system, and is representative of the whole system that gives it its identity. Non-coffee drinkers tell us a lot about coffee drinkers; men tell us a lot about women, children about parents, and vice versa.

Cultural forces and archetypes are forms rather than substances, defined by the relationships they have with other forces within the cultural system that give them their identities.

Archetypes are what we assimilate when we learn a culture—a set of forms or practices that the culture deposits in those who belong to the same community, the same cultural system, and the same language system.

In analyzing a culture as a system of forces, we are not describing characters, actions, speech, or acts, but determining the units, the forces, and their rules of combination that make up a cultural system—that is, the cultural grammar and syntax. The culture is a system of forces in which the only essential element is the relationship between biological needs and the way forces pre-organize the cultural answers to the biological needs.

Two Perspectives

One can conduct a synchronic study of language (study the linguistic system in a particular state, without reference to time), or a diachronic study of language (study its evolution in time). One can also distinguish between a synchronic study of cultural archetypes (a study of the cultural system of forces in a particular state without reference to time) and a diachronic study of cultural archetypes (a study of their evolution in time).

One might study why some people shake hands when they meet, or how far apart they keep their bodies, comparing the results to those of another culture.

Or, one might study why, in the Western world, a man should always give his left arm to the lady he is escorting, especially in the street, comparing that tradition to that of the Japanese woman who is always supposed to walk behind the man she is accompanying (synchronic study). Examining the origins of these traditions might also prove very revealing (diachronic study).

Studying the Relationship

In studying language, linguists explore two types of relationships. On the one hand, there are those relationships that produce distinct, alternative terms (opposition); on the other hand, there are the relationships between units that combine to form sequences. In a linguistic sequence, a term's value depends not only on the contrast between it and others that might have been chosen in its stead, but also on it relations with the term that precedes and follows it in sequence. The former associative relations are now generally called *paradigmatic*. The latter are labeled as *syntagmatic*. Syntagmatic relations define combinatorial possibilities, or the relation between elements that might combine in a sequence. Paradigmatic relations reflect the opposition between elements that can replace one another.

One could speak of paradigmatic and syntagmatic relations between both forces and words. For example, the word "friend" has a paradigmatic relationship with words such as "partner," "dictator," and "professor." A syntagmatic relationship exists between "friend" and its combinatorial possibilities, such as "friendship," "friendly," "friendliness," "friendless," etc.

Culture, like language, is form and not substance. Its elements have only contrastive and combinatorial properties. Culture is not the result of individual behavior, but rather behavior is made possible by a collective social system of active forces that individuals have assimilated.

To explain an action, an individual, or a special behavior is to relate it to the underlying system of forces that makes it possible. This action is then explained as a manifestation of that system. Why do particular individuals commit suicide? Their suicides are manifestations of a weakening in social bond. Crime, too, is a manifestation of the weakening of a certain system of forces defining criminals; our society has switched from a system based on duty and shame to a new one whose forces are organized around rights and victims.

The reasons we do what we do can be discovered not only in the past, but also in the present functioning of our unconscious, both individual and collective. The unconscious becomes the space where any antecedents that have an explanatory function are located.

Structural explanation relates actions to a system of forces—the cultural magnetic field—that includes norms and rules of language, the collective representation of society, and the mechanism of a physical economy. The purpose of the "human sciences" is to explain meaning in terms of a system of forces that escape our conscious grasp, much the same way that the speaker of a language is not consciously aware of the physiological and grammatical systems he uses, although his judgments and perceptions are explained in their terms.

As the subject is broken down into its component forces, it appears more and more as a construct or as a result of systems of forces.

Language speaks through us; even the idea of personal identity emerges through a culture's speech. The self comes to exist through a succession of imprinting experiences that are all fully pre-organized by the cultural system into which we are born.

If a culture is a system of differences in which all forces are defined solely by their relationship to one another, we should look for these differences when exploring the imprint created by a concept or word. We should look for the continuum of variation, for it is in the nature of forces to create tensions (and the sum of these tensions creates the systems).

These forces are organized in axial, or binary, opposition. Each distinctive feature involves a choice between two terms of an opposition that displays a differential property. The use of binary opposition to describe structures is not simply a methodological device, but a reflection of the nature of language and culture; this is why we must be careful as to what is considered an opposition. What might form an opposite in one culture might not in another. Thus, in studying a relationship between two forces, we must accept that our definition of an opposite might have to be redefined. The relationship between Yin and Yang is not the same as the relationship between rich and poor, or between beach and mountain. The meanings of these terms are culturally determined.

Axes do not have to be made of classically opposite forces, in a logical sense; we must accept the logic of emotion of the culture. For example, what is deemed in America as a prohibition of something might be seen in France as a granting of privilege. Each culture has its own logic and its own grammar that are reflected in its axis. This is why no culture can be judged using the axis of another.

Binary opposites are the most natural and economical codes. They are the first operations all children learn as they develop language skills. Thus, all of the different systems of thought, language, cultural forces, norms, values and laws are deeply interrelated.

From Matter to Forces

In his book *Science and the Modern World,* Alfred North Whitehead demonstrates that because new scientific discoveries produce so many complexities, fundamental shifts in perspective are necessary if various disciplines are to come to terms with themselves and their objects.

Physicists discovered that it was difficult to explain electricity and electromagnetic phenomena in terms of discrete units of matter and their movement. The solution seemed to be the reverse of the problem: instead of taking the matter as the prime and trying to define the laws governing its behavior, they took electrical energy as prime and defined matter in terms of electromagnetic forces. This change in perspective led to the discovery of new scientific objects. For example, they learned that an electron was not a positive entity in the traditional sense; it was rather the product of a field of forces, a node in a system of relations, and that it did not exist independently of these relations.

What Whitehead calls the "materialism" of the 19th century, the empiricism that grants ontological primacy to objects, gives way, he submits, to a theory of relativity based on the primacy of relations. "On the materialist theory," Whitehead writes, "there is material that endures. On the organic theory, the only endurance are structures of activity. Emphasis falls on the structures. The event is what it is by reason of the unification within itself of a multiplicity of relationships. Outside these systems of relations, it is nothing."

The primacy of relationships and systems of relationships is the paradigmatic shift that allows us to move into modern thinking. It is *a shift in focus from object to relations*. Relationships create and define objects; it is the relationship that is creative, not the individual. Similarly, biologically, no human can create a new human being without a "relation" of some sort with another human being of the "opposite" sex.

George Braque stated, "I do not believe in things, I believe in relationships." From Saussure and linguistics, to Durkheim and sociology, to Freud and psychology, to Whitehead and physics, and to Braque and painting, we can see the paradigmatic shift that has taken place: moving from the objects of science to the relationships among those objects. Social life and culture are thus products of the relationships existent in a grand field of forces.

For your marketing communications to be effective, you need to shift your focus from objects (products or things) to relationships, as customers seek connections with organizations that reinforce their identities.

SECRET 2:

CULTURES ALSO HAVE AN UNCONSCIOUS: Cultural archetypes have the power to make or break your marketing, sales, or public relations plan.

The power of the archetype is proportional to the power of the imprint—and this is proportional to the strength of the emotion attached to the imprint. Since cultural archetypes determine how people perceive their world and react to it, understanding cultural archetypes is critical to any marketing success in this multi-cultural world. Marketing intelligence depends on an organization's ability to adapt to its environment.

Chapter 5

The Power of Cultural Archetypes

If I get people to laugh, I know I'm right.

Each culture has a collective cultural unconscious—a pool of shared imprints that guides the behaviors of each member of that culture. The collective cultural unconscious present in the American mind is different from that in, say, the Japanese or French mind.

An imprinting is a rapid learning process that takes place early in life and establishes an unconscious behavior pattern. For example, if a wooden box with wheels is shown to a newly hatched duckling at a critical time, it will form an attachment to that object, taking it for its biological mother. Imprinting occurs only during a critical time period, after which it is difficult or impossible to imprint. The unconscious behavior patterns caused by imprints can be put into two categories: universal archetypes and cultural archetypes. The patterns or imprints that enable people to meet their biological survival needs are universal archetypes. Imprints that enable people to better understand human conditions are cultural archetypes.

Cultural archetypes determine how members of a culture perceive their world and react to it. They can be compared to genetics. When two human beings create offspring, they create a human being; they cannot create a fish or a bird because of their genetic codes. This concept also applies to culture. When two Americans have a baby, they have an American baby, not a French or German baby. Since no cultural chromosome exists, parents must transmit their culture to their babies through cultural archetypes.

Every element of a culture has an archetype, and members of a culture interpret that archetype by using a code. The cultural archetype and its code are like a lock and its combination: we must have all of the right numbers, in the proper order (the code), to open the lock (the archetype). Since archetypes and their codes exist at the unconscious level, we need a process to decode them. Likewise, the subconscious nature of archetypes also means that members of a culture can't decide what they should be.

To know how archetypes are formed, we must know how the brain functions. The brain is composed of billions of neurons. When a neurotransmitter passes a nervous impulse from one neuron to another (a synapse), a neural pathway—or a learning connection—is created. These pathways are reinforced through repetition.

Early in my career, I discovered that emotion is directly related to learning. Emotion is the energy that creates biologically released transmitters in the brain, thereby establishing these neural pathways. I ascertained this 25 years ago during my work with autistic children. Autistic children have difficulty learning because they don't experience emotion, or they experience it in a different way than the average child does. For example, in the movie *Rain Man*, the autistic character, Raymond, doesn't feel emotion when he is in an elevator and a beautiful girl kisses him. She asks him, "What do you feel?" and he replies, "Wet." When his brother says goodbye at the end of the film, Ray is already playing with his video games, oblivious to the fact that his brother is full of emotion.

Emotion is the crucial energy required for the imprinting of cultural archetypes and, in general, for learning. The stronger the emotion associated with an imprint, the stronger the archetype. Events imprinted with strong emotion at an early age are usually remembered forever. Once the archetype and its emotion are imprinted, repetition reinforces the neural pathway or mental highway, a process directly associated with memory. If a person begins losing memory, he usually loses the most recent memories first. He can't remember what he did with his glasses, but he does remember something that happened 20 years ago. The reason for this is that the 20-year-old memory involves more emotion and has been further reinforced, so its mental highway is better established.

Process of Revealing Archetypes and Codes

To discover cultural archetypes and their codes, I developed the archetype discovery process. It centers on 10 imprinting sessions that help participants remember their imprintings of the subject being studied. About 25 people attend each imprinting session. Participants are chosen based on the archetype. For example, if an American archetype is being studied, the 250 people would be at least second-generation Americans who spent the first 15 years of their lives in the United States and whose mother or primary caregivers spoke American English. Participants would be chosen from random locations throughout the United States.

I begin an imprinting session by introducing myself as an anthropologist from another planet sent to study the subject being researched, i.e., "cheese," in the tribe of Paris (or whatever city the session is conducted in). The participants are there to help me understand the concept of "cheese."

During the first hour, I lead a discussion of what "cheese" means to the participants. Rather than discussing types of cheese (i.e., Limburger), participants discuss their ideas and feelings about cheese (i.e., "I like the pungent smell of Limburger").

In the second hour, I use free association and storytelling exercises to learn about the unconscious dimensions, or latent structures, of cheese. In the final hour, I use relaxation techniques to get participants into an alpha mental state (wakeful relaxation) in order to help them remember their imprinting experiences involving cheese. When they come out of this state, they write down what they remember. For example, a participant might remember the first time she went to the farmer's market with her mother to buy cheese. The three-hour imprinting session is tape-recorded and transcribed. The transcript and imprinting stories are analyzed for structures and relationships—not for content.

When playing the piano, a melody can be played on one end of the keyboard or the other. Either way, the tune will be recognized as, for example, "Jingle Bells." Recognition of the melody obviously has nothing to do with exact notes, since the tune can be identified both ways. Notes are like the content of a melody. What a person really recognizes are the spaces between the notes; in other words, rhythm, or the way the notes are organized in relation to one another. In structural analysis, elements are not studied, but rather the forces that bind the different elements together.

Cultural Intelligence

Cultural archetypes enable participants to interact with their environment. Cognitive structure results from both biological maturation and cumulative experience. Likewise, cultural archetypes are the results of biological schemata, dependent on biological maturation of a child, as well as on the cumulative experience of a culture developed over centuries. Not only is cognitive structure affected by experience, but it also determines what can be experienced. Similarly, cultural cognition is not only affected by a culture's experience (such as a major war, a recession, a revolution), but it also determines what can be experienced by pre-organizing the way members of a given culture perceive reality. In other words, cultural cognition defines what is true for a given culture at a given time, according to that culture's tentative perception of reality.

Intelligence is accommodation and assimilation. If accommodation is modification of cognitive structure as a result of an experience that could not be assimilated, accommodation is roughly equivalent with learning. Cultures learn at a very slow, almost glacial pace. They take a long time to modify cultural archetypes. Assimilation, responding to a physical environment in accordance with existing cognitive structure, can be roughly equated with recognition of knowledge. Acceptance of cultural cognitive structure creates strong assimilation within a culture, and by using a cultural archetype, participants of a culture manage to become assimilated and be part of a culture.

Equilibrium is the innate need for balance between an organism and its environment, as well as within the organism itself. This primal need for balance motivates an organism to do whatever is necessary to regain balance. Equilibrium is also an invariant because it is present at all stages of intellectual development. In fact, it is actually responsible for continuous intellectual development. At certain times, cultures are in search of equilibrium, or a balance between what its members want or need and its environment.

Cultural intelligence tends to create optimal conditions for survival under existing circumstances. This type of intelligence is reached through adaptation to an environment. Over time, cultural archetypes are solidified or crystallized, even if existing circumstances change. This is called *senility*, or the senile stage of a culture.

I see different stages of cultures. In the beginning, a culture develops in relation to its biological needs as well as its environment, and it uses innate reflexes. Secondly, a culture begins rudimentary concept formation. The third stage is concrete operation, when a culture uses internalized actions or thoughts. Finally, there are formal operations where a culture can thoroughly ponder hypothetical situations. In more advanced cultures, these hypothetical situations have been formalized into rules and rituals.

Intelligence can be understood as existing between two forces: first, perpetuation and repetition of structure, and second, the need for accommodation, or the integration of new learning and new experiences that cannot be assimilated into existing cultural cognitive structures. The intelligence of a culture can thus be understood as its ability to accommodate. If a culture is incapable of adapting its cognitive structure, it is in a "senile" phase, and the end of the culture is near.

Several cultures, such as the Roman, Greek, British, Japanese, Chinese, and American cultures, reflect different phases of this process. At various times in every culture's history, a certain rigidity will appear, reflected in bureaucracy and an overall cultural slow-down.

Another way cultural archetypes are crystallized is that they are made sacred through a ruler, a dogma, or an ideology. When nobody can challenge the cultural archetype, accommodation becomes impossible, leading to rigidity. Again, this is the beginning of senility, and the mark of a culture that will soon disappear.

By viewing cultures as biological entities, we can understand where they come from, where they are going, and how they disappear. We can also comprehend the process by which a culture acquires knowledge. Likewise, intelligence should be perceived not just as individual, but as a cultural trait, or in other words, as all acts that tend to help a culture's survival under existing circumstances.

Marketing Intelligence

Just as cultural intelligence is always related to a culture's ability to adapt to its environment, marketing intelligence depends on an organization's ability to adapt to its environment.

Progressive equilibrium (a living organism constantly seeking a balance between itself and its environment) means changing as a result of maturation and experience. Thus, a balance can never be absolute but rather must be a circumstance. As circumstances change, optimal balance must change accordingly. Cultures should constantly be searching for a new equilibrium, and marketers must lead the way.

Strong, rigid cultures are most likely too close to senility to adapt; young cultures have a better chance of survival. Cultures such as the Japanese, Russian, British, and French are less likely to adapt in this constantly changing world than young, adolescent cultures, such as the United States, which is constantly in search of its identity and thus views change as good. The relative lack of sophistication of the American culture means that it can be re-balanced, moving quickly from one equilibrium to another. The American culture can therefore accommodate, whereas older cultures can only assimilate.

Do archetypes change as a result of biological maturation and sensory experience, or is that experience organized according to pre-organized abstract laws? I submit that neither of these notions is correct, and that we need to consider a third theory: *experience is pre-organized by the cultural archetype*. Biological factors partially determine how we see the world. For example, we have eyes on the front of our heads. This biological structure determines, to some degree, how we do many things. For example, we design cars around frontal, not rear vision.

The design of the human body is reflected in aesthetic creations, as well, such as the use of left/right symmetry and heart imagery.

Likewise, cultural structures also influence, in a more subjective manner, how we view the world. A culture's logic depends on its history and geography (time and space). We need to understand what stage a given culture is in, in order to understand how it (or its individual members) will react to various situations or stimuli. Many people judge cultures without taking into account what stage of growth it is in. Just as an individual is influenced by his physical or biological condition, he is also influenced by the cultural cognitive structures that are available to him at a given time.

Mental Highways

Mental highways refer to the mental connections that are imprinted and reinforced, and represent the collective "software" that people use to relate to and understand the world. By understanding these highways, we could predict how Americans would react, for example, to the disintegration of the Soviet Union, or to what happens in Russia today.

Knowing that the Japanese have a different cultural cognitive structure and different mental highways, we could anticipate that they would react differently to the same events. The Japanese culture is already in a rigid phase, in that it can only assimilate what doesn't challenge its structure. In other words, that culture reacts in a very traditional way. The American culture, on the other hand, is very open and adolescent, without a completely fixed identity. As a result, it can accommodate, change, and modify its cultural cognitive structure.

We have often seen the "sleeping giant structure" at work in American culture. Americans are slow to react and take a long time to decide what they will do, reflecting that culture's absence of a strong identity. Thus, they waited until December 1941 and Pearl Harbor to decide to declare war against Japan and Germany, an event necessary to wake the "sleeping giant."

The Japanese, on the other hand, tend to attack without warning, as they did in 1905 against the Russians, and in 1941 against the Americans, reflecting a very different cultural archetype, or quality of intelligence. The way the Japanese reacted to the economic crisis in America and the conclusions they drew—that this situation was brought about because American workers were lazy, as well as because of the "melting pot" make-up of the United States—is again a reflection of their own cultural archetypes. The Japanese were incapable of adapting their archetypes in order to accept the fact that they were partners with the United States. They could not understand American principles, and thus remained ignorant to the fact that by making these declarations, they went against American cultural archetypes. Clearly, Japan can only assimilate, while the United States can accommodate.

Verification of the Process

Sponsors of archetypal discoveries are actively involved in them. Representatives from sponsoring organizations form an "archetype team." Team members attend at least one imprinting session and three information-sharing meetings called "recap sessions." Four to six members of the "archetype team" form a "core team." The "core team" performs the planning and tasks involved in setting up the imprinting and recap sessions. Each member attends all 10 imprinting sessions and three recap sessions. The "core team" analyzes the data to discover hidden archetypes.

The people at Procter &Gamble helped me refine this process. When I started working with them, they showed great trust in what I was doing, but also helped me see that I needed to improve my program. I realized that team members needed to feel ownership of the code, especially when it challenged what they did before.

Some people are skeptical about cultural archetypes—some even challenge my work. My research, though, is legitimized in three ways: 1) archetypes are based on biology; they are a response to biological needs; 2) several archetypal discoveries have been quantified and verified by research from independent groups; and 3) acting on the results of my discoveries has yielded benefits for many clients, such as Procter & Gamble, AT&T, and the California Forestry Association. Many might disagree with or be surprised by my approach, but hundreds of studies over the past 25 years have proven that it works.

For me, it is not an extensive clientele list, quantitative studies, or biology-based research that best verifies my work; instead, it's people being able to laugh at themselves and at their cultures. I'll often comment about a particular code, and everyone chuckles spontaneously, reacting to gut feeling. When this happens again and again, this pattern of repetition becomes, in its own right, verification. If I get people to laugh, I know I'm right.

Intelligent marketers will pick up signals of cultural archetypes from comedians, journalists, politicians, and advertisers and put these codes to work in their efforts to move their products and services along the mental highways already paved in each culture.

CHAPTER 6

THE LOGIC OF EMOTION

The reptilian always wins.

Understanding a cultural code includes comprehending the emotions used to imprint its first connection in the brain. These emotions follow a logic; they do not occur at random. We have seen how powerful it is to understand the window in time, or the moment and age, at which imprinting occurs. The order of the emotional energy that fires up the mental highways is what I call *the logic of emotion*.

Emotions provide the energy necessary to create an imprint. After emotional experiences forge mental highways, these highways will be unconsciously traveled and re-traveled throughout our lives. Each time they are used, we re-experience the same kind of emotion that was originally used to imprint them. Understanding this logic of emotion is an integral part of decoding the cultural mind and breaking into the collective unconscious. This process requires logic, because the imprinting moment creates a specific order and rationale that can be decoded and understood. Emotion comes into play because the emotional energy that creates the imprint dictates the new logical order.

When experiencing emotion, we use three parts of the brain: 1) the primitive, or reptilian brain, which deals mainly with instinctive and automatic behaviors; 2) the amygdalian brain, home of the sympatic system, which is the center of the emotional world; and 3) the cortex, where conscious thoughts, language, and vision are located.

The reptilian brain mainly deals with instinct and basic survival and reproduction. The reptilian brain tells you when you need to eat, sleep, go to the bathroom, remove yourself from a harmful situation, or perform another task needed for survival. The reaction time of the reptilian brain is extremely quick, almost instantaneous. For example, when you touch something hot, your first instinct is to pull away. This message to pull away can be described as a "reptilian hot button". You have a reptilian hot button for everything you do. When a hot button is activated, you do something out of instinct.

The limbic system deals mainly with emotion. Emotion is a vital part of the learning process because the way in which the brain imprints relies on emotion. The brain is composed of billions of neurons. When a neurotransmitter passes a nervous impulse from one neuron to another (a synapse), a neutral pathway or learning connection is created. These pathways are reinforced through repetition. Emotion produces the neurotransmitters that enable this learning process. The ability to learn is key to intelligence. People with no emotions have problems with intelligence. In the limbic system there is a logic of emotion, meaning there is logic behind the particular emotion that you are experiencing. The logic of emotion is related to the way (the order) in which the emotion was initially imprinted in the unconscious. For example, when you were born, your parents took care of your reptilian needs by feeding you, loving you, and protecting you. Thus, the emotion of being loved and cared for—which can generally be described as a warm, fuzzy feeling or simply feeling "good"—is directly related to meeting biological needs. So now when someone takes care of your needs, you feel good.

The third part of the brain, the cortex, deals with intelligence. The cortex is completely formed only after age seven. Younger children are unable to grasp the concept of conversation or quality. If a child is older than seven, however, he or she will likely look at you and say "Why are you asking? Do you think I'm dumb?" The intellect is a luxury. A person first needs to survive in order to think. If your basic instincts are not working and you forget to eat or drink, you will be dead. So the priority in the functioning of the brain is the reptilian brain, followed by the emotion of the limbic system, and then the intellect of the cortex.

Most energy or pressure to act comes from the reptilian brain. How the pressure is dealt with, however, depends on the intellectual cortex. Every day of your life, you experience pressure. Pressure is a need at a certain time. It can be the need for anything, from the need to go to the bathroom to the need to gain control. You can deal with this pressure in several ways. You can "express" yourself, which means to put the pressure to the exterior or the outside. When you express, you want to accomplish something. One way to express yourself is through sublimation, such as making money, creating art, or writing books. Another form of expression is violence. Rather than express yourself, you can choose repression, keeping the pressure inside. Repressed people can become depressed or violent. When a person has a strong pressure coming from the reptilian brain and strong repression from the cortex; this person will become neurotic.

The ideal situation is when all three parts of the brain are in sync. When they are in harmony, the person will know where the pressure is coming from (the reptilian brain), feel good about it (the limbic system), and look for the means to achieve expression (the cortex). When biology, the culture, and the persona are in sync—when your biological scheme, your cultural archetype, and your personal script are together—the ideal environment in which to live and work is produced.

Emotional Imprints

How do we inherit our culture? Each culture has a collective unconscious—a pool of shared imprints that guide the behaviors of members. Again, an imprinting is a rapid learning process that takes place early in life and establishes an unconscious behavior pattern. Imprinting occurs only during a critical time period, after which it is difficult or impossible to imprint. The unconscious behavior patterns caused by imprinting can be put into two categories: universal archetypes and cultural archetypes. Universal archetypes are those imprints that enable us to meet our biological needs. Cultural archetypes are those that enable us to understand human conditions. As we assimilate language, cultural archetypes, and the emotions associated with them, we assign different weights and values to the experiences. Some experiences slip from memory, but linger in the unconscious. These forgotten experiences help shape our conscious behaviors and thoughts. For example, our expectations of quality relationships stem directly from our cultural archetype. The first imprint we have of a relationship is the one we have with a mother and father; so our imprint of a quality relationship involves being nurtured and cared for. In business, customers expect companies to take care of their needs and look out for their well-being.

Because cultural archetypes are imprinted through emotion, they are primarily located in the second part of the brain, and are generally beyond our awareness. They are formed very early in life, and are thus more powerful than the intellectual and cortical activity of the brain. It is here that we experience emotionally what we must imprint in a certain order and at a certain time. This order then forms our mental highways.

A nation's laws express a level of systematization of its archetypal "grammar." This is why laws vary so much from one culture to another, or from one religion to another, and why they often seem outrageous to outsiders. How do we feel when female adulterers are stoned to death in the Middle East, or when teenagers are caned in Singapore for spraying paint on cars? How do other cultures feel when we release a woman after she castrates her husband, or when a jury can't reach a verdict for brothers who do not deny killing their parents in cold blood? These practices, whether we perceive them as right or wrong, are dictated by the logic of emotion for each culture's archetypes. Thus, the seeming "irrationality" of some actions can be understood if the archetypal code behind them is broken and the logic of emotion is revealed. The awareness of this logic and the axes and forces at work on an unconscious level should not be used to excuse behavior, but rather it can help allow for change on an effective level that doesn't offend a culture's archetypes.

Why Is the Logic of Emotion So Important?

Strong emotional imprints do not change quickly. Very few of us can see the relationship between our childhood experiences and our country's foreign policy. However, when we start viewing things in light of cultural archetypes, we can see the amazing consistency of cultural behaviors. The Americans warning their enemies before attacking is in keeping with American archetypes, whose logic of emotion necessitates being the moral, good guy.

Statistics on teenage pregnancy and violence in America, political orientation in France, or neo-Nazi activity in Germany take on new meaning when viewed in light of deep, unconscious archetypes. The only way to effectively change these statistics is to understand their archetypal roots and then work at the real problems.

Also, comparison between figures in other countries becomes less important, because these nations have another logic of emotion and use different mental highways, so we are no longer speaking about the same things, but rather comparing behaviors that do not belong in the same category.

Understanding codes and their corresponding logic of emotion is vital to cultural comprehension. The decoding process is not complete unless we understand the forces and tensions that archetypes create and the axes upon which our actions are organized.

The Archetype Axis

This axis is a crucial part of understanding the cultural unconscious. When we explore the cultural unconscious, we become aware of tensions; any tension can be visualized along an axis. The axes are derived from archetypes and their latent structures, and these axes thus vary among cultures. If collective behaviors are shaped permanently by these axes, we need to understand them. No foreign policy, global economic strategy, or multi-cultural marketing communications are possible without a deep understanding of why people behave the way they behave (the archetype) and what the possibilities are for the range of that archetype (the axis).

Axes are not opposites, paradoxes, or contradictions. Although the forces being organized might be dictionary opposites of one another, they do not have to be opposites; in fact, they really rarely are. For example, one American axis organizes the opposites of freedom and prohibition, while the corresponding axis in France concerns freedom and privilege, which do not have an opposite relationship. Forces must be present at the same time in order to be on the same axis, and it is only a matter of which force is currently latent and which is dominant that gives a situation a certain flavor. Forces need not be set in juxtaposition—they simply exist and organize.

In other words, different forces are different aspects of the same reality. In America, each time we speak about freedom, we are also speaking about prohibition. When the French, in the name of equality, claim to abolish all privileges, it's like the yin claiming to abolish the yang. These concepts need each other to exist; they define each other, and are part of the same reality.

Latent structures. Elements that define one another are often called "flip sides" or "shadow sides." The clinical term for this concept is "latent structures." In latent structures, one element is usually seen first, and the object that emerges second—the element of reality that is not consciously perceived, despite the fact that it is present—is the latent structure. My methodology reveals the latent structures of cultures. These could be just out of awareness, or hidden as a result of a process of rejection. Consciously rejected latent structures become cultural shadows. Today it is crucial to explore cultural shadows, because they tend to reappear during extreme times, such as wars, natural disasters, or economic cataclysms, and also manifest themselves as reactionary forces in the face of change. The study of latent structures is what will keep us from repeating historical mistakes we've already made.

The field of tension. Tensions have biological origins, and are sometimes expressed as needs. Each culture deals with these biological tensions differently. For example, one American axis is created by the tension between doing (as salvation), and procrastinating (as sin). This tension organizes our personal, political, social, and psychological lives.

Seven Laws of Axes

There can be any number of axes within a given culture (though some govern or inform others), and these axes are created by forces that do not need to fit into a set relationship. However, there are certain laws that govern the actions and patterns of a culture on the axes.

1. Attractors. In every culture, attractors are ideal goals or an ideal position on the axis that will bring equilibrium and rest. However, this position really represents immobility and eventual death, because there is no tension or call for movement. Our conscious minds need an attractor, or inner vision of peace and quietness. Our unconscious minds know, however, that life is movement, tension, and forces in action.

2. Pendulum. The pendulum law specifies that when we go in one direction, it does not mean the disappearance of the other end of that axis. The pendulum law is proof that both forces remain.

3. Length and range. Some cultures, such as American culture, are characterized by extremes. This means that their axes are very long; there is great distance between one force and another. Other cultures, like the British culture, are characterized by subtleties, and their axes are very short. The length and range of an axis translates into the possibility for a limited or vast range of movement.

4. Permanence. Do cultures change? How do they change? How quickly do they change? The fourth law of axes gives us some answers to these questions. Axes are an essential element of a culture; they do not change. They represent the fundamental organization of the forces in a culture. The axis of prohibition and freedom is a basic element of American culture; this axis will not change or disappear. What does change is which force (which end of the axis) is dominant and which is latent. During the 15 years of prohibition, the force of freedom was always present, but simply latent. The tension itself did not change, but the circumstances creating this tension changed over time.

5. Balance. For a culture to survive, the axes must be balanced. Over time, each force on an axis must have equal time share; an axis must keep moving. If an axis remains unbalanced for too long, it loses its tension, and the original culture dies.

6. Axis interrelation. A culture can have unlimited axes and archetypal manifestations, and these are all interrelated. Creativity relates to technology, technology to destruction, destruction to violence, and violence to religion. A culture is the result of a web of axes creating a complex system of forces similar to a magnetic field. Our lives consist of being permanently influenced by these tensions. The ways in which we are materialistic can only be understood through the ways in which we are idealistic.

If we consider any of these forces in isolation, we fall into the trap of stereotypes and clichés. Yes, the Japanese are humble, but they are also arrogant; polite, but also rude; hierarchical, but also independent. They are the unique mixture of these tensions and forces. To isolate any one force and analyze it without understanding its connection with the others is like trying to understand the function of blood without understanding the heart, lungs, and oxygen. Any element of a system draws meaning from its relationship with other elements. Can we know what a child is without understanding birth, aging, and dying? These elements are part of the system that we call life. And because life is made up of tension and movement, cultures also experience continual tension and movement.

7. Quaternities. This network of cultural tensions and forces does not work like a telephone system, but rather like the brain. There is parallel programming, or groups of forces that are activated simultaneously. The way to map the cultural mind is to map these tensions by using quaternities that show the field of tensions created by several forces, themselves organized on axes. A quaternity is formed by four components, similar to north, south, east and west.

These tensions are permanent, but what can change is the balance or position along their axis. At certain times, one is dominant and the other is latent; after a while this balance reverses itself for the good of a cultural personality. Quaternities allow us to measure and monitor such changes.

By understanding the laws that govern the patterns of various cultures, we learn the secrets of marketing in a multi-cultural world.

CHAPTER 7

EMOTIONAL IMPRINTS

Emotion is the energy that creates the mental highway.

Cultures, like individuals, have an unconscious that sculpts their thinking. The collective cultural unconscious can be distinguished from a personal unconscious, as well as from the universal unconscious common to us all.

The personal unconscious owes its existence to personal experience. It is made up of contents that have previously been conscious but then forgotten or repressed. The contents of the universal, or biological, unconscious have not been individually acquired, but rather owe their existence exclusively to heredity. Then, whereas the personal unconscious consists mostly of scripts, the contents of the universal unconscious are made up primarily of biological schemata.

The collective cultural unconscious is an indispensable correlate of the individual and universal unconscious, as it indicates definite mental forms that are common to members of the same culture.

In addition to our immediate conscious, which is of a thoroughly personal nature, and to our universal or impersonal nature, which is identical to all members of the same species, there exists a third psychic system that is inherited, but not congenital. It consists of pre-existent forms, cultural archetypes, that can only become conscious secondarily and that give definite form to certain contents of the psyche.

These archetypes are imprinted at various times in different cultures. Emotion is the energy used to perform this imprinting. Emotion follows a certain logic, order, or critical path, and a certain *logic of emotion* is unique to each culture. Once we break the code of this logic of emotion, we can understand the formula or recipe of this element of a cultural mind.

Archetypes are the unconscious cultural answers to biological tensions. Cultural archetypology addresses how various cultures, at different times and places, deal with survival—in other words, how cultural forces control, organize, and ritualize our basic biological needs.

We readily admit that we are highly influenced by our instincts, apart from the rational motivation of the conscious mind. Imagination, perception, and thinking are likewise influenced by inborn biological forces, but also by factors such as when and where we were born.

Also, just as species are biologically programmed to reproduce, cultures are likewise designed to perpetuate themselves. Thus, archetypes are actually an inherited mode of functioning available to all members of the same culture. They exist before the individual perceives anything, and must be present if experience is to be possible, just as language exists before the individual speaks, and must be present if speaking is to be possible. Archetypes are patterns of instinctive cultural behavior, transmitted unconsciously from one generation to another. Archetypes are also empty and purely formal; they are not determined by their content, but rather by their structure. In this respect, they correspond in every way to instincts that are also determined only by their form.

What we are is a combination of our individual unconscious, universal unconscious, and cultural unconscious. Sanity is achieved when these three elements are in harmony, when the dynamic structure generates growth, and when tensions permit the survival of the individual, culture, and species. This relationship is the subject of archetypology.

Differences do exist between biology and culture, however. For example, biological schemata are not dependent on a learning process because they are not acquired; they are instinctive patterns. Cultural archetypes, however, are acquired, and after a while, they begin to sculpt our brain, transforming our physiological and biochemical reality. For example, the brain of a person who speaks only English does not have the same connections (quantity and quality) as a person who speaks German or Japanese.

So, as we have seen, the brain evolves from its embryonic state into a well-organized network of mental highways (archetypes) that can be decoded. These mental highways are procedures or potential connections that are activated by cultural stimuli. The biochemical and physiological reality of people possessing these cultural archetypes can be analyzed and described.

How the Brain is Shaped by Culture

There are some 10 billion, perhaps as many as 100 billion, neurons in our heads, each making between 5,000 and 50,000 contacts with its neighbors. Even using a most conservative estimate of 10 billion cells with 10,000 connections each, 100 trillion synaptic connections take place. Although we start with approximately 100 billion cells, we age and lose 50,000 nerve cells each day. At the same time, we learn how to function in the world, imprint new experiences, acquire a language or two, go to school, and get jobs. How do we manage to function this way when losing 50,000 nerve cells a day?

The brain activity of older people (measured in glucose consumption) is not less than that of young people. They have fewer neurons, but not less brain energy or activity. Intelligent people use less of their brain than less intelligent people (fewer nerves, fewer connections). Intelligent and older people use more mental highways and fewer little roads. They use less of their brain, but the traffic on the main highway is more important.

For example, suppose that you don't know your way between New York and Buffalo. You try different roads, directions, and freeways, often making mistakes, perhaps even returning to where you started and having to start again. Each time, you have to start the engine, run, brake, stop, and run again. You use a lot of energy, and use more gas than necessary. Your car is wearing down, getting higher mileage, and losing its resale value. If you know the way, however, perhaps because you've made the trip before, you know exactly where to go, which exit to take, and which highway to use. You engage your cruise control and relax. You use a lot less gas and waste less time and energy.

Mental highways are very similar. Intelligent people go directly to the correct mental highways, recognition, or procedures. Older people are familiar with more mental highways than younger people. Both use more mental highways (more traffic), but waste less time.

How We Create Mental Highways

Mental highways are created in five ways: 1) by atrophy of connections not used; 2) by modification at the synaptic level; 3) by reinforcement of connections and procedures that are used; 4) by production of biochemical substances that liberate the neurotransmitter and create bridges; and 5) by different combinations of the first four methods.

Let's explore three different possibilities:

1. The sculpture theory. The learning or imprinting process sculpts the brain in the same way an artist shapes a piece of marble: through elimination. In other words, we create mental highways by eliminating unused cells and connections.

2. The maintenance theory. The reinforcement of mental highways is, of course, done through repetition, but there is also a "maintenance team" at work in our brains, made up of dreams, subliminal thinking, parallel and lateral thinking, etc. This team is programmed to selectively maintain the principal highways, or important procedures. The team has its priorities, and keeping up the main highways is at the top of the list.

3. The brain's reality. The brain has its own principle of reality, mainly developed through recognition and recreation procedures. If the appropriate zone of the brain is stimulated, a person smells, sees, and feels, even if there is nothing there to actually smell, see, or feel. Thus, one can "learn" to ski, play tennis, or swim without direct experience. How? By creating, activating and reinforcing the procedures or connections associated with successful movement. What is called "visualization" is in fact activation of the mental highways without direct experience. If the mental highway is the one of successful movement, the brain is being trained to succeed. In other words, mental procedures are preparing the body for success, because the person already "knows" how to do these activities. The person is already "intelligent," using direct mental highways without wasting energy or time, without contradiction or unnecessary exploration. Therefore, it isn't necessary to experience X in order to have an imprint of X. One can have an internal experience, or visualization, which prepares the same mental highways that are used in real experience.

This is why we can have archetypes of things before experiencing them. To learn a word and its meaning, one must create mental connections and establish mental procedures or mental highways. Outside experience might or might not come later.

Internal archetypes are imprinted through internalized words and verbal communication with others (what you are told, read, see on TV, imagine, dream, or rehearse in your mind). External archetypes are imprinted through direct experience, sometimes a series of events or imprints. For example, every woman has an idea of what it means to be a mother before actually becoming one herself. The way in which she performs as a mother is partially pre-organized by her culture. She has played with dolls, watched her own mother, watched TV, read books, and played with friends. The procedure for recognition, identification, and experience of motherhood is in place.

Internal archetypes are sometimes not followed by real external archetypes, as in the situation of a woman who never gets pregnant. Four situations involving internal and external archetypes are possible: 1) an internal archetype is imprinted but never followed by an external archetype; 2) an internal archetype is imprinted and followed by an external archetype; 3) an external archetype occurs without preparation (without a previous internal archetype); and 4) an internal archetype is imprinted, followed by a contradictory external archetype, resulting in trauma, confusion, or contradiction.

The Process of Imprinting

The process of imprinting is reinforced through repetition, progresses from an internal archetype to an external archetype, and is finalized in the process of crystallization when other cells and connections have been eliminated (atrophy). This process includes plasticity, which means the remaining axons grow more dendrites, thus enhancing communication throughout the brain. Thus, sculpture (elimination), maintenance (language, dream, actions), and plasticity are the three main components of crystallization, or the creation of mental highways (procedures).

Emotion. We use emotion to create and categorize memories; we interpret the world through our mental models. In a sense, we create reality in our brains and, to a large extent, we see what we expect to see and hear what we expect to hear. Language is the first level of crystallization of these mental models. It affects brain organization and how we interpret what others say. The Chinese brain handles language in a different manner than the brain of a Canadian. There is a powerful connection between not only language and the mind, but also between language and the formation of mind. Language shapes the mind, physically sculpting the brain.

Emotion is the energy required to imprint any new experience. We need emotion to learn anything, including language. Understanding how emotion works and how it is processed by the brain is therefore crucial.

For example, suppose that a woman is alone in a room in an unfamiliar house. The door to the room is open. Suddenly, she can hear a dog running wildly down the corridor leading to her room. She immediately turns toward the door, her heart beating, her blood pressure rising, and her muscles tense. Her brain and body are working together to prepare her to defend herself, all within a second, as quickly as a reflex (reptilian brain). Her anxiety adds to the tension, and memories start rushing to her head. She has a flashback of when she was a child and a big, ugly dog bit her, scaring her to death. She remembers feeling lonely and helpless, as well as angry at her parents who had left her alone. She is now deep into the world of emotion and parallel thinking (amygdalian brain, limbic system). The dog is still not in the room. She starts thinking. Her host is a canine expert, and there's no reason why he would have let a mad dog run loose in his house. Maybe he is with the dog, or perhaps it is on a leash; maybe there is no reason to be afraid (cortical brain). Then her host arrives at the door with the dog under his control. Her cerebral cortex analyzes the situation; all is clear, but she is still somewhat afraid. Herr heart is still pumping blood as if she were preparing for a marathon. She can also still feel anger toward her parents for leaving her alone with the dog.

Amygdalian Archetypes

Emotion is the energy necessary to release neurotransmitters. If emotions are vital to learning and memory, where is the emotional part of the brain located? The amygdala play an important role in our emotional lives. If we distinguish the cortex as the "thinking" brain and the reptilian brain as the "instinctive" brain, then the amygdala becomes the "emotional" brain. Since emotion is the energy used to imprint cultural archetypes, we could call them "amygdalian archetypes."

If "reptilian" schemata are congenital and can be considered as fixed biological survival programs, amygdalian archetypes, too, seem difficult to change. They are the cultural answers to biological needs, the "survival kit" necessary to fill the gap between birth and the time when we can survive independently from any parental figure. The amygdala cultural archetype is a set of nerve cell pathways connected to other brain structures that create basic survival procedures (memory connections) in order to maximize the chance of survival. Since the amygdala doesn't have an eraser, these are permanent emotional and mental highways (or memories and procedures) that play a crucial role in the way we perceive the world, react, think, love, hate, memorize, and create.

Two Levels of Archetypes

Within the brain, there are two levels of archetypes. One is very direct, emotional, and deeply imprinted, which we will call "emotional archetypes." The other is cortical, and a more sophisticated, complex level of archetype. We will term these "intellectual archetypes." My research has demonstrated that the structure of our emotional archetypes does not change. Intellectual archetypes, though, can be influenced and delayed, and are generally used to control emotional archetypes.

Reflexes are inherited and cannot be changed; we are still reptilian in many ways. The amygdalian brain scrutinizes information in order to determine its emotional weight and then permanently records most emotional information. This unconscious emotional record can exert a strong influence on conscious behavior; the reptilian brain provides the body with the instinctive behavior necessary to fight, flee, catch, and perform sex. The amygdala provide the energy needed to imprint everything that we need to learn and to survive. Humans do need this amygdalian brain to survive, however; reptilian instincts are not enough. Then there is the cortex, a third part of the brain which generates a more complex picture. The cortex lets us know that things are never as they seem. It might override signals sent by the amygdala or the reptilian brain, acting as a sort of appeals court.

Parallel Processing

The brain is not an electric machine, a computer, or a complex network of telephone lines. Neurons don't operate according to a binary on-off code. We do not store images, but procedures. What one nerve cell "tells" to the next depends on the "conversation" occurring between groups of hundreds and thousands of cells at the same time, all at varying distances from one another in the brain. We can call this kind of conversation "parallel processing." While we are reading a book, we can also drink tea, hear the doorbell, think of the impending arrival of a friend for dinner, and monitor the weather on the radio. This type of situation reflects the process of parallel imprinting.

Any two cells or systems of cells that are repeatedly simultaneously active tend to become associated so that activity in one facilitates activity in the other. The brain does not deal with information serially, that is, one bit at a time. Rather, it operates via constantly working subsystems of complex alliances and parallel thinking processes. Imprinting should be understood not as a process of paving solitary mental pathways, but also as the establishment of all procedures for reactivating cellular "conversations" associated with the imprinting moment. Then this group of procedures is enriched with all new associations coming from repetition, maintenance, and different "conversations" connected with it.

Decoding an archetype thus involves discovering not only the logic of emotion associated with the moment of imprint, but also the interconnecting network of associations. When exploring an archetype, we put on several of these interconnected networks on alert. This is what we are trying to do through using the latent structures approach and free association. This interconnecting circuit is stimulated each time we try to remember something; our memory system does not conduct a linear search. Instead, it reaches out in many directions at the same time, pulling in information from many different networks or alliances. Cellular "conversation" will happen all over, and recollection is the result of this complex procedure based on archetypal imprints.

110,000 Rapailles

How much energy-supplying emotion is required for imprinting? How much emotion is necessary to imprint "coffee," and how much to imprint "love?" Do we need positive or negative energy? Do we need more emotional energy when we are adults than when we are children? Can we change people without using the same energy that was originally used to create and maintain the mental highways we want to alter? To address these questions, we need to define the unit of emotional energy. I like to refer to a unit of emotional energy used for imprinting as a "Rapaille."

A baby is born "unfinished," or unable to survive without others and their existing "survival kit," culture. A child must quickly learn how to survive on its own. The first strong emotion in one's life might result from the trauma of birth and physical separation from the mother.

Life begins with a strong emotional experience because we need this emotion to learn and to imprint that learning. There is no production of neurotransmitters without emotion, and, as we have seen, neurotransmitters are crucial to the imprinting process. Strong emotions release more neurotransmitters than weak ones, and the issue of negative or positive energy is irrelevant. The amount of energy is what is important (i.e., the number of Rapailles). The earlier an imprint occurs, the stronger and more powerful is the emotion associated with it, and the more crucial it is for our survival. Maintenance and repetition programs require emotion, too, although they need less of it.

As we have seen, little learning (or memory) takes place without emotion. When people want to change—to create new mental highways through paradigm shifts, expecting new attitudes and new behaviors to follow—they sometimes don't understand that they can't accomplish such a change without emotion. They come up with well-designed training programs including books and how-to manuals that make sense intellectually, but these do not center on the generation of neurotransmitters.

The concept of quality is imprinted at a very early age, and this imprint is generally a negative one, occurring when one is supposed to do something and fails. The resulting feelings of shame and remorse imprint the idea of poor quality. This experience might involve 50,000 Rapailles imprinted at the age of four. For the next 30 years, this imprint is going to be reinforced by everyday culture (i.e., "no pain no gain," "never give up," "try again," "the more mistakes you make, the better person you become," etc.). This reinforcement program might represent 1,000 Rapailles a year, adding up to another 30,000. Film and media such as "Rocky," representing American heroes who obviously do not do it right the first time, serve as a "maintenance program," adding another 1,000 Rapailles per year. After 30 years, then, 110,000 Rapailles related to the attainment of quality, reached after repeated efforts have accumulated.

Then, suppose this person, at the age of 35, attends a quality program based on Japanese mental highways and centered on "doing it right the first time." Of course, the program makes intellectual sense, and this person understands it. The whole program, though, might represent 500 Rapailles. There is no way that 500 Rapailles will change what has been pounded in by 110,000 Rapailles over 30 years, just as two days of rain will not change the course of the Grand Canyon's riverbed.

Memory. As stated earlier, deterioration of memory begins with recent memories and progresses to distant ones. This is because older memories have been reinforced with more Rapailles.

Rigidity. Older people get rigid; they keep using the same mental highways again and again and making it impossible for new paths to compete with them. New experiences have very little chance to create new mental highways because they involve so few Rapailles in comparison to past experience.

Children. The popular notion that the first five years of a child's life are the most crucial for development can be better understood in light of the Rapaille hypothesis. Children are very emotional; they laugh, cry, play, laugh and cry again several times a day, sometimes to the exhaustion of their parents. This high emotional level is why they learn so much in such a short time. For example, they learn to speak their native language within two years, and are also extremely receptive to learning multiple languages, more so than at any other age.

Psychoanalysis. Why do some people need to go through 10 years of psychoanalysis? It is because humans cannot stand an overdose of Rapailles (transference, reactivation of unfinished business, bringing to consciousness strong emotions that have been repressed, etc.). We need time to digest and to integrate. We need time to produce the same amount of Rapailles in a positive way in order to balance the negative ones we have accumulated.

Electro-shock. This is a way to "blow up" some of these mental highways, using a lot of energy in a very short time. Using dynamite to open a door might work, but you won't be able to close the door afterward. The ineffective electro-shock approach is the artificial transference of 100,000 Rapailles at once with the hope of fixing an emotional problem.

Outbound experiences. Why do people pay to be thrown off of bridges with only a cord attached to them? Because this type of activity produces a lot of Rapailles. It creates unforgettable memories, opens up new mental circuitry, and adds unknown procedures to the mind. Why is the reaction to this type of event so strong? Because these activities relate directly to survival and to primitive fears.

Adolescence. Why is adolescence such an emotional stage? Children are very emotional until they are eight (the "age of reason"). They are then quite stable until they reach the teen years. At this point, they return to a very emotional state. Why? Because they need the greater quantity of Rapailles in order to imprint all of the new issues and changes associated with this transitional stage of life. Because this stage is not clearly defined in many modern societies (i.e. rites of passage, etc.), the room for anxiety becomes even greater. In many cultures, the initiation to sex is well-organized and ritualized. In Western culture, teens are left with no exact rituals and often no guidance. Sex education is clearly approached in a very unsatisfactory manner by Western culture.

Emotion is the key to understanding how we become who we are. Emotion makes learning and memory possible. Our logic of emotion is our deepest identity, both individually and culturally. This identity is based on the procedures used to satisfy our biological needs. Decoding this logic of emotion is necessary to market products effectively and to communicate cross-culturally.

Secret 3:

If You Don't Know the Code, You Can't Open the Door:

Decoding the mindset of the target market opens doors of opportunity.

When a door is not just a door.

Instead of just listening to what people say, we can try to understand why they do what they do—and thereby open new doors to the minds of cultures. Each culture has an unconscious or a code that can be decoded.

Certain doors will remain closed to us until we decode the concept and the culture—and then we need the vision to see and the courage to seize our new marketing opportunities.

Chapter 8

Opening Doors

When a door is not just a door.

Let's see how the logic of emotion works for several basic elements of our lives such as doors, food, and the body. Once we understand the archetypes, we can open many doors of opportunity for ourselves and our companies.

Doors. The success or failure of an advertising campaign often hinges on early, long-forgotten childhood memories. Simpson, a Seattle-based company that makes and markets high-quality wood doors, found that its sales were plummeting. The company blamed rival steel door companies and their ads that featured the allegedly superior strength and security of their products. Simpson wanted to understand the archetype of a door in its relationship to security in order to know how to design and advertise new products.

Our archetypal study discovered that in America, a young child is often left alone by his or her mother in a room with the door closed. The archetype of the door was an interesting one: probably the earliest memory of many small American children is that of being taken upstairs to bed by mother and told to go to sleep. She then closes the bedroom door. In the earliest consciousness of babies, something no longer seen no longer exists. The closed door thus evoked memories of considerable anxiety, fear, loneliness, and insecurity.

With this information, the old presentation of a door closed from inside was replaced in Simpson's marketing communication with a new door designed with a little window of transparent glass. This door became Simpson's best-selling new product. They redesigned their advertising campaign, which had previously featured closed doors, to show open doors with people on either side in communication with one another to enhance the feeling of consumer comfort with the product. Another new ad campaign featuring an open door with children emerging from it rather than entering the house also led to an immediate rise in sales.

The American code for door is "welcome" and "being welcomed." Another ritual unique to America is that upon return to the States, customs officers often say, "Welcome home." No one in France says, "Welcome home." "Welcome" forms a strong mental structure, especially for Americans. So a door in America, then, is associated with *danger* if it is perceived as closed from the inside, and with *welcome* if perceived from the outside, particularly if it is open.

Quality. Most American business corporations have adopted the Japanese quality precept of doing it right the first time. However, my study revealed an unexpected archetype of quality: while we pay lip service to the Japanese concept of first-time perfection, all "imprints" show that Americans don't want to "do it right" the first time. The deeply ingrained American mental highway is very different and can be summarized in the maxim, "No pain, no gain." There is wisdom in the American culture's approach. Americans need to try and fail and try again in order to learn. And, if allowed to follow this "mental highway," Americans actually learn much faster than the Japanese.

Rewards. The main focus of one of the archetypal studies I conducted was rewards; that is, the different ways in which American businesses reward employees and officers. I found that rewards fall into two basic categories: those rooted in the past (scrolls, diplomas, certificates, checks), and those that project into the future (new tools for workers, a more sophisticated laptop for a promising employee, an ambitious night school course, training programs). The rewards rooted in the past led nowhere, offering no hope of movement or change. The rewards projected into the future, though, were full of the "buzz" of change, enhanced activity, and excitement—and for

Americans, change is good. The lesson to American businesses is that past-oriented rewards are counter-productive and should be eliminated in favor of forward-looking rewards.

Cars. Years ago, in a product-related archetypal quest, I found myself clashing with most Detroit experts over the kinds of cars American industry should be building. Conventional wisdom said that Detroit should compete with Japan in the production of small cars. In a worldwide study, however, I found that imprinting sessions indicated otherwise: recurring buzzwords included "space" and "keep moving." Americans, even those living in completely circumscribed urban environments, longed to emulate their adventurous ancestors and "go west." My study showed that by far, the kind of car Americans most craved was the minivan. Indeed, during the desperate years that were to follow in Detroit, Chrysler survived solely because of its foresight in designing and marketing minivans.

Toilet paper. A product-related study of a different kind interested me because it revealed a particularly vivid childhood imprint that had escaped my attention until then. Procter & Gamble asked me to study toilet paper in order to determine a suitable form of advertising. Imprint studies were expected to reveal the importance of toilet training, but what they revealed was that toilet training was only part of the imprint. The more important moment in time was not when the child was simply toilet trained, but when he or she was "toilet paper trained." The first time a child uses toilet paper on his or her own is an extraordinarily vivid, emotional experience. This is because in a single occasion, the child is able to reject her parents (lock the bathroom door), act responsibly and independently, and also earn her parents' praise and approval.

When Procter & Gamble was able to understand the emotional conflict taking place inside a mother due to relief that her child is fully "toilet paper trained," and therefore independent of her, but at the same time now capable of rejecting her, the company modified its advertising to take this new understanding into account by emphasizing a child's new growth rather than simply the softness of the product.

Shampoo. Roger Brookin, marketing manager for Nipponlever (Uniliver Japan) had a problem. The sales of his Sun Silk shampoo brand were dropping, and the company was losing marketshare. He wanted to know why this was happening and what to do about it. The company had done traditional consumer research and was not satisfied with the contradictory results. Roger, an experienced marketer, called the contradictions "double talk," explaining that consumers often say one thing and do something else. However, he was less interested in what people said or did than in why they said and did those things.

Roger informed me that the sales of Sun Silk shampoo were strong for a while. Then, they suddenly started dropping dramatically. I asked him if, at that turning point, he had tried anything new or changed anything, such as positioning or packaging. "We did a new commercial, but it was done by a Japanese ad agency. I think they know their own culture pretty well, so I wouldn't expect that to be a factor," he explained. I asked to see the commercial.

The ad was fascinating. The theme was sensual: a sexy young Japanese woman was shown washing, and then drying her hair. A slow-motion effect added to the sensuality, giving her hair a floating, liquid appearance. Suddenly, the doorbell rings, and the viewer sees a close-up of a male hand opening the woman's door. Then comes the tag: "Sun Silk shampoo," and that's the end of the commercial. The audience is supposed to understand that the couple is about to have a date, and that the woman is washing her hair before going out.

We went through a series of "imprinting sessions," in which groups of women were asked to go back to their first experience with shampoo, allowing them to enter the world of emotions, since we knew how to open that door.

Shampoo is not just shampoo. Instead, it is an element of culture, and the way it is used in Japan reinforces Japanese culture. No object in a given culture is isolated; all objects have systemic relationships with one another, and determining this structure is the key to decoding cultures.

We ran the commercial again, asking the participants to write down what they thought happened next after the man's hand was seen. The results were astonishing and powerful. Many of the women wrote, "He takes out his sword and cuts off her head." No wonder sales were going down! I immediately recommended that Sun Silk stop running the ad and create another one emphasizing cleanliness, rather than seduction. The company heeded my advice, creating a new campaign stressing "safe" values (cleanliness, anti-dandruff, duty, and pride) that we had recommended. Sales immediately began to climb.

The Archetype for Food

Decoding food in any culture is a big first step toward decoding the culture itself. Obviously, food is one of the priorities for survival, and how a culture deals with food and drink determines many other behaviors. Because we all eat every day, we are all concerned about food. My purpose is to give you a new set of glasses to help you see the way your culture deals with food. As you gain greater awareness, you might even increase your possibilities, and freedom of choice. You might also be disturbed by some provocative truths that you don't want to hear. Either way, decoding your culture's perception of food will not leave you indifferent.

American code for food: Never too rich or too thin also means never too poor or too fat. We each have our stereotypes of rich people, as well as poor. In many cultures, to be fat is proof of wealth, because it takes money to buy food. Several studies have shown that over-eating is an unconscious way of accumulating food for tomorrow. If a person considers himself to be poor, he might unconsciously program himself to eat as much as he can, when he can, just in case he doesn't have food tomorrow. He is in "animal time," grabbing as much as he can, as quickly as he can, before others arrive and steal his prey.

If a person thinks that she is poor, she may also think that she doesn't have time to sit and enjoy her food. So she eats all the time, whenever and wherever she can (walking in the street, watching TV, driving, working) She always has food with her. What is the ideal restaurant to attract those of this mindset? "All you can eat for $9.99."

Extra luggage. This archetype extends to luggage, as well. People who are anxious often carry too many things with them and end up not using them. This "just in case" mentality finds its place among all of the brown corrugated cardboard boxes that you have in your basement or attic which have been following you for years from one house to another, each time you move. You may not even know what is inside them or why you keep them, but you worry that one day you might need what has been preciously stored for years. Not only poor people can be frightened into this kind of need. The accumulation of extra food is common to some small animals who have to store as much as they can to survive the difficult winter time; Americans, too, from the pioneers to those who went through the Great Depression, are culturally trained to prepare for harsh times. This is why they store so much.

The storage law. In one discovery I conducted on storage habits, I found that the American mindset obeys a basic law: each time you throw something away, you can be sure that the next day you will need it. This "just in case" attitude tells us to keep everything, and manifests itself in numerous places, from the garage to the basement to the desktop. This pattern correlates with the need to "store" food when one is poor, just as a bag lady carries all of her belongings with her wherever she goes. At the other extreme, a rich person can go around the world with no luggage other than a credit card, for she can buy anything she might need. When someone goes to the airport struggling with five bags for a two-day trip, he is most likely afraid of the unexpected and feels the need to be prepared for any occasion. He thinks "poor," and that is why he travels "fat."

The power to get rich and thin. America has the fattest "poor" in the world, and its best-selling books are diet books. "Get-rich-quick" books are a close second. If we understand this preference of the American consumer, we can imagine the success of a book combining the two, such as *How to Get Rich and Thin in 25 Days*. This what Anthony Robbins' *Unlimited Power* did. Robbins is a self-proclaimed guru and successful author whose main credentials are that he was once fat and poor. He is now thin and rich, and we can supposedly accomplish the same things simply by buying his books. But beyond the "rich and thin" mindset, what actually is the code for food in America?

Food is "fun fuel." The American code for food is "fuel." Americans have other things to do than indulge in the sensuous, erotic, or artistic experience of food. This code of "fuel" can be seen in such concepts as the drive-through, fast food, and being "full."

Americans don't want to know how their food arrived where it did, only that someone has certified it as safe. Americans are not generally concerned with discovering or expanding a wide range of palatial pleasures, but rather with working hard to create a better world for the next generation. Of course, Americans like food, and a few revel in its delights. But as a culture, they stress speed and quantity more than anything: the average American dinner is a 12-minute process served around 6 p.m., all on one plate. When dinner is finished, Americans say, "Thank you, I'm full," as if they were vehicles into whom gas was being pumped. Americans have thus invented fast food, but it has brought many problems along with it; 60 percent of Americans are overweight, more than any other nation.

Cheese. Another archetypal discovery was done for Dannon, a French corporation that wanted to sell French cheese in America. At first, the company did things the French way, emphasizing the smell and sensuousness of the cheese. Dannon used a sensual TV advertising campaign that had been very effective in France, juxtaposing the delights of cheese and wine. In the ad, feminine fingers caressed, poked and pinched the cheese, then the woman smelled the cheese with great enthusiasm and delight.

That campaign turned out to be a complete disaster in America. When Dannon failed at its marketing attempt, it came to me to find out what to do next. I was asked to uncover the archetypes of cheese in both France and America. In both countries, we conducted imprinting groups that evoked early childhood memories of cheese. The French group's findings were very similar: participants recalled how, as children, they had watched their mothers feel the cheeses in shops and markets, sniffing them, poking them, and weighing them as French women do. Their mothers' purpose was to determine the cheese's age: a "young" cheese could be kept until needed, and a "ripe" cheese was for immediate consumption. The code is that within the French culture, cheese has a life span; it is "alive." No self-respecting French person would keep cheese in a refrigerator for long. Rather, the cheese must be allowed to "mature" until it arrives at its best "age" for eating.

In the American imprinting groups, the earliest imprints of cheese were completely different. First, cheese was definitely associated with meat (cheeseburgers). Also, it was always tightly wrapped in plastic and invariably kept until needed in the refrigerator. According to the emotional logic of Americans, the cheese was safe because it was germ-free and pasteurized, or in other words, dead. Because of this unconscious viewpoint, Americans rejected the French-designed TV ad. After all, who wants to feel or smell a corpse?

By understanding the American archetype for cheese, the safety of pasteurized cheese has become a primary element of communication, and a special "dead" French cheese was created for the American market that could not have been sold in France, but that has been very successful in America. Of course, the code "dead" cheese is not actually used in communication, but rather as a concept for understanding how cheese should be packaged (in plastic), stored (refrigerated), and presented (as a safe item). For Dannon, realizing that in America cheese had to be "dead" to be acceptable allowed the company to package and advertise its product in such a way as to communicate this underlying message without ever directly referencing it.

Coffee. When I explored the imprint for coffee in America, I saw tremendous possibilities for those who market it. Real estate agents always tell me that it's difficult to sell an empty house. That same empty house, however, can be turned into a sellable home with the simple addition of freshly brewed coffee. Why does coffee hold such magic power? It all goes back to archetypes.

However, unlike the findings in my previous studies, coffee is actually imprinted at two different moments in American life.

The first imprint occurs when we are about two years old. It's time to wake up. You're still in your bed and can smell the aroma of freshly brewed coffee. You know this home, and know somebody cares and thinks about you. This is a positive feeling associated with the sensation that family is near, preparing breakfast and caring about us. Because of this very positive first imprint, most Americans love the aroma of coffee, whether they drink it or not. But this is not the only imprint of coffee that occurs in America

The second imprint of coffee occurs when we are teenagers. Yielding to peer pressure, we try it. We usually don't like the taste, which is generally an acquired one. We may think that the coffee is bitter, so we add milk, sugar, and sometimes cream, in order to try to hide the taste. Taking it black is a proof of strength and virility. Thus, the flavor of coffee is not associated with home, but with strong peer pressure, and we hide the bitterness of both the coffee and the situation with milk, sugar, and cream.

While Americans often have a type of morning ritual associated with coffee, there are no symbolic meanings or mythical stories on a level equivalent with tea for the Japanese. The attempt to persuade the Japanese to switch over quickly from tea to coffee was the wrong strategy. First, we had to create a completely new set of experiences that started at an early age in order to get the next generation accustomed to the taste of coffee. This strategy was the right one, and has been reinforced by fashion and media culture.

Champagne. Champagne is not simply a beverage—it is part of the French collective unconscious. Even though I am now an American, the fact that I was born and raised in France gave me a special relationship with champagne. When my son was only three, he already loved champagne; each time we drank it, Dorian (my son) wanted to celebrate with us. This is obviously not the way normal American boys imprint alcohol for the first time, especially not champagne.

We discovered that the imprint of alcohol in America is very different from the European imprint. Kids usually don't drink until they reach high school age. There, under peer pressure, they drink too much, become sick, and spend two days with their heads in a toilet, throwing up. This first imprint of alcohol is associated with losing control, sickness, and peer pressure, all at a time when adolescents are experiencing a constant shift between emotional highs and lows.

The first imprint of champagne in French culture, on the other hand, is associated with celebration and family, at an early age, when one is not yet rebellious. Rather, it is an age of discovery, of belonging, and of strong family identity. The whole cultural statement made by people drinking alcohol in these two cultures is obviously very different.

Wine. On one of my first visits to California, I went to a restaurant, sat down, and before I even looked at the menu, the waitress asked me what I wanted to drink. I was not in the restaurant to drink, but to eat. I thought I was supposed to order the meal first, and then choose the wine, because the French code for wine is that its purpose is to enhance the taste of food. Thus, you chose your wine only when you know what you are going to eat, and then select the wine that will best complement the food. You are not supposed to drink wine if you are thirsty or on an empty stomach. I was therefore confused. Only after conducting a study on alcohol did I became aware of the different codes in action.

Alcohol. In America, alcohol is a "before" beverage—something one drinks prior to dinner, before meeting someone, during "happy hour," or often, sadly, sometimes before driving. In the French culture, alcohol, and especially wine, is an "after" beverage consumed after eating food in order to enhance its taste.

In Tokyo, I was once asked to discover why alcohol plays a completely different role in the Japanese culture than in any other. Like most outsiders, I was charmed by the Japanese people's elaborate politeness, bowing, and rituals. I quickly discovered, however, that these things are merely a single aspect of the Japanese culture. One day after work, my two male Japanese assistants asked me to join them for a drink. We went to a bar, had a few drinks, and my very respectful colleagues suddenly became loud, obnoxious, provocative, and even rude, climbing up on a podium to sing a drunken version of the French national anthem in my honor. I was astonished.

The next day, I asked them to explain to me what happened the night before. "What do you mean?," they asked. "Nothing happened last night. We don't understand the question." Obviously, I was missing something; that missing piece was the code.

The opportunity to break the code of this behavior was soon afforded me by Jardins Mathewson. This company wanted me to unlock the unconscious code of whiskey in Japan, where they were selling White Horse whiskey at the time.

During the imprinting session, participants were asked to go back to their first experience with alcohol, and to describe all they could remember related to this moment.

Comments included, "You need courage to drink alone," and "Don't drink unless you are ready to face your emotions." Story after story, the same pattern appeared: a "before" in the world of appearances, an "after" in the world of emotions, and courage to pass between these two worlds. Alcohol provides that passage for many Japanese people, rapidly transporting them from the day-to-day world of appearances to the "night world" of true feelings and emotions. Getting drunk is therefore not perceived as shameful or bad by the Japanese people; they aren't losing control—they're choosing to enter the world of their deepest emotions, a journey that requires courage and strength.

The American Code for Body: Machine

If food is fuel, the body must be a machine. As a culture, Americans are fascinated by Robo Cop, the 6 Million Dollar Man, and R2D2. We indulge in cosmetic surgery because we want a machine that works well and looks good. We want power, and we get our pleasure from developing that power, which is why we revere technology so much. This perception of the body also helps explain the tendency to blame our actions on hormones, the equivalent of a power surge or mechanical malfunction.

The beauty of the body-machine. Though beauty standards may not seem a survival tactic from a biological viewpoint, methods of attracting the opposite sex are part of the perpetuation of the species. In some cultures, only very heavy women are considered attractive, often in cultures where fat signifies wealth, good health, and time for leisure. In other cultures, the perspective on weight is quite the opposite.

The American obsession with cleanliness and health is related to the American relationship with sensuality and sex. Both food and sex are dangerous in American culture; calories and cholesterol are equatable to herpes and AIDS. Food is supposed to be clean, controlled, and all labels must disclose the ingredients contained therein; taste is subordinate to appearance and safety. In many ways, we function with a similar code regarding sex, as we should be free of disease or infection ourselves, as well as investigate the condition of our partners (safe sex).

Keeping the body-machine healthy and clean. Killing germs is almost a national sport in America. Sports often serve as a form of torture, and gyms thus have large windows so that the public can witness the suffering. No pain, no gain. If you want to be beautiful, you have to suffer.

We are bombarded daily by the virtues of scrubbed floors, ziplocked bags, and ring-free collars. No orifice of our bodies is beyond the reach of a clever marketer with a message aimed at triggering our cleanliness fetish. Even the names of the products—Vanquish, Ban, Raid, Mr. Clean—serve as reflections of our collective unconscious and of the fact that Americans are enlisted as foot soldiers in the holy war against germs and their animal (dirty) selves.

By the same token, the French mind thinks that some bacteria is indispensable to human life, and that excessive bathing causes the skin to lose its natural protection. When I conducted a study on seduction for L'Oréal, French men did not rate high with American women. Most of the women said that French men might be okay to date, as long as they took baths first.

In the course of my discoveries, some American women have told me that food is in fact better than sex. "Food is safe sex," according to one woman. Links between food and sex are ancient, but the American archetype remains consistent: although food may be "dangerous," it is often considered safe sex because it doesn't include unauthorized sensuality.

Americans want to get filled up as fast as possible; similarly, the purpose of a "quickie" is to "fill" oneself up as fast as possible. The feelings of being sexually fulfilled and of being filled with food are analogous; thus, sexually frustrated people often eat too much to try to compensate. But eating being perceived as "safe sex" is more complex. Food is a means of fulfilling one's duty to get lots of fuel as fast as possible without experiencing unauthorized pleasure. There is also the notion that if one gets too much pleasure, a price must be paid, such as being overweight or unattractive. Going even further, becoming overweight is also a twisted "solution" to sexual problems, since being what is socially considered to be unattractive eliminates the risk of attracting a mate.

Body odors are erotic. Several discoveries on perfume conducted for Dior and L'Oréal have shown a distinct gap between French and American cultures. For the French, natural odors are erotic and should either be protected or enhanced. When a French woman chooses a perfume, she is looking for the best combination between the perfume and her natural odor; therefore, she tries the perfume on her skin and waits a while to smell the result. The American mind functions differently. Killing germs and destroying all negative body odors with showers and deodorants are of utmost concern. The main function of perfume, then, is to act as a screen between the natural animal side and the fabricated public side. American women often look for a perfume with a strong smell that lasts all day. Of course, they often test a perfume on their skin, as well, but this is generally thought of as checking for a chemical compatibility.

Becoming aware of disparities such as this one between cultures is the key to successful marketing of a product, as well as accurate evaluations of ongoing or current campaigns.

CHAPTER 9

THE BIG THREE: SEX, MONEY, AND POWER

American popular culture dominates the world.

To say that Americans are obsessed with sex, money, and power is to state the obvious. Indeed, about 150 years ago, Alexis de Tocqueville observed, "The love of wealth is to be traced, as either a principal or accessory motive, at the bottom of all the Americans do; this gives to their passions a sort of family likeness." What Tocqueville did not say is that we have hopelessly confused money with sex and power.

The most powerful man is the one who has the most women (quantity). The most powerful woman is the one who gets the richest (most powerful) man.

America's Anti-sex Culture

"Big Brother" knows best: the super-parent (the state, the law) is always watching you, even in your bedroom (because in America, even if you are 35, you are still an adolescent). In some respects, there is no private life in America. In 1988 in Georgia, James Moseley was sent to prison for five years for having consensual oral sex with his wife; he served 19 months. Sodomy is prohibited in 25 states and in the District of Columbia. Adultery is still against the law in half of the 50 states. Prostitution is illegal in almost every state. We also average 374 rapes per 100,000 inhabitants in the United States (there are only 1.4 rapes per 100,000 inhabitants in Japan). In my research of America, one word resurfaces again and again among women: control.

Control: American Code for Power

Women want control more than anything else. They don't want to lose control or to give it up. They want to control their lives, their children, their husbands, their hair, their diets, their bodies, and their bank accounts. Control is the magic word. In meeting with women who are executives in advertising agencies, I have often experienced that after five minutes, the word "control" turns out to be the key explanation for everything. Why do women buy toilet paper, cosmetics, or peanut butter? Control.

The power game is, in fact, a control game. We did not want to defeat the Russians; we wanted to control their expansion. Women don't want to win against men; they want to control them, to contain them. To be out of control is the most dangerous situation, and rape is even more horrifying in America than it is anywhere else, because it represents a total loss of control.

We are not partners in fun; rather, we are enemies in a war over power and control. And, as usual, money is the proof of who is legally right, or who has "won."

Thinking has been replaced by slogans, with the result that we respond like machines. In medicine, the more you use a prosthesis, the more you atrophy a muscle. Likewise, the less we use our judgment, our talents, and our intuitions to enjoy our fantasies, have a private life, and have fun in the bedroom, the more we atrophy our minds. This is a vicious cycle.

Battle of the Sexes

In the domain of gender relationships, America is a threatened culture. All imprinting sessions disclosed that the situation between American men and women is nothing short of catastrophic. My archetypal study of seduction in America, in complete contrast to similar studies conducted in France and Italy, showed that far from containing pleasurable elements, seduction was regarded not only as dangerous, but as something to be avoided at all costs.

American archetypes related to seduction—and the way American men and women communicate—show the latent impact of the still dominant Puritan ethic: America may be efficient and even pleasurable in other ways, but the prevailing "mental highway" is that life is not to be enjoyed. Seduction is seen, overwhelmingly, as something intrinsically evil, as an unwelcome and unprofitable distraction from the main purpose in life—work and the accumulation of wealth—but never the enjoyment of it.

Male imprinting sessions revealed that for males, seduction is not a priority, as sex is seen in terms of a "quick fix" or a "score." Men's attitude toward women "acting seductively" was overwhelmingly hostile, and even violent in the eyes of many males.

Female "imprinting" sessions were even less encouraging: for all the acceptance of their biological differences and specific child-bearing, family-raising capacities, American women are conditioned from birth to believe that men and women are equal and to reject anything related to a "culture of sensuousness." Wanting to be treated like men, theirs is an especially frustrating predicament: distrust of males predominates, together with a fear of violence. Many of the same women who are prepared to call the police when approached by a stranger in America are prepared, once on Italian soil, to respond favorably and flirtatiously to an unknown stranger's advances.

The seeds of this conflict are planted very early in life. Parents inculcate into their children the very "mental highways" that prove so mutually destructive. The other side of this hostility is its primitive idealistic dimension: both men and women have unrealistic expectations: the belief that the "ideal mate" must exist leads to constant experimentation, undeterred by failure.

Teenage Pregnancy and Sexual Disassociation

In men, frustration breeds aggression, which is exacerbated by the absence of family constraints. This explains the importance of the gang in America, whose rules replace the absent rules of the family. The lack of anything resembling a "culture of sensuousness," together with adolescents' belief in total freedom, also results in one of the highest teenage pregnancy rates in the world.

Having sex is part of this system. How can we emphasize safe sex, when nothing in life is safe? "When people tell me I should have safe sex, they don't realize that I might never get to be 14. I might get killed long before that time," said a 12-year-old boy in Detroit. "Three of my boyfriends have been killed already," said a 13-year-old girl in Chicago. Safe sex becomes like safe violence. You take a chance in life, and you take a chance in sex. Sex becomes a hobby, a form of entertainment that involves neither love nor fear. Love is the part of the game that becomes too dangerous.

In a world where love is perceived as dangerous, and where, in fact there is no love ("my parents never loved me," "boys just want my body"), how do girls find the love that as human beings, they need? If you are a teenage girl who wants to love and to be loved before she dies, but your mother is a drug addict, boys are "dogs," and you have no father, what are your options?

To girls in these types of situations, having a child means "safe" love. Somebody will love them, and they can finally love someone unconditionally. You don't choose your child, and the child does not choose you, either. This is "safe," because if there is no choice, there can be no rejection, at least not for a long while.

Because we learn the facts of life in a special chronology of imprints and with an appropriate logic of emotion, we, in America, imprint pregnancy long before sex. Pregnancy is associated with fulfillment (to be "full" of someone).

Pregnancy is also a stronger emotional imprint than sex. Teens learn about pregnancy at a very early age, usually younger than seven, and almost always associate it with someone they were close to, such as a mother, sister, or aunt. Their first memories of this occasion are without embarrassment and often have overtones of a connection with love. What can we do about teenage pregnancy? First, we must accept that everything that we have tried so far has failed. It's time for a new approach. Sex education will not do the job, because sex is not the issue; in the teenage mind, sex really has nothing to do with pregnancy. This disassociation is even stronger when we can use the body machine to reproduce without love. Artificial insemination, surrogate motherhood, and sperm banks are all concepts that further confuse America's teenagers. Whose child is it when a grandmother can give birth to her daughter's baby?

When a girl of 13 wants to have a child, it does not mean she wants to have sex. It is necessary to conceive, but there is no emotion in it. The emotion is in the desperate need to have something to love, and something that will love her back. We have to accept that we have created a culture where sex, love, and procreation are deeply disassociated.

We need to reunite what has been separated: the body and the soul, sex and love, and action and emotion. We need "love education," not more classes on how the body-machine works. We need to address the real dangers of love. We need to communicate to our children that love is dangerous, but that it's possible. The notions of "safe sex" and "saying no to sex" are irrelevant; they simply don't address the real problem, so they will never bring real solutions. Love is where energy is, where motivation resides, and where the source for radical change can be tapped into.

Multiplication of Powers

In the adolescent American mind, the multiple power game is always on. We like to switch from one power to another to try them all. Everyone is in the power game. We even extend this power game to other countries. For example, in our desire to spread the gospel of democracy worldwide, we refuse to recognize that our brand of democracy is unique to us and not exportable.

The American code for power comes from sexual energy being repressed and then transformed into either unrealistic expectations (impossible dreams, rights to happiness) or depression and self-destruction (violence, rape, control, litigation, political correctness).

Other cultures see power as a means of achieving harmony, attaining pleasure, mastering one's mind and body, and reaching higher states of consciousness without drugs. Americans see power as a way to control their hormones, the economy, men, women, Blacks, Hispanics, drug dealers, gangs, rich people, and immigrants.

American Code for Money: Proof

Since we are in permanent search of an identity and living in a culture where there is no nobility and no real class or caste system, we need proof of who we are and where we stand in relation to our fellow men. Women make less money than men, so men have more power. Blacks make less money than whites, so whites have more power. In the American mind, money serves as proof, and "proof" is thus the code for money.

This is why in America we do not speak of nobility or of old families, but of "old money," as opposed to "new money," or those with comparatively recently acquired wealth. The question is not who are you, but how much you have. The best-selling issues of *Forbes* and *Fortune* are those that list the richest people in the world. They are not scientists, artists, intellectuals, farmers, or carpenters, but only "millionaires" or "billionaires." This also explains why American girls talk about "marrying money" (a uniquely American expression). To complete the identity, fame arrives, and you reach the pinnacle of proof of your powers: you are rich and famous.

* * *

We are prisoners of this simplistic dichotomous vision typical to our culture's adolescent age. Japanese men and women explore the fascination of submissiveness as an exercise of power, whereas Americans are afraid of losing control. We do not understand the classic relationship between master and slave. The Japanese believe that there is no master without a slave, or, in other words, that a slave has as much power in a relationship as a master; Americans just don't get this concept. We don't see that a relationship means two parties. Men are what they are because of women, and women are what they are because of men.

Americans believe in a more simplistic world. You are either good or bad. Because we are good, we always give a second chance to the bad people. This "protect the criminal" attitude is actually a show of superiority. If we are the good ones, we can give the bad guys a second chance, thereby controlling their lives.

In the end, the name of the game is not accumulation for the sake of accumulation. It is not power per se. It's a puritan demonstration to God that we are the chosen ones, and that we have reached a point where there is proof that we are good. The American ego is the biggest in the world.

So the American mind strives to control the world, for better or for worse. Popular culture, created in Hollywood, has already influenced the old world, mainly through its adolescent appeal to young people. Disney appeals to children using very simple archetypes. Mainstream "shoot-em-up" Hollywood movies appeal to the adolescent, using the same core of the adolescent mind, the Big Three: sex, power, and money. The recipe works perfectly; American popular culture dominates the world. No other nation even comes close to matching American genius for making and selling fantasies, icons, and attitudes.

Chapter 10

We Never Get a Second Chance to Have a First Experience

The fish does not understand the water.

First experiences are very powerful. As I stated earlier, when we experience something for the first time, a "mental highway" is created in the nervous system, and from then on, we use this pathway, or chain of neurons in the brain.

Our first experience is unique to our culture, whether that is American, French, Japanese, or Italian. The emotions associated with a first experience are also unique to our culture. For example, I once worked with an American company that was trying to open a business in Spain. When my client arrived in Spain, I said, "We're having dinner with one of our major customers."

My American client said, "Dinner. Good, I'll see you at 6:00."

"No," I said, "This is Spain. Dinner is not at 6:00."

"Oh, 6:30 then?"

"No, not really."

"You mean 7:00?"

"No, not 7:00 either."

"Well, what do you mean?" he finally asked.

I replied, "Dinner is at 10 p.m. It will last two hours, and you'll eat 12 dishes and drink three kinds of wine."

"My God, am I allowed to have a sandwich now so I can last until 10 p.m.?" he exclaimed.

My client now understood that we were dealing with a different cultural code. We don't question our own codes, because they're second nature to us. In fact, we're often not even aware that we're acting according to a code.

The Cultural Trance

When I was at the Sorbonne, I became acquainted with American scientist Lawrence Wyllie. Wyllie had dedicated his life to studying a tiny village in the south of France, and would tell me about French culture. At first, I would say, "Oh, no! That can't be." Then, "Well, maybe you're right." Through Wyllie, an American, I discovered things about my own culture that no French person could have taught me. It requires an objective or outside viewpoint to see many of a culture's archetypes and behavioral elements.

Culture is a learned response that becomes so deeply ingrained in us that we can mistake our cultural reactions and behaviors for "natural" or "moral" responses, even though they are largely conditioned upon the circumstances and environment of our upbringing.

No culture is an open book, especially to its own citizens. Each culture is an intensive collection of recurring patterns. As members of a specific culture, we live our lives so closely to these patterns, and operate so automatically within them, that, for the most part, they remain invisible to us.

As we grow, we receive little formal training on how to read and follow these cultural patterns; generally, they are imprinted as part of the process of becoming a citizen of a culture. This imprinting occurs naturally and without effort, so that we rarely think to question it and are barely aware of its awesome power. Sociologists call this phenomenon a "cultural trance."

Just as we can speak English without understanding its grammatical rules, we can also function within a culture without a conscious awareness of its rules. However, the moment we step into another culture, we notice the differences. In spite of a shared language and cultural and historical ties, anyone who has been to

England immediately knows he is not in America, without being conscious of exactly what is telling him he is in a different country; he "just knows."

Foreign cultures, even those that appear familiar on the surface, are literally alien nations. Without understanding national or cultural archetypes, we can't understand the meaning of our experiences within a foreign culture. If we move far from our local culture, we might find that life in a foreign locale appears as a chaotic jumble of behaviors, objects, and events that might seem either quaint or threatening. The success of worldwide hotel chains is based on the approach of providing something is "safe" to travelers.

Archetypes and the Future

Cultural archetypes—more than fashion, food, language, or logic—differentiate and divide one culture from another. Understanding them intuitively or through research is the crucial element in operating successfully in our own culture and in dealing peacefully with others.

Once these archetypal patterns are outlined and tracked, they can actually be used to "forecast" the future. And because cultures remain remarkably stable over time, they can also be projected backward through history to explain past events. There is no crystal ball that reveals the future more readily or reliably than the examination of cultural forces. It tells us nothing less than who we were, who we are, and who we will become. Such a study can also indicate who our allies and enemies will be, what we will regard as indispensable to our well-being in the future, and what trade-offs we are willing to make to protect, maintain, and further the status quo.

The application of cultural archetypal research is thus very far-reaching. Like the act of learning to read, the whole world can be opened up with this key. Archetypal studies are a way of reading culture by looking beneath the bewildering multitude of surface details to see the framework underneath. These types of studies can explain why corruption does not mean the end of a political career for American public figures (the "comeback" archetype), as well as why Americans willingly take risks that other nations simply cannot consider (the "frontier" archetype).

Once we understand the structure of an archetype, we can predict the forms that it will take within a culture in many different areas and how a nation's laws will crystallize out of these attitudes. The archetype then becomes the passkey to opening numerous cultural vaults.

Basics of Decoding Cultures

When we learn the basic principles of decoding cultures, we can use these rules as tools to help us recognize cultural archetypes. Among these analytic tools are the tenets of archetypal research.

1. Cultural forces come in pairs. Cultural archetypes are balanced; that is, they come in pairs. This balance gives a culture the illusion of immobility or of permanence, when in fact these forces are dynamic and usually pulling in opposite directions. These opposing forces are sometimes perceived by outside observers as contradictions or paradoxes, when they are actually two sides of the same coin.

For example, one of these balanced pairs of forces in the American mind runs along an axis of individualism versus uniformity. Americans believe that they are unique and that they have the right to actualize their own unique potential; however, the apparent American uniformity is evident to outside observers. For example, commercial standards of food, hotels, and clothing are extreme; also, the need to fit in and be integrated and accepted is a priority of all new immigrants. This standardization is beyond conscious awareness. Therefore, in any discussion of American archetypes, a predictable statement would be, "There is no American cultural archetype—we are all different." Ironically, this belief is part of the American archetype of their own country.

Each culture has its own conflicting internal forces. In Japan, we find such opposing cultural forces in arrogance and humility. Within the Japanese culture, one of these forces will usually be dominant, but the other will always remain, awaiting its resurgence. For example, after World War II, the Japanese were extremely humble and exhibited little arrogance. Now, mostly due to technological advances, the Japanese culture of arrogance is dominant. By understanding these complementary forces, we begin to break the code to the mind of this culture.

2. The logic of emotion. The logic of emotion is the predictable set of feelings that result from the way we experience events for the first time. These emotions become neurological imprints, and our culture becomes, as it were, part of us. Our cultural logic of emotion dictates most of our reactions to new experiences because it brings all of our prior history related to that event into the present moment. When we understand a logic of emotion that is culturally, rather than individually, based, we can predict how a culture and its members will respond to new stimuli.

3. Cultural structure and content. The concepts of cultural structure and content explain cultural stability amid change. Cultural research tools enable us to read trends, and chronologies allow us to see when forces are imprinted. Recipes focus on the forces that shape different generations. All of these elements make up what I call *The Archetyposcope,* which is similar to a microscope in that it can be used to view in detail the components of culturally based behavior.

Cultural Rights

The role archetypes play in international affairs could not be more significant. Through archetypal studies, we learn to "speak the language" of other cultures. Just as we would be unable to negotiate differences between countries if we did not speak foreign languages, we likewise need to be familiar with different cultural meanings and definitions.

Archetypal studies take us deeper than surface language can in order to understand underlying unconscious cultural assumptions and perceptions. By familiarizing ourselves with the unconscious language of both our own and other cultures, we can discover ways in which nations can work together to avoid misunderstandings as well as develop successful marketing tools. For example, we can understand a culture in which torture is an accepted means of eliciting information, one in which the taking of hostages is an acceptable means of political action, and one in which focus on the individual is suspect and where only teamwork is prized.

I must emphasize the notion of cultural partnership, rather than cultural imperialism. Partnership means that as an American I am proud to be an American; I am aware of my own culture, and am assertive about it. At the same time, though, I accept that other people come from different cultures, and that they can be assertive and proud of those cultures, as I am of mine.

I must also stress the rights of the individual culture and the benefits that will come from the preservation of cultural diversity to all people through honoring cultural archetypes worldwide. In this view, cultures are seen as our most precious treasures, and the rights of cultures must be a high concern, as primary as the preservation of wildlife and the environment.

Cultures Need to Be Respected

The globalization of the economy does not have to be at the cost of the disappearance of individual cultures. They represent the emotions of generations and a unique collective reality; in a global economy, we need this diversity of cultures. For each culture to have a chance to survive, we must build collective respect for all of the world's cultures.

"If our own culture is a text, then we should seek to understand its structure to identify its strengths—with an eye toward consolidating them—and to identify its flaws with an eye toward alleviating them," wrote John L. Caughey in *Symbolizing America.*

I'm suspicious of those who think they have the only truth, and that all others are inferior. Decoding cultures helps illuminate the need for respect of every culture, and the best way to do that is to become aware of our own cultural archetypes. These biases and familiarities within our own culture are the reasons why even when we are on a great vacation in a foreign paradise, we will often get homesick. We miss our normal mental highways. I remember meeting an American couple in Venice who told me that they couldn't wait to go back home—to Akron, Ohio, of all places! Even if people have an enjoyable time in a foreign country, it is still a foreign country, requiring a special mental and cultural gymnastics. Visitors are not used to foreign mental highways, and after a while grow tired of having to decode everything natives say or do. The important thing is to recognize that to others, our own mental highways can be frustrating or incomprehensible, and that their cultures (or mental highways) deserve as much respect from us as we give to our own.

Five American Forces

Several forces shape American culture. Without a deep understanding of these forces, our comprehension of American people, values, and products will remain fragmented.

1. The escape. Americans see the escape as a means of avoiding a certain reality, accompanied by the desire to and hope of creating another, better reality. America was created by "escape artists," or those who escaped religious persecution; rigid social systems of nobility, cast and class; decay resulting from lives dedicated to the senses and to pleasure; restraints of space, and restraints of time (i.e., too much emphasis on past history and traditions).

When Europeans complain about what they call "an absence of culture" in America, they simply don't understand the essence of the American culture. Of course, what they mean is the absence of European culture in America; but that is why the first Americans escaped from Europe, to create something different, with fewer restraints. In other words, they left to escape the confining dimensions of small European nations and states, and to create a culture of space unique to America.

If Europeans like "le juste milieu," or the right balance and harmony, Americans prefer extremes and tensions. While Europeans can stay in the same place for generations, Americans prefer mobility, a reflection of the force that "escape" has in their culture.

Many aspects of American society can be understood as manifestations of their need for escape. For example, in America it's possible to change one's name, file for bankruptcy, move to another state, and try again. There is almost always the possibility of a second chance.

2. The choice. America is, for many, the "chosen" country. Although I was born in France, I did not choose that country, much like I did not choose my mother. I did choose the woman I love, however, just as I chose to become an American. Americans who choose to become Americans are in some ways more "American" than the second- or third-generation Americans who are born here and who dream of things such as going to Europe. The new blood, which has been immigrating for centuries, is what keeps the American spirit alive. No citizens believe in the American Dream, but many people all over the world are ready to die in their attempts to reach America. This great attractive power is unique to America; no other country accepts people the way America does.

The force of choice is also why Americans are not very interested in history. They don't want to be limited by the past, names, religion, tradition, castes, or systems of values. Immigrants do not choose America because of its "culture" in the European sense of history, art, or tradition; rather, they choose America because of its absence of such culture. They choose the dream, the potential, the possibility, the open space, the absence of historical constraints, the frontier spirit, the challenge, and, most of all, the chance given to them to prove themselves.

3. Dreaming the impossible dream. The impossible dream is at the very root of American history. Franklin, Jefferson, Adams, and Washington persevered against opposition at home and abroad to forge a new nation based on explicitly utopian ideals. Lincoln held to his vision of a slave-free "noble experiment," leading the nation into a bloody Civil War in order to preserve the dream of 1776.

From the transcontinental railroad to the Manhattan Project, from the building of the Panama Canal to the first moon landing, American cultural milestones can be viewed as the realization one "impossible dream" after another. All of these are great achievements in the face of apparently overwhelming odds, and this spirit is what Americans cherish, as can be seen in their popular culture. The "Fantastic Four," "Superman," and the "Dream Team" all represent the American superhero who can perform seemingly impossible feats using personal superpowers.

4. Just doing it. Americans believe that a person can do anything she wants if she just believes that she can. It doesn't matter where she comes from, who she once was, or what she has done before. All that is needed is a dream or a vision and hard work, courage, and faith.

The counterpart of this myth is that if you fail it is your own fault. There is a moral dimension behind this, which is that taking action is the moral option, while not striving for anything is immoral and even dangerous. Because of this bias for action, Americans will often start off on quests without knowing where they will end up. The first pioneers didn't know what they were going to find, but they went anyway, and ended up finding a new world. And how do you know when you have "done it?" Money is generally considered as proof of accomplishment in America.

5. Quantifying. Numbers are sacred in America. Americans always want to be the best, and how do you know that you are the best? Because you have more than others; action and performance are measured in numbers. Thus, art is judged by its monetary value. Americans feel comfortable with numbers, even if they are not good at math: we count calories during dinner, measure our blood pressure at the supermarket, and watch our weight in the bathroom. Other cultures do not perceive the beauty and romanticism of numbers as Americans do.

Codes Are Consistent

Any code is interconnected with all the other aspects of a culture. Each code is also consistent with the other cultural archetypes of a culture. As in biology, every element of your body, has your biological identity carried within it on its DNA. The same is true in any culture; every element of a culture contains a cultural identity. The way we eat, sleep, make love, raise our children, or choose our cheese, is all filled with purely American archetypes. This does not mean that we don't have similarities with other cultures, but rather that we have our own unique identity or code that is engraved in every aspect of our cultural lives.

This type of consistency exists in every culture; we all have the same knowledge, but the way in which we use our knowledge varies according to cultural codes.

Clichés, Stereotypes, and their Marketing Application

Clichés and stereotypes are not archetypes or codes. They can reveal codes, but are part of a conscious superficial culture. If we react against stereotypes, it's because we are aware of them. Codes, on the other hand, generally exist on an unconscious level.

From the marketer's perspective, we need not make judgments about cultural fears and preferences—it is only necessary to know that these fears and preferences exist and are waiting to be turned into purchasing decisions. By the same token, those of us who aren't marketers don't need to decide whether these attitudes are good or bad in order to identify how they affect our attitudes and habits.

Everything we do and every product or service we buy are the results of many cultural forces that can be understood through codes and through the logic of emotion.

We imprint a whole culture each time we learn a new element of that culture, because each element contains the whole culture within it. Of course, wearing blue jeans does not make you an American, but when you are raised in America, every step in the growing process is loaded with the same structure, cultural message, and logic of emotion. Each experience reinforces the next and contributes to the process of acculturation. From waking up in the morning and smelling the aroma of coffee to being toilet trained, each element serves to create an American instead of a Japanese or British or German person. No element in a culture is isolated; they are all interrelated, and each contributes to the meaning of the others. This is why, whatever I study—from alcohol and shampoo to forests and nuclear energy—I discover part of the fundamental forces of a culture and its collective unconscious. We might learn more about American violence by studying trees or teenage pregnancy than we would by studying guns and prisoners (and indeed we have). We might learn more about American families by studying coffee and doors that by studying marriage and relationships.

When looking for archetypes, you discover unconscious connections that are more candid than conscious ones. The American obsession with cleanliness tells us more about sex and food in that culture than one could possibly imagine, yet few Americans believe, at first, that they are talking about food and sex when they speak about cleanliness. The key is not to listen to what people say, but rather to the structures underlying the content of what they say. To think in terms of structure is a mental gymnastic move that, when practiced with accuracy and precision, allows us to see the hidden collective unconscious.

To know a culture in the sense of being "fluent" in it is not the same as understanding its underlying structure; natives may not recognize the existence of linguistic and cultural structures that govern their lives. They may even deny the existence of such structures because the structures are so familiar that natives cannot see them.

Strangers in Our Own Cultures

Americans don't understand American culture, and Brazilians don't understand Brazilian culture. This is why we either need strangers, or to become strangers ourselves, when we study our cultures. The "professional stranger" can give us a new view of our culture. The stranger can see things that we are not even aware of. The "collective conspiracy" occurs when we all know that something is either true or not true, but it is so much a part of our culture that no one will dare to say it.

Alexis de Tocqueville, in his *Démocratie dans l'Amérique,* was another professional stranger. However, one doesn't have to be French to decode the Americans or vice versa. Once you train your mind to this type of approach, you can start to apply it to your own culture, or to any other.

If the fish does not understand the water, we need professional strangers to show us what we cannot see about ourselves, our organizations, our products, our services, and our marketing opportunities.

SECRET 4:
TIME, SPACE, AND ENERGY ARE THE BUILDING BLOCKS OF ALL CULTURES: Each culture has a DNA, and you can encode your culture for top marketing and sales performance.

The more global awareness you gain, the more you become sensitive to local codes—and the more your marketing reflects this intelligence. You gain market leadership by going global with sensitivity to local codes.

CHAPTER 11

THE CORE CODE OR CNA

CNA is to a culture what DNA is to a species.

Every cultural element contains a core of the most fundamental forces that a whole culture needs to perpetuate itself and to transmit its life force. This "survival kit" that ensures the life of the species is the Cultural Nuclear Archetype, or CNA. It underlies all other structures of a culture; it is to a culture what DNA is to a species. It represents the simplest elements required to duplicate and perpetuate a culture. Every element of a culture contains its CNA, just as every human cell contains DNA, the genetic code. The CNA, though, contains the basic cultural code, or core code.

The CNA occupies a different cultural level. It is unconscious and made of core components that pattern our thinking and give us sets of assumptions for arriving at our cultural truth. The CNA is highly resistant to attempts to manipulate it from the outside.

Around the CNA, there are different cultural levels that can be categorized by the degree to which people are aware of them. The archetypal level is the unconscious level of hidden forces that permanently organize the material of a second level, in which words, symbols, clichés, stereotypes, myths, heroes, and rituals play a key role.

The nucleus contains the minimum information necessary to reproduce a culture. At the heart of a culture is its core code, including the CNA and its three primary components: time, space, and energy. Next comes the archetypal level, with its codes, forces, axes, quaternities, logic of emotion, and chronology. In the outer ring lies the conscious culture, whose manifestations include clichés, stereotypes, symbols, heroes, rituals, myths, icons, patterns, truths, laws and procedures.

Life is Movement: Time, Space, Energy

We know from biology that life is movement and rigidity is death. We are living beings, and so we must breathe, drink liquids, and eliminate constantly. If one of these movements stops, we are in trouble. If they all stop, we are beyond help.

Movement has three elements: time, space, and energy. These elements form the core code of a culture. Their relationship can be expressed in the following formula:

CNA=(TxS)+(ExS)+(TxE)=Movement.

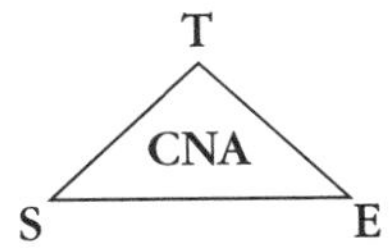

T

CNA

S E

An analogy can be used to explain these three axes: if you want to move from one city to another by car, you need time and space to determine that the distance is 50 miles and that it will take you one hour if you drive at an average speed of 50 miles per hour. But you will also need gas (energy) for the trip. If your car gets 10 miles per gallon, you will need five gallons.

The first part of the formula (TxS) is a definition of speed. How fast do you want to go? How fast is a culture going? The second part of the formula (ExS) is consumption. How much energy will you burn going from point A to point B? How much can you afford? How much can you produce or buy? The third part of the formula (TxE) is the time dimension of consumption. How much fuel (energy) will you burn in one hour? To understand the CNA, we must understand these components. They are at a culture's core, and they vary from one culture to another.

Let's explore these three components of the CNA of American culture, and how the notions of time, space, and energy represent the CNA of everything that is considered to be American:

Time: Part of the Culture

Time is a language, an organizer of activities, a synthesizer, and an integrator. But it is even more than this; time is part of the core systems of all cultures, and because culture plays such a prominent role in our perception of time, it's virtually impossible to separate time from culture at any level. This is particularly true of primary level culture.

Animal time. The American code for time is an animal one that emphasizes the immediate present. Everyone is aware of the cultural clichés concerning Americans and "nowness": "Just Do It," instant gratification, greed, absence of planning, short-term solutions. This American time code does not have to be seen as negative, however. Americans want to see results now because they are not going to sacrifice a generation in hopes of a better future. They are the future, and they want a better life now.

Thus, a large number of myths exist about Americans achieving instant success: "rags to riches," the door-to-door salesman who becomes president of the company, and myths concerning California, nouveau riches, Wall Street, and real estate. But what is important to see here is the length of time envisioned as necessary to accomplish a radical change in one's life. In other cultures, this type of change might take generations, or even sound impossible if one is born in, for example, a caste system. America has accumulated more than one billion foreign citizens during its short history, and most have found a better life in America than the one they left behind. So, these myths have some basis in reality.

From Donald and Ivana Trump to Sam Walton, anyone can make it in America. The fact is, you can make it in your lifetime, no matter what your name, place of birth, or education. You can make it, lose it, and make it again; American millionaires, on average, lose all of their fortune 5.2 times, which means they recreate it that many times, as well. This is a fascinating statistic. In other cultures, it usually takes several generations to reach the dimensions of wealth and power of a millionaire. In the United States, it can happen right now.

This notion of time being very short has to be taken into account in everything we do in America. Nothing lasts forever. If the new buzzword in the factory is quality, workers know that it's not going to last; in no time it will be history, so they wait to see what the next buzzword will be. The present, the now, or the fleeting moment is what we call *animal time*. Animals don't comprehend history or the distant future; rather, they function according to the food chain, eating or being eaten. Animal time is thus immediate.

What is popular today might be obsolete tomorrow. This frame of mind explains why it is difficult for Americans to become deeply and emotionally involved (highly motivated) with something (a notion, a concept, a new technique) that they perceive as running on animal time, or as fads, trends, or gimmicks.

Founding time. Every obvious structure has a latent strategy, however. If we are aware of the "nowness" of American culture and society, are we conscious of its other dimension? Several studies on American time have revealed that the other side of the American time axis is "founding time."

Americans like change, but at the same time, they like what lasts forever, or what will never change. For example, America has the oldest written constitution in the world, mainly because the British did not write theirs down and because the other countries have changed their constitutions repeatedly. The American constitution is highly successful; it is more than 200 years old, and almost no one is against it.

In France, on the other hand, every new politician, from Napoleon to De Gaulle to Mitterand has used altering the existing constitution as part of his campaign. We cannot imagine anybody being elected in America who is anti-Constitution. In America, however, the Constitution is considered sacred and somewhat untouchable. Its truths are self-evident, and its principles universal. So much for people who say they like change!

What must be clarified is that Americans do like change, as long as certain fundamentals are not altered. I call this dimension of American time *founding time*, because it goes back to the founding fathers and the discovery of the New World. Founding time cannot be questioned, because its principles (freedom, equal opportunity, etc.) are inherently untouchable. That people are born equal is an obvious and unquestionable principle to most Americans because it's a belief associated with founding time. This same concept does not pass the test of reality for many other cultures, which see inequality in biology (race, gender, handicaps, etc.) or in socio-economics (clan, place of birth, class, castes, names, etc.).

Founding time provides Americans with a certain security and stability. Because we are certain that our foundation is solid and unshakable, we are able to enjoy our animal time, as well. We can indulge our bias for action, spend our cash, and live in the present because we know that underneath it all are the unchanging principles that we cherish most.

Time differs in every culture. The way Americans watch TV is another manifestation of their perception of time and space. We want to have as many channels as possible (unlimited choice), and we keep zapping from one to another with the remote control. A program is only worth watching if it is a succession of "nows" that are good. If there is a short "now" that is not satisfactory, we don't wait. That is why TV is a non-cumulative medium; every program must be a "now." Series are written to be seen in random order, each episode containing a beginning, a middle, and an end. Even within a program, each section of the show (between commercials) should be a self-contained unit. Our TV habits reveal a very schizophrenic perception of the time and space elements of our culture.

When the Japanese see American television programs promising them that they can become multimillionaires in real estate overnight, they can't believe it. Why? Because they don't want to become multimillionaires (change their identities) overnight; that would be rude to their family and neighbors. While Americans often want to do better materially than their parents, the Japanese see this as a lack of respect for their parents. "What was wrong with your parents?" they would ask. Self-actualization is not a need in other cultures, and certainly not a priority. In Japan, giri ("to fulfill one's duties") is top priority.

American companies are devoting great energy and time to quality improvement. Their approach has been to copy the Japanese success in this area. In so doing, they have neglected founding time and tried to install quality in animal time (thus, people wait to see the current emphasis fade and watch for the next "program of the month"). Not only have we denied our own founding time, but we have asked Americans to behave like the Japanese. Americans have translated this in their unconscious to mean that is no longer good to be an American.

This is where understanding the American axis of time is vital. Opposing forces on the axis create a dynamic tension; if we try to focus too much on one dimension, a culture will spontaneously generate energy in the other direction. Trying to copy the Japanese has resulted in books such as *More Like Us*, by James Fallows, and *America First*, by Pat Buchanan, which promote going back to basic American principles of founding time.

Animal time, by its nature, does not last. The Gulf War is a good example of an action based on founding time (basic princi-pals, "God's job," we were "just, right, and moral" in George Bush's words) as well as on animal time (the war lasted 100 days). It was the overwhelming pressure of animal time that caused America not to finish the job (thus, a campaign bumper criticizing George Bush asked, "Saddam still has a job, do you?"). A victory in animal time is just that; you can't continue to capitalize on it.

After the Gulf War, Bush tried to capitalize on family values, a pro-life stance, and "grandmother Barbara," without understanding that these values were not universal ones associated with founding time. Another slogan used against Bush was very clear: "It's the economy, stupid." In understanding one of the crucial axes which structures the American mind, Bush might have understood that if the American people were concerned with the economy, it was because the American success ideal was being threatened and disappearing. A return to traditional American family values, when only 17 percent of Americans live in a structure that could be called a traditional American family, was obviously a mistake.

Bush's second mistake was in thinking that he could continue to capitalize on a success that took place in animal time. The Iraq war was on animal time; once it was finished, it was gone. These mistakes cost him the presidency.

Understanding founding time and animal time is not enough; one must be fully aware of the relationship between them.

Maintaining tensions between forces is what perpetuates a culture, and what makes a successful American leader.

Space in America: Go West, Young Man

The concept of space is, of course, rooted in biology and physiology. The first notion of space might be a closed one inside the womb, followed by the infant's release to the outside world. This basic notion of skin, borders, and separation between inner space and outer space is crucial. Decoding a cultural system of space is basic to understanding a culture. How we deal with the concept of space, how much space is available, and what a culture tells us to do with it are considerations that influence everything we do, from our private lives to business relations. These concepts represent the grammar of space for a given culture.

People sometimes ask me where I live, and my answer is always "in airplanes," covering an average of 8,000 miles a week. Looking out an airplane's window as I cross the United States, I am fascinated by the beauty of the landscape and scenery. On one of these flights, I was heading west toward California, and even though I'm no longer young, I could feel the magic of the experience in the mountains, lakes, plains, and deserts. What really struck me most was that for hours I didn't see anything but beautiful, empty, raw land. I couldn't help but wonder at that incredible, powerful experience of space.

The stories of the American pioneers discovering the beauty of the west for the first time came to mind. I remembered looking at the statue of the Mormon pioneers in Salt Lake City. Those pioneers had to pull their handcarts themselves, because their horses and oxen died. Half of the people who crossed the continent died in the attempt. Suddenly I realized the power and magnitude of such a task. It became clear to me that we cannot understand the American mind without considering the notion of space.

The number one code for space in America is the cosmos. Americans like and feel comfortable with space; we also like to own space. This is why we put an American flag on the moon while the whole world was watching. It symbolized the idea that the universe was ours. Americans deeply believe that the rest of the world is made of under-developed future Americans. We are not imperialistic or trying to invade other parts of the world; we simply believe that the principles by which we live are universal.

The American mind feels at ease in vast space; we have the ability to move easily from city to city, from state to state, and soon from planet to planet. This well-known American mobility comes from our very special relationship with space. It is important to note that Americans use the same term for a "shuttle" that goes between cities and a "shuttle" that goes to the moon, reflecting their perception of space.

No European culture has had the experience of settlers filling up wagons, waiting for a signal, and then making a mad dash to grab a piece of land that was theirs for the taking. Space was free in America. As we pushed the new frontier farther west, we had the feeling that we were at the beginning, creating a new world with the space God had given us. The same force is in action when we go into outer space. Americans have a mission to be first to the moon, the first to Mars, and the first to the entire universe. Star Trek is a manifestation of the American mind. We were the first to conquer the West, and using the same cultural script, we were the first to go to the moon. It's safe to predict that this same script will be used again in the future.

If cosmos is the dominant code for space in America, what is the latent force of that axis? The answer is "home," as seen in the line written by Paul Simon, "Homeward bound, I wish I was," or in Dorothy's statement, "There's no place like home." Or in baseball, for example, you score when you come back home. Also, a popular phrase during wartime is, "Bring the boys home." Celebrations take place when we come back home. These two contradictory forces, home and movement or exploration, are always in action.

We can often see these apparent contradictions embodied in behavior that would not make sense in any other culture. For example, America is the only country where people have mobile homes that never move. Why? Because people like the idea that if they want to, they can move or go to another state, but they also like home, so they tend to stay in one place.

Another example of this contradiction is seen in the fact that Americans will move from Boston to San Diego without any problem. The uniformity of American life makes it easy to recreate our homes wherever we go. We already know the supermarket, the coffee shop, and our long distance telephone company; it's like we've been there before. No matter where we go, we're still at home; it's all part of our concept of space.

One other American symbol that proves that space is home is the 24-hour convenience store. Wherever I go, I can always find such a place where I can buy a Coke, coffee, or a newspaper. It's a type of home. When Americans arrive in Europe, where everything closes at 5 p.m., where Bruce Willis speaks French on TV, and where they need another visa if they drive more than three hours in the same direction, they feel homesick. They wonder, "What is wrong with these people? Why are they trying so hard to make my life difficult?"

Cultural archetypes for space also influence personal space. The first time I took the subway in Tokyo, I was amazed at how well the Japanese accept crowding. The job of some uniformed employees is to crush people inside subway cars so that the doors will close. People there will spend two hours commuting with someone else's elbow up their nose without saying anything. In contrast, when I came back to America and waited in line for a customs officer, I noticed red lines on the floor designed to keep each person at a distance from the person ahead of him. The message was clear: don't get too close to other people and invade their personal space. Cultural personal space (the space around you that no one can invade without your authorization) is larger in America than in most other countries. Having never been invaded or occupied, Americans deeply believe that their unlimited space is their natural space, or their home.

The American experiment needs space, and we have plenty of it. We have so many choices, so much space available, and such a variety of climates, landscape, and beauty. But because space here has been free and abundant, our culture does not have a strong imprint of respect for the value of land. Land is still relatively cheap in America. Even if it is very expensive in some elite places, such as Beverly Hills or midtown Manhattan, in the Midwest you can still buy 5,000 acres for a few thousand dollars, something that would never happen in Japan or in Switzerland.

Americans also have a tendency to want to make the world their home. This is the other force that balances the unlimited cosmos space. Just as we put an American flag on the moon, we believe will one day install the first Holiday Inn there.

The experience of space, of course, varies from culture to culture. For example, when I lived in Geneva, I could start my car and in five minutes be shopping in France, or drive a couple of hours and attend Rigoletto at La Scala in Milan, or drive another few hours in the opposite direction and visit Ludwig the Second's castle in Munich. That was my spatial experience.

Shortly after I came to America, I rented a car in New York to drive to California. I drove for a week and was still in America; I couldn't believe it! Throughout that week, I could clearly tell that I was in the same country with the same language and without borders or customs. Every night I could stay in the same hotel chain with the same green carpet in the same room, and eat the same beautiful salad with no taste.

That was my first experience with American space, as well as with American uniformity and standardization. Every night I watched Johnny Carson in English and used the same procedure to make a phone call. I realized I was in a new world, a place bigger than anything I had experienced before. These conveniences that Americans take for granted, Europeans are still trying to achieve.

Europe: Invade Thy Neighbor. Europeans have always had to fight for space. Every European state has tried to conquer the others, and these wars have always been about space (territory). The Spaniards occupied Holland, the French occupied Moscow, the British and the Arabs occupied France for 100 years, and the Swiss identity was forged in the face of Austrian invaders. Europeans have a long, unfortunate tradition of killing one another to steal space. In Europe, size is somewhat irrelevant. If you can say that a little space is yours, you can form a country. Luxembourg, for example, has only 450,000 inhabitants, but it has its own laws and is one of the 12 independent nations making up the new European community. The American mind cannot relate to these small ranches that call themselves nations. If Texas sometimes feels like another planet, it may be because you can fit France into its territory.

Japan: Small Is Beautiful. The Japanese notion of space is almost the opposite of the American concept. The Japanese have no space. For centuries they have known that their islands are the limited space available to them. With half the population of the United States, Japan has space equivalent to one-fourth of the area of Oregon. It is no wonder that the Japanese therefore relate to size and space in a very different way. Their notions of beauty and aesthetics show how space has pre-organized the Japanese mind. Every square inch of a Japanese garden is supposed to be beautiful. Women are supposed to have small feet, small mouths, and small eyes, completely the opposite of the western concept of beauty, where women use makeup to make their eyes look larger or their mouths fuller. Japanese surgeons are excellent at microsurgery, and Japanese manufacturers are the best at minifying everything. The Japanese notion of food is another difference. Food, for the Japanese, is made of little pieces that receive a lot of attention, and as a result are much like art. Some of my Japanese friends openly tell me, "It's not much, and it might not taste very good, but it's so beautiful to look at." For Americans, on the other hand, the quantity of food is most important; plates are big, servings are enormous ("all you can eat"), and obesity is prevalent.

The Japanese also have little furniture because they have no space. Beds are futons that roll away during the day to make more room. The Japanese do not have a word for "intimacy." They don't need one; there is no room for intimacy when a family of a minimum of five (two grandparents, two parents, and a child) live together in a small two-room apartment. As a result of limited space, their culture has developed strong rules of cohabitation, politeness, and "the mask" in order to create the harmony and anesthetics that make life possible in such crowded quarters.

Time and space axes are crucial to understanding foreign policy, or perhaps more accurately, America's absence of foreign policy. If Americans must go outside of their borders to fight for a just and moral cause, they don't want to stay there. After the job is done or the fighting is over, they have no desire to occupy Japan, Kuwait, or Somalia. They want to go home.

Energy: Essential to Movement

How a culture regards energy is another crucial element of decoding its collective unconscious mind. Some cultures get their energy from man, some others from technology; some value high energy, others low energy. Energy is essential to movement. As there is no life without movement, there is no movement without energy. We need fuel to do anything, including going from one place to another, breathing, fighting, building, and reproducing. You could say that there is no life without energy. Knowing how a culture deals with energy as a concept is as crucial as understanding its perception of time and space. How a culture symbolizes energy is also very important. If the fuel of life is money, money becomes the symbol of energy—a very superficial and remote source. If energy is inside of you, in your hara ("stomach," in Japanese), your perception of it will be completely different.

History, geography, and geology pre-organize the way a culture deals with the notion of energy. As a result, the production, consumption, and price of energy, are always interesting indicators of how a culture's collective unconscious deals with movement, life, and change. For example, if we compare the United States, Saudi Arabia, and France, we find three different models: Saudi Arabia produces the most energy per capita in the world, the U.S. consumes the most per capita, and France pays the highest price per capita. Obviously these facts are going to shape each culture's mind in a different way.

What is the code of energy in America? Oil. Its energy is dormant, underground, and centuries old; it is the energy that has been frozen, waiting to be tapped. When unleashed, this energy has no limits.

American oil reserves are among the most important in the world. Exxon is the number one oil company in the world, as well as the oil company earning the most profit. Its name symbolizes energy. Thus, in many respects, America is number one in energy.

The American code for energy, oil, is also a symbol for the incredible resources that are inside of each citizen. We have enormous energy inside, and simply need to find a way to express it. When we have the opportunity, we show the world what we have inside. Thus, "You never know unless you try," is part the American logic of emotion.

The Sleeping Giant Syndrome. However, America is also a "sleeping giant," due to our tendency to procrastinate. This is the "don't fix it if it ain't broke" attitude. It is a form of avoidance, of not wanting to understand or to face a problem, hoping it will fade away. Often, Americans can be beaten on the head for years before they start reacting. There is a limit, however; if the wrong button gets pushed, the "sleeping giant" awakens, and then ordinary people can do extraordinary things (such as defeating the Germans and the Japanese in different wars). If the recipe is just right, there is no limit to what American energy can accomplish. If some elements are missing, though (as in Vietnam), we move toward a zone of self-destruction.

The Superman Syndrome. The "Superman" syndrome is the opposite of the "sleeping giant" syndrome, and it is actually a cultural script. The ordinary man can transform himself if he has a noble cause to inspire him (saving a child, rescuing a family, etc.). When the job is done, though, he flies away and comes back as the ordinary man he was before. Americans need a noble crisis to conjure up Superman-like energy. More money, 15 percent higher profit, or more market share are not enough. The American energy axis can be seen as having the "sleeping giant" on one end, and Superman on the other.

The Adolescent Culture

The adolescent dimension of American culture accentuates this tension between the "sleeping giant" and Superman. Depression that besets some Americans is sometimes painful and desperate, but we also know that our destiny is to never give up and to try again. These powerful forces are always in action inside of us.

This culture has the strong hormonal and energetic dimension of an adolescent, as well as the powerful repressive dimension of Calvinism, with its very demanding laws of self-control (in Calvinism, there is no possibility of absolution through confession, as in the Catholic religion). This tension may explain why we see in many Americans a fascination with the forbidden, a projection of unbearable limits and restraints, and a transference of the need for pleasure into more acceptable dimensions such as violence, food, and drugs.

Never Attack First. Americans generally feel that to mobilize their energy, they need a moral cause. We need to feel that what we are doing is just and right. Therefore, Americans never attack first; they only respond. The Japanese, in contrast, always attack first, in order to maximize the advantage of surprise. Americans are moral warriors; Japanese are Machiavellian warriors. Americans need to have God, justice, and morality on their side before they can inflict destruction. They need to be provoked. Then they will explain in detail their "secret attack" on CNN so that their enemy can get ready, and then they might attack.

John Wayne, a classic American hero, doesn't shoot without his opponent being aware that he's going to shoot him. Good guys don't shoot people in the back. So the "best," the one who draws the fastest and shoots the straightest, will survive. The Japanese, though, will kill an enemy while he sleeps, simply because he is the enemy and they must destroy the enemy. If they don't succeed in killing their country's enemy, then they have failed, and they have to kill themselves.

The difference between American energy and Japanese energy is dramatically apparent in a scene from the movie *Raiders of the Lost Ark*. The American hero faces an intimidating Japanese warrior, who has spent all his life training, in order to learn how to use his interior energy (hara) and his intuition to move his sword with all the power necessary to kill; he has prepared his mind by practicing

Zen Buddhism. What does our American hero do? He takes out his weapon—a gun—and shoots him.

Our high-energy American culture helps explain why we are also a gun culture. With a gun, we have quick firepower available, which also connects to the concept of unlimited space; we like to shoot guns from planes (i.e., Top Gun) or fire rockets and go to the moon (the gun is a symbolic way of saying that just as we have the right to pursue happiness, we have the right to access unlimited energy (the gun) in order to get what we want here (space) and now (time).

Japan is a blade culture (blades are used for harakiri, for preparing sushi, for performing Caesarean sections, for practicing the martial arts of Kendo, etc.), and the United States is a gun culture (Colt 45's, Winchesters, armed school kids, 2.5 guns per family, the NRA, the right to bear arms).

America's Unlikely Success

American culture is shaped by the cumulative influences of the three components of the CNA. Each force also has its shadow, the other polarity of the axis, which is also an important aspect of the American psyche: space and home, time and eternity, and energy and inaction.

An analysis of movement in America explains why we have created 50 states with no limits of movement between them. In a similar situation, the Canadians have created a very difficult system of red tape, and the Europeans have been unable to create the same kind of movement among only 12 states.

The vitality of America is evident in its time (bias of action), its unlimited space (i.e., going to the moon), and its incredible energy (the new blood of immigrants constantly arriving). None of the other countries or cultures of the world has these. Australians have space, but not new blood, which is limited by immigration controls and the law of the whites. The Japanese have no space and thus no immigration. The Europeans are divided and have no movement or unity, and seem far from achieving either of these things.

As an adolescent culture, America is always up and down, but we are quick to move from the downs to the ups, and vice versa.

Europeans have been predicting the end of America for decades; some of them chose the USSR as the likely winner of the Cold War. These people were judging America by only one side of the axis, ignoring the other or perceiving it as a contradiction.

Europe does not have freedom of movement, freedom from the past, new blood constantly arriving, or open space, such as Americans are endowed with. Europeans are like elderly people who fear they might die from a strong cough.

Americans, though, are young adolescent extremists who enjoy ups and downs, who learn from their pain, and who never give up. Europeans are always surprised to see the country they chose as a "winner" (Russia, Japan, etc.) is always, in the end, beaten by the Americans.

Knowing how different cultures deal with time, space, and energy provides insights that are very valuable in marketing products and services in this multi-cultural world.

Chapter 12

Elements of Encoding a Culture

We need to look at cultures as if we just arrived from another planet.

As you go through the mental pathways of your memories, you might remember some crucial events in your life that have shaped your personality and identity. This chapter is about more than mere memories and individual experiences, however. This is about cultural imprints and the way concepts, objects, and relationships are engraved in a collective mind. This is about how we encode and perpetuate our cultures.

My belief in the importance of my first imprint of America was intuitive. Today it is clear to me that if a childhood experience could have that much influence on my own life, there must exist in all children's early lives a series of emotional experiences that are far more important in shaping their later lives than any formal schooling or religious instruction they might have undergone.

How, then, do we encode a culture? There are four basic elements. First, there is the imprinting moment; this is usually our first conscious experience with something. This moment is drenched with the emotion that performs the imprinting. Second, there must be repetition. Repetition reinforces initial mental connections and transforms mental pathways into mental highways. Third, there is a maintenance program. Every night while we sleep, we use our mental highways. Dreams and thoughts that contain the objects of imprints are used and reused, like a maintenance team removing obstructions and cleaning roads for daytime use. The fourth element is the crystallization of an imprint in language and law. Let's review these four elements in more detail.

1. The imprinting moment—our first experience. Children are archetypal experts. They learn their cultures long before they learn the language of their cultures; they encode most of the mental connections that they will use later in life long before they are able to speak. To be able to function and communicate in a given group of people requires an ability to encode and then utilize these unconscious representations of reality. Children become experts of a culture in just a few years, including the use of language; they deduce the rules of a culture from the regularities or patterns they experience in their relationships with others, just as they learn the language of their parents. Each child is a student of archetypes who must decode his or her native culture and the rules of that culture's native language.

Imprints are the keys to the collective unconscious. Imprints of various kinds, at every stage of our experience, strongly condition our thoughts, prejudices, hates, loves, and emotions. If we could bring to awareness the imprints in our collective cultural unconscious, we would have at our disposal a new tool to understand, interpret, and explain behaviors of all kinds. We would have the means to comprehend the very fabric of a culture, even one as rich and diverse as American culture.

Imprinting is essential to normal psychological development, and imprints are produced by emotional experiences, usually in early childhood. Many of these imprints are forgotten in adulthood. Nonetheless, these imprints serve as the foundation for our beliefs throughout our lives.

2. Repetition. It is fascinating to observe little children as they play, because they enjoy repeating the same thing over and over again and don't get bored. Once when my son was three years old, he intentionally broke a glass. His mother was upset, of course, and told him not to break glasses because he could hurt himself or others. But the minute she left the room, he broke another one.

Why? Because he was establishing some major principles, reinforcing mental highways, and finding out about important concepts such as breakability, the nature of glass, and the limits of parents. Repetition allows for a test of consistency, and hence of truth. Just as a scientist repeats his experiment a hundred times to test his hypothesis, a child also repeats his experiences to solidify the mental highways created by his first imprints.

3. Maintenance. Reinforcement can also take place through contrast, rather than consistency. Children are often fascinated by magic tricks, because they create a new category in the mind for the things that are inconsistent with already solidified mental highways. With magic, birds can talk, have a second life, or be transformed into other animals. The child then experiences reality by understanding magic, or what is not reality.

Thus, if "magic" is important to understanding reality, when do we as adults experience this magic? In other words, how do we maintain those mental highways? Again, it is in our dreams. We know our dreams to be separate from reality and hence can solidify our understanding of reality by contrast. Everyone dreams, whether he or she remembers the dreams or not. Dreams are an important part of our mental health. They allow for reinforcement and delineation of our mental highways within ourselves. As for our cultural health, language reinforces our culture's mental highways.

4. Crystallization in language and law. When you learn a language, you learn more than words; you learn a way of looking at the world. You see the world through the cultural glasses that you acquire as a child; this is reality as your culture perceives it. Without decoding archetypes, this is the only reality that you and all members of your culture can see. The problem is that other cultures often view the world through a different set of glasses, and they are just as convinced as you are that their view is the true one.

Taxonomy is the science of classification. Language serves as a sort of cultural taxonomy, where we are given a set of categories with which to look at the world, and it is the categorization with which we communicate. For example, if you learned French as your first language, you know without a doubt that the sun (le soleil) is masculine. All associations with the sun, such as an aggressive nature and the ability to burn, reinforce that perception. In contrast, the moon (la lune) is feminine. She has mysterious powers and comes out at night.

If your first language is German, you know that this is complete nonsense. Clearly, the sun (die sonne) is feminine. Only a female could bring such light and warmth, and only a female could shine and radiate. The moon (der mund), of course, masculine, and resembles German males who are always vacillating up and down.

Language is not only a means of communication but also a way of defining the realities of a culture. The Japanese, for example, have many ways to say "I." The "I" that one uses when talking to a boss is not the same "I" that one uses when speaking to a spouse or a child. The choice of which "I" to use defines the nature of the relationship; everyone in the Japanese culture understands this. The Japanese also use different words when counting long objects or round ones. The Swedes have two neutral systems, one for moving objects and the other for stationary objects. Eskimos have at least 20 words for "snow." They obviously perceive snow in a very different way than we do, distinguishing between snow they can and can't walk on, can build a house with, can and can't eat, and so on.

Despite all of these lingual differences, it is important to note that a child, for biological reasons, first experiences the world without having the use of language. He can then start using American, Japanese, or French taxonomy to sort out cultural experiences. Further crystallization occurs on an even broader scale through the enactment of law.

Laws, in many cultures, also define categories. The very delineation of misdemeanors versus felonies places crimes into different categories. We all possess these mental categories, and sometimes they are so unconscious that they become second nature, pre-organizing the way we look at the world.

Take Off Your Glasses

Mental highways were once necessary for physical survival. They served almost as culturally created instincts that became second nature. Sometimes these mental highways become obsolete, and over time we forget what they were for. We perceive them as the "natural" or only way to do things, but the essence of their construction is long forgotten. It's like wearing sunglasses after the sun has gone down simply because you forgot that you had them on. It becomes crucial to decode these forces in our cultural unconscious in order to rid a culture of obsolete solutions and instead create working solutions.

The process towards awareness can start with any element of our daily lives. Because a whole culture is manifest in every element therein, studying even the most mundane objects such as toilet paper or coffee can reveal the framework of an entire culture.

Studying Modern Tribes

We all know that American coffee doesn't taste the same as Italian coffee; in actuality, they aren't even in the same mental category. It's a mistake to use the same word to describe too many objects and products that might seem to be universal but that are really quite different things to different cultures. We need a complete paradigmatic shift to understand the way different cultures relate to and perceive things.

To some people, a dolphin is a fish. It swims, has fins, and travels in schools, so it seems to belong in the fish category. For others, the dolphin is perceived as a mammal, for obvious biological reasons. Our behavior towards dolphins might be greatly influenced by which categorization one uses. If a dolphin is a fish, our main concern may be how to cook it. If it is a mammal, our concern may be to teach it language and communication skills. Categorization, or taxonomy, makes an enormous difference (especially for the dolphin!).

Another example of categorical differences would be the perception of coffee in France versus its perception in the United States. After dinner, French adults get up and go to another room (le salon) to have coffee. The ritual is always the same, and coffee therefore signals the end of the dinner time.

The first time they dined in France, some of my American friends asked for coffee right in the middle of dinner. The hostess, in a worried tone of voice, asked, "You don't want any salad, cheese, or dessert?"

We often think we know what we are speaking about when we use common words in different languages, when in fact, what we need are the codes behind these words. Without codes, we might make big mistakes and even lose millions of dollars while trying to sell our products or services to those of other cultures. Though the difference between coffee in America and coffee in France may seem insignificant, these differences could obviously have a huge effect on the marketing of coffee in either of these countries.

Similarly, when we try to implement quality in America, we cannot use Japanese or German principles, because their codes for quality may not fit with our own archetypes. Rather, we must decode what quality means to Americans. Anthropology has been associated with the study of primitive people or remote tribes, but one pursuit of cultural anthropology is decoding the American tribe, the Canadian tribe, the French tribe, and the British tribe. Western customs, languages, and societies are just as "foreign" and worthy of study as non-Western cultures. Just because these cultures all watch CNN does not mean that each of them is not a very different tribe with very different unconscious codes.

Discovering the Window in Time

We see how important emotion, repetition, and maintenance are in the imprinting process. Another element is important too, if we want to understand imprinting, and the way we encode cultures: the moment that a culture tells us to engrave what we learn. I call this moment the "window of time" for imprinting. The uncovering of archetypes and their imprinting moments are at the root of the cultural resources available to us. But in the encoding process of the imprinting moment, there are special constraints at work that are the keys to the eventual decoding of a culture. Let's explore this cultural window in time.

The window of time when we encode is actually part of the code itself. Ducklings, for example, have a very small window of time during which they can be imprinted by the "mother." Whoever or whatever is near the ducklings during that time will be permanently regarded by the ducklings as their mother. This imprint is so strong and lasting that the ducklings will follow that mother figure everywhere, regardless of whether it is really their biological mother. The "mother" needn't even be a living thing—the ducklings will follow anything near them that moves.

Such an imprinting moment exists in the human species as well. The window in time for humans has even more powerful results when it occurs at a very early age. At that time, a child is very emotional and has a great deal of energy, always discovering new things, exploring new territories, and requiring attention. Parents know that their children need to discover the world, but at the same time they are afraid and protective. Their emotional reactions charge the imprinting situation even more, keeping the child from danger; this serves as an ideal condition for imprinting.

Each culture provides a different window in time for imprinting different things. Of course, some imprinting windows are dictated by biology. For example, a child has to learn a language before she is 10, or she will never speak more than a few disjointed words. Similarly, a child must learn to control his sphincters before age three, or he is in big trouble. Things like language and bowel control can't wait. But the window of time in which peanut butter or cars are imprinted are much more flexible, and can vary from one culture to the next (or even be omitted), without dire consequence. Even toilet training imprints have a little leeway. In Japan, for example, children are toilet trained an average of six months earlier than American children, and in a much shorter time period. Toilet training in Japan in more linked to societal obligation, whereas American toilet training is linked to autonomy.

Some elements are not imprinted at all in certain cultures, or they are imprinted much later in life; the Dutch don't imprint chopsticks in childhood, nor do Americans imprint alcohol in infancy. The culture not only determines what will be imprinted and when, but also how it will be imprinted—in other words, what kind of emotion will be the energy necessary to perform the imprinting. Going through different growth stages creates different conditions for imprinting. Not only is it crucial to know what is and is not imprinted in a culture, but the age at which these imprints take place is also of great importance.

Encoding at Different Ages

A child is a different person at age two than he or she is at age seven. This may sound obvious, but it is often less clear that, at different ages, children have very different mental tools for apprehending the world. One observable phenomenon that marks stage development is the explanation of the conservation of matter. After most mental tools are in place (around age seven), a child will be able to comprehend that an amount of liquid remains constant no matter what vessel it is poured into.

Cognitive Stages. A child goes through a series of cognitive stages. At a certain age, a child can use only limited intellectual tools; later he will have more tools available to him. Logic is only one aspect of child's growth. Emotions, too, go through stages of development. Discovering at what stage and age a culture imprints coffee or toilet paper might have an important effect on our decoding process, as well as give us an in-depth understanding of what those elements represent in a certain culture.

Emotional Stages. We know that children are very different at age two than they are at age eight. We also know that little children are very emotional, while those past age seven are generally more logical. In the teen years, kids are once again highly emotional and difficult to understand. Anything imprinted during this emotional period will be strongly associated with the emotion generated during this stage. Children will use whatever they can to imprint; in other words, they'll use the emotion or energy available to them at the time. Whatever emotion we associate with our first experience will be the energy we use to imprint.

The Result of All These Elements Is the Code.

Discovering the window of time is important to understand the relative importance of the various elements of the imprinting process. The energy and emotion used to imprint a mental highway will be of a different nature and intensity, depending on the age of a child and the context of the child's culture. Repetition by the culture, the existence of rituals and myths, reinforcement by the media, and crystallization by language are the elements that create a code and imprint it deeply into the part of our unconscious that is common to all members of our culture. Once it is there, it is difficult to access or to change an imprint. Indeed, what we learn at an early age generally stays with us forever.

Second nature. Soon these imprints become so second nature to us that we do not question them any more. If we are aware of different and strange ways of people from other cultures, we are very rarely aware that our own ways might appear strange to them to. Even more, it is extremely difficult to view our own culture with the eyes of a foreigner. So how can we not only decode other cultures, but also our own? What are the new glasses that will enable us to see our own collective unconscious, and give us the key to understanding why we do what we do, why we think the way we think, and why we keep repeating the same patterns?

Studying the window of time not only gives us the context of the imprinting moment, but also the cultural stage, or the normal age in a culture at which this element of the culture is imprinted.

Notwithstanding the difficulties facing an outsider when attempting to penetrate another culture's surface, being a "stranger in a strange land" can also have definite advantages. One can look at everything with astonishment. Outsiders to a culture can often see elements of that culture from a more objective perspective because these things are not "normal" to them.

We need to look at other cultures as if we were arriving from an another planet, without any prejudgment and without using our own value systems, but rather with humility and respect. It often takes a stranger to show us things about ourselves that we do not see, as we are too close to have a clear view of our own cultures.

Chapter 13

Culture as a Survival Kit

Your culture is likely the best one for you.

When we look at collective behavior, we need a code to make sense out of what people do. Decoding cultures can explain our own collective unconscious behavior with more accuracy than statistics or surveys and lead us to an understanding that not only provides a tremendous competitive edge for business marketers, but also helps us cope with such problems as teenage pregnancy and drug use, avoid conflicts between cultures, and enhance education.

If simple elements of a culture, such as shampoo and alcohol, can have such surprising unconscious significance in a culture, imagine how powerful and different the cultural significance would be of such psychological and emotional concepts as love, freedom, prohibition, peace, quality, and caring.

Content is not what matters, but the forces that organize this content are what is crucial, especially when these forces are unconscious. Expressions of content are like metal filings on a magnetic field; it is not the filings that are important, but the way in which they are organized by the invisible forces.

Like a magnetic field, the culture organizes generation after generation, from the way we feel and love to the way we hate, function, and ultimately survive. To understand our collective behavior, we must first understand what divides us into our cultures, or how we become "cultural animals." No matter how hard we try, we can't rid ourselves of our own culture, for it penetrates to the roots of our nervous systems and determines how we perceive the world. Most effects of culture lie hidden and are outside of voluntary control. Even when small fragments of culture are elevated to awareness they are difficult to change, not only because they are so personally experienced, but because people cannot act or interact in any meaningful way except through the medium of culture.

Most animals are developed enough to survive on their own soon after birth. People are not. This is why we are "cultural animals." Our culture serves as a survival kit provided by adults to their newborns to help them survive and grow; this is a characteristic of all human cultures. We are fragile beings: we cannot stand drastic variations in temperature, we have no real natural protection, and we have no natural weapons except our intellect.

Culture Is an Answer to Biological Needs

Our lack of natural defense provides a unique human need for collective survival. If we construct a survival kit that succeeds, we will survive; if we don't, we will disappear.

The animal kingdom provides us with some models of basic culture. On a fundamental level, animals, too, can learn new ways of dealing with their everyday needs and share these new methods with other members of their group. For example, monkeys eat potatoes, but they don't like the skin. One monkey discovered by chance that when potatoes are floated down a mountain stream, the skin is peeled off by the rocks by the time the potatoes reach the bottom of the mountain. This monkey, then, started to throw potatoes into the current at the top of the mountain and waited at the bottom for his lunch. That innovation, though, cannot make a culture in and of itself. What makes a culture is when, several years later, all of the monkeys on the island regularly throw their potatoes into the river on the mountaintop and wait for them at the bottom. A survival tool must be transferred to future generations in order to manifest itself as a culture. If you came back several generations later, and saw that the monkeys continued to prepare potatoes in this rather ingenious way, then you could conclude that they have developed a basic culture, passing down techniques of survival to their young.

Obviously, many factors contribute to the specifics of a culture. On an extremely general level, differences in geographic location and resource availability will affects these specifics. For example, using a bush or tree to one's advantage and staying away from big lions are part of the culture in regions of Africa, while building igloos and ice fishing take precedence in Eskimo country. A culture need not be sophisticated; it only has to work. If, from one generation to another, it keeps working as a survival mechanism, it is then internalized and becomes "second nature." These inherited patterns or mental structures are used as if they were "natural ways" of functioning; they become so deeply ingrained that they are transmitted without question and often without awareness.

Priorities and the Logic of Life

Culture is a system of crystallized answers to biological needs. If a culture succeeds in addressing these survival needs in a satisfactory way, the species will survive and the culture with it. So, in speaking of "culture," I am not talking about opera or ballet, but rather the basic survival kit that every one needs; if you are alive, you have a culture. If that culture does not meet your biological needs, either it must change or you will die.

Biology is the logic of survival, the "logic of life" that we share with all members of our species, and even, in some areas, with many other species. Biology is, in a sense, the science of priorities, as certain priorities must be met in order to survive.

Understanding priorities is the key to understanding survival. For example, breathing is more important than drinking. If you can't breathe, you won't have much time to think about drinking (or anything else, for that matter). Drinking is more important than eating; you can stay alive longer without eating than you can without drinking. Liquids play a crucial role in the body's survival, and the brain cannot stay alive for more than a few minutes without an influx of oxygen, carried by the flow of fresh blood. Learning these priorities allows a physician to take the proper order of action to save a life. If a physician doesn't respect these priorities, his patient will die.

This order of priorities is what I call the "logic of life." We are all programmed to survive, and priorities form our biological program. Corresponding to this biological program is the unconscious cultural program that organizes the collective answers to basic survival needs (or "questions"), such as food, water, fresh air, shelter, procreation, and territory.

At an individual level, we are all unique. Not only are children distinctly different from their parents, but parents, too, can change dramatically within their lifetimes through a restructuring of will, determination, courage, counseling, or simply by "growing up."

However, all people share the universal biological program of needs. Certain groups share the same collective response to those needs (culture). From that shared base of biology and common pool of culture, individuals choose their tools for creating and exerting their own individuality.

The Pyramid

The quest for identity is aeons old, and knowing about universal biological needs and the collective cultural response to those needs puts any individual ahead in the quest for his or her own identity. To know where we are going or where we have been, we consult a map. In understanding ourselves and our actions, we can also consult a cultural map of where we are coming from and where we can go. This map is easily visualized as a pyramid, as shown on the facing page.

This pyramid explores the relationship between biological needs and how cultures deal with those needs, use unconscious forces to address survival, and how these forces determine the way we function as individuals.

Life Is Tension

Sometimes people spend their whole lives trying to ease tensions or avoid them. This is a misunderstanding of the purpose of life. Without tensions, there is no life. Biological priorities create

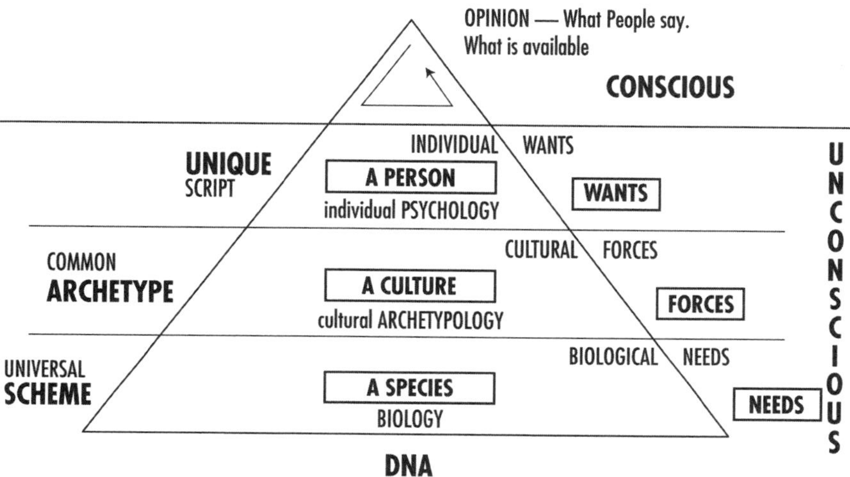

tensions, so these tensions are the very impetus and movement of life. When the movement ends, there is no more life.

For example, pleasure and pain are two sides of the same reality. The sensitive system that communicates pain from my fingers to my brain is the same one that communicates the pleasure of stroking my cat. The network is independent of the message; a telephone wire is not affected by whether you are in love and desperately want to call your beloved, or whether you are upset with your neighbors and need to call them to move their car out of your driveway.

Tensions are messages sent by our bodies which call our attention to needs. Let's suppose you're fascinated by a book, and you've been reading it for several hours straight. You are undoubtably still fascinated, but you begin to feel some persuasive tensions, suggesting that it might be time to go to the bathroom. The book is so interesting that you ignore this tension, and keep reading. After another hour, however, the tension becomes painful, and you can't concentrate on the book anymore. You rush to the bathroom and release the tension with a smile of pleasure. You can then come back to the book and enjoy it.

What happened was a switch in priority created by the pain. The release of tension then created pleasure. The pleasure then disappeared, and you returned to your former priority. This ability of tensions to bring to the foreground an element once in the background is indispensable to our survival.

Adapt or Die

I call this flexibility a "gestalt," the German word for structure—in this case, the structures upon which a person relies to inform his or her behavior. How flexible are your gestalts? Do you listen to your body telling you again and again to stop eating a certain type of food, for example, or is your gestalt frozen in a destructive pattern? Some cultures, like individuals, can become "frozen" in gestalts that can eventually destroy them.

Let us suppose, for example, that one of my ancestors is the chief of a small nomadic tribe in the Middle East 3,000 years ago. One day, the chief decides that the tribe needs to expand its territory, and to do so, it needs to attack another tribe on the other side of the desert. The desert is very expansive, however, and it will take several weeks to cross it. They have to pack enough food for the trip. But there is a problem: they're good soldiers, but their favorite and most abundant food is a little animal called the marsupilamy. This animal is found only on this tribe's side of the desert, and the little creatures need so much water to survive that it is impossible to bring some along alive. They have no idea how to preserve meat in a safe way, so it is equally impossible to think of killing some marsupilamies to take as food across the desert.

In the middle of the desert, the chief discovers that some of his best soldiers are sick. Quick investigation reveals that these soldiers have brought some dead marsupilamies along, which have of course gone rancid, and they have been eating them. So the chief, who does not want to lose any warriors, declares that it is illegal to eat marsupilamies in the desert. The next day, during a battle against another tribe, he dies.

His son takes over and has to face the same problem: his soldiers like the tender and delicate forbidden meat, and even break the law and risk their health to eat marsupilamies. So the son cleverly says: "My father, who was a wise man, and who is now with God, said you should not eat this meat. So the rule is now coming from beyond. It is not only illegal to eat this meat, but it is against God's law." To reinforce the "divine law," the son makes it clear that not only will you lose your life if you are caught eating the forbidden gourmet dish, but your whole family will be banished and you will lose eternal life. This is now serious business, and the warriors consider twice the possibility of ingesting damnation. The established system thus works: the chief keeps his warriors healthy, and they win the ensuing battle.

The problem is that 3,000 years later, the same tribe now has freezers. They have deep-frozen marsupilamies, but are starving because of the divine law that prohibits them from eating this meat. Of course, the origin of the law has been lost over time. This is what I call the "reversal law" of culture: a solution that was well-adapted to a certain situation at a certain time has now been crystallized and is no longer challenged. When a culture becomes too rigid and cannot adapt to new circumstances, its chances of survival are limited. We know that powerful cultures can disappear this way: the Egyptians, Greeks, and Romans, to name several, are good examples of what happens to dominant cultures that have no flexibility of gestalt or cultural structure.

Old Dragons Never Die

The time frame for changes within cultures varies—some changes can even take centuries. Americans like to think that people can change quickly. In my research, I often hear that "the new generation of Japanese is different—they eat hot dogs and wear blue jeans" or that "the Germans are not like their ancestors." But recent incidents in Yugoslavia, the resurgence of fascist activities in Germany, or even the trade war with Japan, are all reminders of the phrase, "old dragons never die."

After three generations of Soviet repression, the Serbs are more Serbian than ever, the Croates more Croatian, and they are all ready to die for their cultures. It might take centuries to change a culture, and when one is in danger, we see an incredible resurgence of old archetypes.

Thus, we are presented with a paradox: cultures can survive only with a flexible gestalt, and yet their archetypes often remain unchanged, despite tremendous pressure or oppression, even over hundreds of years. This situation is really not as irreconcilable as it seems, for although cultures change at a glacial pace, they can also sometimes experience tremendous quakes. Of course, all changes occur on an axis, and the axes themselves do not change, as I noted earlier. Where we are on an axis, or the focus on one side as opposed to the other, will change over time. Cultures can change the way they use their forces and the way they position themselves on an axis, and awareness of archetypes and forces allows for informed change.

The survival and success of your marketing campaign will depend on your awareness of cultural archetypes.

Chapter 14

Old Leaders, New World

The global world is more and more a local world.

Many leaders think that being global means being strong enough to impose their way on the rest of the world. But humanity as a whole has become more and more resistant to this monolithic world vision.

Today's reality is quite different. What is currently happening in the former Yugoslavia is a good example. As soon as the Soviet leadership there weakened, nations and cultures that were repressed for three generations started emerging and fighting for their survival. The more we assist in the globalization of the economy, the more we see this type of resurgence of local cultures. Thus, the global world is more and more a local world. This is not a contradiction in terms; modern technology, especially the Internet, allows members of the same culture to reinforce their own local identities and to become players in the global market.

So who are the new leaders? Few CEOs are multi-cultural and at the same time literate in the technology of globalization. Many are still fighting old battles that are completely irrelevant to survival in the 21st century. Some, for example, seek to preserve jobs of the past, when they should instead lead toward the creation of jobs of the future.

Many leaders, in struggling to find the best route to globalization, miss their chance to compete globally. Several executives have told me, "If only we knew the code for 21st Century leadership, we would find the leaders of the future, train them, and keep them."

The Great Connector

Today it is already extremely difficult to find a leader for a local American company operating in the United States. But when you must find a global leader for the unpredictable and bumpy ride ahead, the task becomes even more difficult. It is impossible to lead a car manufacturing company, without understanding how to deal with the Germans and the Japanese, or without being aware of the cultural differences of South America and Europe.

It is painfully obvious that a global world needs global leaders. Detroit car makers might be very well prepared to deal with Detroit's challenges, but how well do they negotiate and manage in Tokyo, Stuttgart, Paris, or Milan?

Breaking the Code

In 1997, I decided to start an archetype discovery program in order to break the unconscious code of what "leader" and "leadership" really mean in today's world. General Motors, Kellogg, Canada Trust, and Royal Bank joined forces with our team at Archetype Discoveries Worldwide. The results were astonishing. We heard much about consensus, commissions, and committees, leaders as facilitators, and leaders as creators of the right environment. We discovered four basic traits or responsibilities that a leader must have.

1. Leaders lead. Deep down, what people want and need are leaders who are able to guide them. Sadly, few people actually have the courage and ability to be leaders on that basis.

2. Leaders read. Leaders should know how to read various situations, the emotions of their employees, and the intentions of their enemies or competitors.

3. Leaders model. Leaders are archetypal, meaning they constitute an original pattern, design, standard, or model. That is an important insight: the archetypal leader is the one we need today. Only he or she had the power required to lead companies and cultures through the mutation of the global world.

4. Leaders connect. So what is an archetypal leader? The code of an archetypal leader is "connector." Such a leader is one who connects who you are and what you do with an overall mission and vision. People rebel and revoke their commitment when they feel disconnected or useless.

Example: The Crusade

If your boss tells you to buy a horse you might do it simply because you have to obey, even if you don't know why you are buying the horse. If he tells you that you have to buy a horse because you're going to ride it, you become concerned. You might be more careful in buying the horse, knowing that you are going to have to ride it.

If the leader tells you that you are going to ride the horse in front of an army, and that you are going to be the army's commander, you will definitely be sure to buy the right horse for the job, because the boss has clearly connected the horse to you personally (you are going to ride the horse) and to your function (you will be the commander on the horse in front of the army.) But, you still don't know what you will accomplish with this horse and army.

Then the leader tells you that he's giving you a mission: you must liberate Jerusalem before the end of the year. You now have a deadline (the end of the year) and a specific goal (to liberate Jerusalem). You can now measure for yourself whether or not you achieve your goal.

You might still wonder why you have to liberate Jerusalem. The leader tells you, "We have a vision of a world where everyone will be safe and happy in the same religion and with the same god." This vision is the reason for the crusade you are about to embark upon.

Finally, the ultimate connection has been made. You are not simply buying a horse, you are saving the world, and a clear reward, eternal life, is in sight.

When President John F. Kennedy decided in 1961 that America needed to put a man on the moon before 1970, a mission was created. When any person working at Cape Canaveral was asked what she was doing, she could answer, "I'm putting a man on the moon before the end of the decade." All of the simple but useful tasks of thousands of people were therefore connected. That's leadership!

Numbers don't lead; a 10 percent increase in profit is not a mission, and certainly not a vision. Medieval crusaders traveled mostly on foot from Europe to Jerusalem without being paid, because they were motivated. Workers in Detroit, however, will not be motivated to work harder simply for a better percentage return to shareholders. If GM workers go on strike, it is because no meaningful connection is made between what they are personally doing and a greater vision or mission; they feel disconnected, and that they have nothing to lose by striking. Real leaders do not lead with the cortex (rationality, numbers, statistics); they lead with the heart, by connecting archetypal emotions to instincts of survival.

Four Basic Questions

Now that we have set the stage, let me address four questions I raised earlier.

Who are our global leaders? Global leaders are the men and women who connect a global world vision with their home base culture and with a local mission. Let me go back to the Kennedy example. If America is "the last best hope for mankind," sending a man to the moon becomes a big step for mankind. In this sense, the American flag on the moon is the symbol of mankind, and John F. Kennedy is, at that moment, a global leader, because he is able to connect the American mission with a global vision.

More and more, people around the world are asking the same questions: Where is the world going? Are we going to lose our cultural identities in the process of becoming a global company? Will Daimler-Chrysler become German or American? What does being a global company mean? How can we become one? What is our vision?

Global leaders need to have global vision before they can hope to connect with their employees. I'll go buy a horse if I know it's part of a crusade. The role of the global leader is to show me the connection between what I do every day and the way the world is going. Then I can feel part of it, and it all makes sense.

How do I find global leaders? Some managers already belong to several cultures. They speak several languages and have lived in many countries. They have gut feelings about the relations between cultures. They have used different archetypal glasses to see the world, and have accepted the idea that cultures are not right or wrong, but simply different. These people have the right attitude, and attitude is what matters most, not knowledge. A manager can learn another language or another culture, but if she doesn't have the right attitude, she can't be effective.

At the same time, managers need to have strong roots in local culture. They need to have a cultural home, a place where their hearts are. It's a mistake to think that the next global managers are going to be homeless citizens of the world. Leaders need to have roots in one culture in order to accept that other people have strong roots in their own cultures.

How do I train a global leader? Future leaders need to be immersed in different cultures. Learning a language is not enough; you have to learn a culture and the logic of emotion of that culture. Discovering the cultural archetypes is the best training for global managers. Knowing the code for "loyalty" for Americans, Germans, British, Japanese, French, and Chinese is essential if you want to create a global organization, as well as the codes for "reward," "recognition," "quality," and "leadership." Only those with a deep understanding of these cultural unconscious forces will be able to lead the way toward a global world.

How do I retain global leaders? Always take into account two sides, local and global. Future leaders need opportunities to grow on a global scale and get more responsibility worldwide. But at the same time, they need to go back to their cultural home bases where they have their roots and memories. Companies should have a home base fund to help managers maintain their homes and reconnect by going home every once in a while. These future leaders need to know that from their home cultural bases they can explore the new global world. Over time, these capable men and women will become global archetypal leaders; they will connect all of the world's cultures with their global approaches and will be priceless to your company.

SECRET 5:

SOLVE THE RIGHT PROBLEM: You must design and create new products or services to solve the right customer problems.

Americans are not bored with cars. They just can't find the kind of cars they want—so they buy trucks, vans, and SUVs.

Many marketers have the right answers to the wrong questions. To get real innovation and creativity, you need to address the real problems and design products to solve them. Competitive advantage begins by addressing the real customer problem.

Chapter 15

The Creativity Archetype

Often the true problem is different from the original evaluation.

In the rapid change that is currently taking place in the global economy, American business is falling behind. It's time to wake up the sleeping giant and become creative and innovative again—the American way. Historically, America has excelled in the area of creativity, shown in its ability to create new products, new methods, and even a new form of government. Today, seeing the rapid development of business in other countries, many Americans feel that they should imitate Japanese or European methods to become more creative and innovative.

I believe, however, that Americans are uniquely creative; America, because it is made up of so many cultures, has a culture of creativity all its own. It is a nation that can meet global challenges by understanding and better using its own creativity and innovation.

To better understand how American businessmen and scientists are naturally creative, I studied the American archetype of creativity and innovation and its application in American business. Results of this study are used to train American business people to be more creative and innovative, and thus to compete worldwide and regain a leading position.

An archetypal discovery uncovers the unconscious meanings and associations that a concept or a product has within a culture. It is the most advanced way to "break the code," to understand cultural logic, and to use this logic to make a company very competitive.

Here are some of the questions that must be addressed: How do I select, keep, and motivate creative and innovative people? How do I increase the creativity and innovation of my company? How do I structure, organize, and manage permanent creativity and innovation within my organization? When do people stop being creative? Why? How can we prevent that burn-out from happening? What is the relationship between creativity or innovation and quality, teams, reward, leadership, ownership, production, service, distribution, globalization, cultures, markets, crisis, routine, communication, motivation, training, and events?

The Chrysler Experiment

The PT (Personal Transportation) Cruiser is Chrysler's first vehicle designed entirely through our market-research process known as archetypal discovery. Since first learning of this process five years ago, Chrysler, now effectively the American arm of Daimler-Chrysler, has shifted much of its market-research program over to archetypal studies. In a business with billions of dollars of product investment on the line, Daimler-Chrysler hopes this process will help the company "institutionalize the insight," says David P. Bostwick, director of corporate market research. "Being successful by chance is Las Vegas," he says. "Being able to replicate your success by understanding it is good business."

The goal of the PT Cruiser development team, which began work before Chrysler merged with Daimler-Benz AG, was a sizeable one: to create a vehicle that mixed past and future and attracted a "cult" following, much like Volkswagen's redesigned Beetle.

The process began with a series of free-wheeling, three-hour focus group sessions in the U.S. and Europe. We asked participants, with lights dimmed and mood music playing, to drift back to their childhoods and jot down the memories evoked by the prototype PT Cruiser parked in the room. After the sessions, we analyzed the stories, looking for the emotion—and the "reptilian hot buttons"—sparked by the vehicle.

When Chrysler hired me, I and about a dozen other members of the PT Cruiser team took the designers' first prototypes and hit the road. Over several months, we held a series of three-hour sessions in cities across the U.S. and Europe. Unlike the traditional focus groups, where participants are chosen because they fit into a particular demographic segment, the members of these groups were picked to represent entire cultures.

In the first hour after showing the group a PT Cruiser, I told the participants, seated in a circle: "I'm from another planet, and I don't even know what you do with this thing. What is the purpose of this thing?" One early prototype was described by many participants as too toy-like. They said, "I'm grown up, so I don't want a toy," and we thus knew that the design was wrong.

In the second hour, participants were asked to sit on the floor, like children, and use scissors and a pile of magazines to cut out collages of words they thought described the vehicle. At that point, their chief concern about the prototype became clear: it looked insubstantial and unsafe. This discomfort was particularly notable with focus groups in the U.S., where hatchbacks don't sell as well as they do in Europe. In the conversation following the collage making, many participants suggested that the rear hatch's large window would let prying outsiders see in and make the car dangerous if hit from behind.

A group in Paris had a different reaction. Accustomed to hatchbacks, the French group was more concerned about the car's utility, rather than its safety. The group described the prototype as a tantalizingly wrapped box under a Christmas tree that promised a great gift, but didn't deliver one.

The result: the Chrysler team went back to the drawing board and, in later sessions, introduced a model with removable rear seats and a front passenger seat that folded forward to make a tray that could hold a laptop. These became the PT Cruiser's most talked-about features.

The third hour was perhaps the most bizarre—but also the most productive. I asked the participants to lie down on the floor. I then dimmed the lights, began playing tapes of soothing music, and told the group to relax their bodies. I wanted to lull them into a semi-sleeping state when the intellectual part of the brain hadn't yet seized control from the instinctive part. The goal was to figure out what "reptilian hot button" the PT Cruiser pushed.

I gave the participants pens and paper and asked them to write down stories triggered by the prototype they had just seen. In the first focus groups, the stories again centered on toys. In later groups, when I asked participants to write about what they hoped the PT Cruiser would become, the stories contrasted the dangerous outside world with the secure interior of a car. The participants wanted more of a sport-utility vehicle. "It's a jungle out there," said one message. "It's a mad world. People want to kill me, rape me." My message to the designers: "Give me a big thing like a tank." So the designers went to work to make the PT Cruiser look tougher. They bulked up the fenders, giving the car a kind of bulldog stance from the rear. They also made the rear window smaller, increasing the amount of sheet metal in the hatch to make it look stronger. The result: a vehicle that thrilled some, and put off others.

Problem Solving: Do We Have the Right Problem?

One difficulty of discovering unconscious codes is understanding that the actual problem may be different than the perceived problem, since the unconscious logic of emotion may be directly counter to conscious logic. For example, most psychologists believe that phobias (irrationally exaggerated fears) have little to do with the thing feared, and more to do with seemingly unrelated subconscious matters. Thus, an intense fear of flying may have more to do with, for example, a childhood trauma than with the physical dangers of flying. People with such phobias, then, often devote tremendous energy and fear to a problem that really isn't the problem.

Before discovering archetypes, many clients feel that they have already identified the problem, when in fact, like a phobia, the true problem is of a different nature.

Many years ago, when Renault was hit by the first oil crisis, they started looking to manufacture a "cheap" car that wouldn't burn much gas. The prime model in this category was the Deux Chevaux, by their competitor, Citroen. It was a difficult champion to beat. The name Deux Chevaux (French for "two horses") alluded to the fact that the car had only two cylinders. It ran on very little gas, but was a "real" car, and Citroen was proud to see customers driving around the world in their surprisingly ugly little automobile. It was easy to take apart, easy to fix, and easy to put back together. But, most importantly, it was economical at a time when the price of oil was rising and people favored value over style. Renault stated their problem this way: how can we create a small, cheap, economical car that consumes very little gas to compete with the Deux Chevaux?

The management thought they had the solution: they knew what cheap and economical meant, and simply had to figure out the logistics of manufacturing a tiny car that used little gas. Renault asked me if I could help them create this new "cheap, economical" car. I agreed, with one stipulation: that we discover what "cheap and economical" meant to the customers (not what we assumed it meant) and let them tell us what they wanted, and what their unspoken needs were. By applying the archetype process, we made some very fascinating discoveries.

The Most Economical Car Is an Egg

The study revealed that most people don't think about the amount of gas they put into their cars. Rather, they want to know what they are getting for their money and the gas that goes into it. "Cheap" and "economical" were relative notions, and did not relate to gas prices or to gas mileage numbers. By going back to the first imprint of a car, we realized that a car is perceived as having two distinct areas: living space and dead space. Dead space is any space that you don't have access to, or where you can't see what's going on in it.

For example, the Corvette was perceived as a car with a lot of dead space and very little living space. Room for passengers and visual access space (the space you can see and control from the inside) was limited. Therefore, even though the Corvette was small, it was not "economical" at any price. The logic of emotion followed that if a car had a lot of dead space, it was not economical, because you had to buy gas to carry all of that dead space around with you. If you put the same amount of gas in a car that had a lot of living space, then the car would be "economical." Within the logic of emotion, then, two cars could have the same exterior size, the same price, and get the same gas mileage and still be perceived as "economically" different if the space of one car was hidden (dead space) and the other was more open and accessible (living space).

An economical car could thus be modeled on an egg with a very thin shell; the egg shape would allow visual access to all parts of the car. Renault believed that they already had egg-shaped cars (their more aerodynamic lines), but those cars were like eggs with a little yolk (living space) and a lot of white (dead space). Instead, Renault needed to make an "egg" with a huge yolk and no whites. In other words, customers wanted the interior space to be as large as possible and visually and physically available to the passengers. Customers wanted more space for their money.

And they got it. Renault built the first minivan and called it L'Espace, or "space." Renault learned that the notions of "cheap" and ""economical" could only be understood once these terms were defined by the archetype that customers wanted a lot of space at a reasonable price. L'Espace, compared to a regular car, was cheap and economical, because for the same price and the same amount of gas, a customer got more space and better access to that space. Some American companies, trying to improve their minivans, came up with the wrong idea in putting a console between the two front seats, thus restricting the "walk through" ability. As anyone familiar with the above archetypes would expect, these models did not sell very well. Renault was close in their original evaluation of its problem; the company had the right substance (the need for a cheap and economical car), but not the correct understanding of its meaning. Often, the true problem is far different from the original evaluation.

Understanding the true problem is the first step in coming up with a creative solution that passes the test in the marketplace.

Chapter 16

Performance Versus Creativity

We have right answers to wrong questions.

When Lego, the famous Danish toy company, wanted to know how to improve their instruction booklets for the American market, they asked me to help. Lego felt that the way to succeed in America was by improving their instruction booklet; American children would then understand how to play with Legos and would want to buy more of them to make all of the things pictured in the booklets. They had already spent a lot of money on research to find out how they could improve their booklets.

As a general rule, I refuse to consider the supposed client problem as the real problem. Most of the time, the real problem is yet to be discovered, as well as its solution.

In this case, Lego wanted to increase sales in America, and they thought that improving their instruction booklet would do the job. The problem was actually far different. Their model was the German market, where they had been successful for many years. They wanted to be as successful in America as they were in Germany, and they didn't see any reason why this success wasn't forthcoming. They believed that the American market was very similar to the German one, because Germans emigrants represented a large and influential group that helped to create the New World.

When we videotaped German kids playing with Legos, however, the tapes showed German children receiving a new box of Legos. The children would very carefully cut the sticker on the side of the box, move the top of the box back, and start sorting out the different elements, putting the red Legos on one side, the blue ones on another, and the white ones in the middle. The process was done with such extreme care and precision, that we observers were rather astonished. They then took the instruction booklet and read it carefully, from start to finish, and proceeded to build an exact replica of what was shown in the booklet.

The process of discovering the imprinting moment with a group of children is more difficult than discovering it in adults. The difficulties of studying children include sustaining their attention span, controlling their tasks, and keeping them focused. That is why videotaping with little adult intervention works best. It allows for direct observation of the logic of emotion process and, if parents are present, often reveals ways of passing archetypes on.

When we observed American children, we got completely different results: American children got the box of Legos, looked at it perfunctorily, and immediately started tearing it apart with great excitement. Once the box was open, they threw everything around in all directions, making an incredible mess in only a few seconds. They then tossed aside the instructions and began to experiment. This is typically American; Americans often don't read instructions.

Lego spent a lot of money creating the best possible instructions for their product, but they never realized that the American kids weren't reading them—they were throwing them away. American children generally never once read any part of the instruction booklets. They simply didn't care about them. Action was more important to them. They were impatient to start making their own things and following their own ideas. They were praised by their mothers for their creativity and unique constructions, completely opposite of the German children who were, on the other hand, praised for following instructions.

The logic of emotion here is that Americans don't read instructions—we don't learn as well from books, processes, or even training, but rather prefer action. We would rather call a friend to get some practical direction than read instructions. We learn by doing and by making mistakes. Legos are perceived by American mothers as a way to develop their children's imaginations and creativity, while in Germany, Legos are a means of learning how to follow instructions and perform tasks in a prescribed manner. The difference here is creativity versus meeting standards, and on the shadow sides, rebellion versus conformity. Of course, some children were different than the others in their cultural group. Some American children conformed by copying others, and some German children were rather creative within the instruction book framework, but the actions of these exceptions were still informed by the overall archetype.

Right Answers to Wrong Questions

Lego had spent a lot of money trying to find out how to improve their instruction booklets for the American market, but the money they spent was wasted because they were addressing the wrong problem. The problem wasn't designing a better booklet, because American children would never read it.

When I presented the results of my study to the president of Lego, I explained that in the archetypal study process, it's important not to have any idea at the beginning about the true nature of the problem. We go through a discovery process together, and we don't know what we will find. But when we discover the right problem, it becomes so obvious that it seems like we knew it all the time.

We have to go back to the original issues. What are we trying to accomplish? Why do we want American children to read instructions? As in the case of Renault, Lego thought they already knew the necessary solution. They thought that by improving their instructions, they would sell more Legos, when actually reading instructions would be disastrous to their American market. American children love a box of Legos because they see it as having infinite possibilities, or precisely because they don't have to follow instructions.

Lego repositioned itself as a source of developing creativity and imagination. If they explained, however, that with one box of Legos there exist infinite possibilities, consumers would only buy one box, creating a loop. Lego needed to create a spiral, with possibilities for children to create more with two boxes than one, and still more with three than two. Instead of an instruction booklet, they needed a growth map, showing how a child's creativity grows from one box to the next. This map could take the form of a framed collection, with stickers that the child put in preset places each time she bought a new box, and that showed her where she was in her creative growth and what was still missing, thereby developing in the child the desire to go further.

The way we look at a problem is crucial. We must always refuse to have any preconceived ideas of what the problem really is. If you have a broken leg and it hurts, you're generally not ready to consider that the problem might be that you are overweight, or that you don't exercise enough. First you want your leg to be fixed and the pain to go away; then you might listen. Clients are the same: they have a problem, and it hurts. They want the pain to go away. I must take their problem into consideration. But my real job is to find the true problem—that is, not to treat the symptoms, but the root causes—to ensure this won't happen again. Getting clients to accept this new paradigm requires a complete change of behavior.

Changing Behaviors

When, in 1989, the Timber Association of California (TAC) was feeling the pressure to change, it didn't know in which direction to go. The TAC had a public image problem, and it asked me to find out why. Their age-old dilemma was created by the steady demand for wood products countered by the need for forest preservation. The problem wasn't whether or not wood products should be made, because even staunch environmentalists need them, nor was the problem to make such products without cutting down trees. Somehow, the process was the issue. But just what aspect of the process was the problem, and how to rectify that problem seemed a mystery.

This dilemma raised some fascinating archetypal questions: What are the American codes for a tree and for a forest? What are the emotions used to imprint these words? What do these words mean at a deep unconscious level in our cultural mind? What will we do with our forests? Will our children still be able to enjoy trees the way we do? What is the future of this industry?

The challenge was to decode the American collective unconscious and its relationship with forestry, and then to see how we could change behaviors to protect the forests while still protecting jobs. We started in California, following the archetypal process by going back to the first experience of a tree and a forest, looking for the common grammar underlying these experiences. We wanted to find out if there was an American way to relate to, learn about, and become emotionally attached to a forest.

We had 10 imprinting sessions where people were asked to go back to their first experience of a forest. We then used a structural analysis approach to decode their stories.

Before long, I was asked to verify these findings by conducting an additional 10 sessions all over the country. After completing these sessions, we had data from more than 500 people, and had collected more than 1,000 imprinting stories. Even though archetypal studies are not meant to be a quantitative business, the Timber Association of California, and the National Forest Product Association felt good about the size of the population studied. They felt even better about the findings. Joyce Kilmer's poem captures the archetype I discovered almost perfectly:

I think that I shall never see
A poem lovely as a tree
A tree whose hungry mouth is pressed
Against the earth's sweet flowing breast;
A tree that looks at God all day
And lifts her leafy arms to pray;
A tree that may in summer wear
A nest of robins in her hair;
Upon whose bosom snow has lain;
Who intimately lives with rain.
Poems are made by fools like me,
But only God can make a tree.

Skeptical of my results, the association conducted its own test. In field polls, Californians were asked to rank, from a list of organizations, which ones they would trust to care for the forests. There were two different lists: one list included the Timber Association of California; the other list included a proposed new name, the California Forestry Association (CFA). In the list with the Timber Association of California, Californians ranked its trustworthiness or credibility very low, at only 16 percent—a ranking only above elected officials. But in the list with the California Forestry Association, Californians ranked its credibility at about 50 percent. We learned that people don't think of the forest as a commodity, even when it's private property. Most people's notion of the forest is deeply engraved with sentiments of camping and hiking when they were children. Thus, when you cut down a tree, even if it's already dying, you are killing it.

Based on the results of the field poll, the organization changed its name to the California Forestry Association. But that's not all it did. Because I also discovered that the code for a seedling is a "human baby," it revamped its public relations campaign.

Previously, in its brochures, the association tried to explain that it was caring for and nurturing forests by showing a big guy with a chain saw, saying, "I care for forests." This message was ineffective. Why? Because caring, nurturing, and making trees grow is a female image, not a male one. Biologically, it takes a few seconds for a man to make a baby. It takes nine months for a woman, though, and then when the baby is born, her work is just beginning. Nurturing and caring are therefore typically feminine, not masculine. The association's message on how it planted trees also contained a negative image. A big guy in boots carries a seedling by its leaves (a baby by the hair) and plants it (the baby) with his feet. In the subconscious mind, the consumer is thinking that you can't do that to a baby. The images were wrong because they lacked sensitivity.

From Quantifying Trees to Caring for Babies

The usual manner of speaking about planting trees came from the male performance-quantity scheme. An industry spokesman would say, "This year we planted 2,425,000 new trees." In isolation from an archetype, however, such figures mean very little. Is this a lot of trees? Did you cut down more than you planted? What does this number mean? Does it mean that you care about the forest and about humans, or does it just mean that you need to plant to cut down even more trees?

After hearing of our findings, the president of one of the companies ran to the phone to tell his advertising agency to halt their present campaign because it didn't respect the archetype. A few weeks later, I received a copy of their new ad; I was thrilled. There were no dead trees, no big numbers, no male quantity-performance kinds of communication. Instead, they used a picture of a mother with a baby in her arms—very simple, very touching, and a universal symbol of nurturing and protecting. The text read: "For every baby born in California, we plant 100 trees."

Every aspect of the archetypal code was addressed in this ad: the caring, the life cycle, the feminine side, the baby associated with the baby tree, the idea of growing together, the notion that both babies and trees need maternal care, as well as an easy representation of the industry's numbers. The new ad brought to the public's awareness the entire life cycle of the forest, which was the side of the industry that had been ignored in the past.

The California Forestry Association also radically changed the images in its communication media. They now depict women speaking about caring, nurturing, seeding, and planting. Women are shown carrying baby trees in their arms. They gently plant the trees with their hands—the way you would treat a baby. The harvesting (cutting down) of trees is downplayed; it is explained using a graphic depicting the life cycle of a forest. Consequently, the California Forestry Association now has a more positive image.

The Code for a Tree: Human Being

In all the stories I gathered in my study for the CFA, the underlying grammar was very clear: a tree is not a plant, it is human. To cut down a tree is to kill a tree. Trees are born, grow old, and die; they have heads, arms, hair, and mouths; they bleed, suffer, and observe. People speak to them and listen to them. They pray. We have roots, just as trees do. We, too, need to feel grounded and yet to branch out. A tree might die, but a forest, like a family, can survive. The public can accept that trees must die, but they cannot stand idly by while forests disappear; such a catastrophe would be equivalent to a holocaust.

If trees are human, it follows that young trees are babies: they need to be fed, spoken to, protected, and loved. Each baby tree is an individual, and thus it is not "natural" to grow baby trees in a line on tree farms, just as it wouldn't be natural to grow babies in labs.

The code for old growth is "grandparents." They have seen so much, and they are wise. Their very presence is a comfort to us in times of trouble. Old trees thus represent the past and our heritage, and though one day they will die, it will be a slow, natural, and quiet end. They deserve peace and are seen as sacred.

The American archetype for "forest" is actually two archetypes: the natural forest and the managed forest. The natural forest has little to do with the reality of nature; the archetype says it is a clean place where everything is in harmony, and there are no bugs or predators and no desperate fight for survival. The "natural forest" is a place to meditate, a playground, and a place we like to know is available to us even if we never use it. It's a dream place, a symbolic place, a sylvan retreat.

To manage the forest is thus to destroy harmony. A managed forest is a natural forest that has been invaded by man. A managed forest means an unnatural intrusion that leads to the destruction of paradise. This archetype explains the now-classic scripts of any Tarzan movie. At the beginning, the forest is in harmony. Everything is beautiful, and everyone loves everyone else. Tarzan flies from one tree to another, kisses a lion, hugs a giraffe, caresses an alligator, swims in clear water, and plays with Chita. Then, suddenly everything changes. The white man arrives, and he puts this harmony in danger, even threatening Tarzan's life. The whole forest must therefore pull together to expel him. After a fight, the white man is eliminated, much like a virus, and harmony is reestablished. This is the logic of emotion that is engaged when we hear, "manage the forest." It is a powerfully negative statement to suggest man is managing Mother Nature.

The code for timber is thus "killer." The word "timber," recalls the archetypal association of "timber!," yelled when a tree is about to fall down after being cut, or killed. In the American mind, this is a strong association.

Application to Communication

When we become aware of cultural archetypes, we need to change the nature of our communication and have this code become part of our everyday practice, or we undercut the message that we are conveying. If we want people to listen to what we have to tell them, we need to use words and attitudes that fit with archetypes and thus clearly express our position and what we want to say.

Clearly, "timber" was the wrong word for the CFA to use. It became clear that the industry should not emphasize the cutting or "killing" aspect of their work but rather focus on the product. Almost everyone enjoys wood. It's a fantastic material because it's warm, natural, and simple. It is also beautiful. It has a quality of its own that no other material can match. When I went to visit a saw mill, however, I saw no indication of the wondrous final product. Instead, I saw that the way the industry was presenting itself to visitors was completely wrong.

They had piles of cut and stripped trees ("dead bodies") outside. They had "killing" machines. They were showing excessively the undesirable aspect of their industry and nothing of the resulting products or cultivation programs. This striking analogy demonstrates what I mean: suppose you are a plastic surgeon who is an expert in rhinoplasty, and you are proud of the results you get. So, to attract more clients, you choose to show a picture of one of your patients: the nose is opened, the skin of the nose is completely folded over on one side on the cheek, the face is covered with blood, and you are holding a hammer and knife, breaking the bones. How many new clients do you think you are going to get with this kind of picture?

This is exactly what the forestry industry was doing. They were communicating an archetypal slaughter of trees with holocaust-like machinery and expected to gain rich and respectful support from the American public. They were exposing their process, ignoring their product, and downplaying the benefits of the industry.

Men, Women, and the Natural Forest

Out of a 70-year cycle, during which they seeded, protected, and made the forest grow, the Timber Association chose to emphasize the six months when they cut down trees. Their real job was protecting and enhancing the natural life cycle of the forest. Why? To produce natural products for the American family.

This came as somewhat of a shock to members of the industry. Of course, they knew this—it was part of the underlying archetype—but it had remained at an unconscious level until my study. Most importantly, they were not aware how important this archetype was for their communication with the American public.

In the phrase, "protecting and enhancing the natural life cycle of the forest," several words are important, but none more than "cycle." The difference between men and women becomes important here. Men don't experience cycles the same way women do; every 28 days, most women are reminded of what a biological cycle is. The biological scheme for a woman is different, too, regarding time and quantity. Men produce billions of sperm during their lifetime. Women, on the other hand, produce only about 400 eggs, which are released one at a time over the course of many days. This difference affects their perception of time, quantity, and the effort required to create something. As a result, women have somewhat of a biological reference for the amount of time and nurturing that babies require. Reflecting on these schemata helped us a great deal in shaping the communication for the forest industry.

It has never become more clear to me that in decoding a culture and helping people to become aware of what they are doing, we are helping them to communicate. The wood industry generally cares about the forest and wants to preserve it. But they were not decoding properly what they were doing and saying, and after this decoding they had to go through a complete change of attitude and behavior.

On a Clear-cutting Day, You can See Forever

One member of the association was practicing clear-cutting. My advice was very clear-cut, as well. "You should never use the term "clear-cutting," because the code for clear-cutting is "holocaust." "But," the man replied, "we can explain why we clear-cut because there are good aspects of it that people should know about." I reemphasized to him that this would be the equivalent of Hitler trying to justify the holocaust.

Regardless, when the manager in charge of public affairs was asked for an interview concerning clear-cutting, he accepted. He did the best he could to justify the practice, but not understanding the code, there was no way it could have worked. And it didn't. Discovering the archetypal code, then, not only explains the past and the present, but it can also inform our perception of the future. The failure of the clear-cutting interview was easy to predict.

This code is as good for environmentalists as it is for the timber industry. When environmental radicals spike trees to save them, it is perceived by the public as an aberration. It's like planting a nail in a child's arm to save him from going to school. Both environmentalists and loggers can learn to respect the archetypal code of the forest.

As seen in the forestry industry, knowledge of an archetype only makes a difference if it is implemented into a change of action and attitude. It is sometimes difficult to accept that you aren't supposed to use certain words, especially when these words have been a part of your everyday life for decades.

What a "forest" is in the American mind has been imprinted for generations with the same code. Our freedom to change things is not situated at this level. Rather, we can free ourselves by knowing these codes and using them according to our vision. If we cannot change *how* we feel, (the logic of our emotions, which is cultural), we might want to change *what* we feel. We need to re-root ourselves into the depth of the archetypal soul of our culture. We must stop imitating the Japanese or the Germans simply because they produce good cars that might have fewer defects. Let's tap into the hidden genius of each country; let's decode the culture in order to frame the right question, discover the right answer, and meet the real needs of people with our products and services.

Chapter 17

Archetypal Answers to Seven Unanswerable Questions

Who wins in the war of the sexes?

Archetypolgy can be used to solve business and marketing problems by providing valuable insights into the collective unconscious. What is clear to us, after more than 25 years of research and field experience, is that archetypology can also be applied to societal problems in a way that provides fresh insight into their causes and cures. These are my responses to seven questions about America that are so complex we need to look at them through archetypal glasses.

1. If violence is our solution, what is the problem? The problem is guilt. Americans love to feel guilty about something. This guilt complex can take different forms (Vietnam, slavery, victory against the Germans or the Japanese). We are always too rich, too powerful, too big. Our enemies, and many of our "friends," manipulate this complex. Thus, in America, the victim must be blamed. That woman was raped because she was too sexy; she dressed too provocatively; she led him on. This man was too rich; that's why he was murdered. This star was too famous; that's why the crazy guy followed her everywhere. Because we feel guilty, we believe that the criminal is somehow the victim, and that the victim is to blame.

In America, it's okay for a teenager to kill a German tourist mother in front of her children, and then get court-supplied lawyers to explain that American culture is actually the guilty party. It's okay for fatherless teenage girls to have five children before the age of 18 and to be paid by the state to do so. It's okay for teenage brothers in Beverly Hills to buy shotguns and kill their father because he was "abusive." It's okay for a teenage girl with mental problems to shoot her boyfriend's wife and then to make millions of dollars on television rights. It's even okay for the wife and boyfriend to make money on the deal.

Every day, lawyers prove that American culture is guilty, and that we are all collectively to be blamed, not their individual clients. By the same token, we punish achievers through taxes and reward failures through welfare, because we feel guilty and responsible for the poor, minorities, and criminals. Because of this neurotic attitude, we are not looking for solutions—we are consciously perpetuating a self-fulfilling prophecy. American culture feels guilty because we don't believe that perfection is possible, and so we must find something to blame for our inevitable failure.

The Japanese have the lowest rate of violence and teenage pregnancy in the world, as well as the highest rate of literacy. Obviously, these two things are related; they form part of a cultural whole. We need to recognize that our social problems are not isolated, but rather part of a whole cultural system of guilt. We think that it's more important to give a second chance to the criminal than to protect everyone's favorite whipping boy—the middle-aged, hard-working man on whom we place all the guilt. By going after this symbol of America, we are destroying many positive aspects of American culture, the same culture that attracts immigrants, that put a man on the moon, that won the Cold War, and that created the freest nation on earth. The neurotic adolescent American mind must feel guilty about all of these achievements that have placed us ahead of every other nation in the world.

If we really want to stop violence in America, we must stop feeling guilty about being the wealthiest and freest nation on earth. We must stop getting stuck in the past; we have tried long enough to pay for the "white man's sins." It doesn't work. We must recognize that guns are not the problem, but rather a symptom. The Swiss all have arms at home because every Swiss is in the military, but there is almost no violence there. Why? Because they realize that they have arms to protect their country, not to rob and kill their neighbors.

We must stop promoting racism in America. Everyone should be treated equally according to the law. When a good legal system says people are guilty, they should be accepted as guilty; when the jury says they are innocent, they should be accepted as innocent. We must also reclaim the war zones that we call "inner cities". If necessary, we should use the military to take back neighborhoods, one block at a time, and take all of the guns away. A local police force of citizens could be trained to maintain order.

We also need to treat teenagers like teenagers. Enforce a curfew of 11 p.m., and hold teens responsible for their actions.

Let's promote the idea that unity is good, and place the guilt on the dividers. Let's be proud to be Americans again. There is no problem we cannot solve, once we wake up the sleeping giant. Let's stop being an adolescent culture, reinforcing and rewarding adolescent behavior. The problem is in the American mind, not in American streets, schools, or inner cities. We simply must decide that enough is enough.

2. Who wins in the war of the sexes? Actually, we are all losers, because all of the energy that is not used to satisfy your partner and yourself becomes frustration, and is used to take revenge and to destroy others. "Make love, not war," we might say, but as a culture, we are obviously better at making war. Ours is not a sensuous, sexual, loving culture. We do not explore these directions as an art. We don't develop talents for pleasure among our children. We experience sex just as we experience food; we don't make love well or enjoy our dinner. That's why we invented fast food.

Because violence is equivalent to sex in America, loneliness is the ultimate winner of the battle of the sexes. Men don't understand women, and women don't understand men. Neither side gets it. Americans are becoming sexually atrophied and losing our capability to have fun and to enjoy each other.

What is needed is a new feminine culture (not feminist, but feminine). The anima of America needs to be awakened. The mission for women should not be to win against men, but rather to bring more feminine dimensions into American life, and to wake up the feminine side of American culture.

With more care, respect, pleasure and fun, we might even begin to like each other, thereby restoring a sense of balance in our relationships. Many cultures look at male-female relationships not as combative, but as complementary and harmonious.

It's time for a return to the sophistication and refinement of the old Hollywood days, when Clark Gable and Errol Flynn, Audrey Hepburn, and Catherine Hepburn ruled the screen. Hollywood must play a role here in moving away from simple cartoon-like figures, such as those portrayed by Stallone or Schwartzeneger, to more sophisticated characters and role models.

Primitive violence is everywhere, and everyone is concerned with survival. By triggering our ancestral fears, Hollywood can always produce a hit. Thoughtful people, though, are fed up with blood-and-guts and special effects. Where is culture, the art of pleasure, and sophistication? There is a strong connection between the level of a society's culture and its degree of violence. Japan has a very sophisticated culture, from flower arranging to food, painting and music; their writing itself is an art. Consequently Japan has the lowest rate of violence in the world. Although they have a strong violence archetype, they control it with a strong culture!

The American mind works in animal time, as I discussed earlier (prey vs. predator). We are always looking for the quick fix and instant gratification, and we do not see that by postponing this immediate gratification, we might achieve higher satisfaction. We need to promote refinement and sophistication; if we must have violence, it should become an art, as many martial arts are, with rules, rituals, and aesthetics.

The male-female relationship can become an art, as well. We need to use American archetypes to create an American ritual of love, to achieve higher levels of satisfaction. We must harness the destructive energy of the battle of the sexes and reorient it towards a vent for pleasure. We must value the relationship more than the contract, pleasure more than power, and exploration more than control.

We have a divine mission to please each other, love each other, and care for each other's needs. We must develop the talents necessary to fulfill this mission. Can you imagine conducting classes in pleasure, instead of creating more frustration and violence? Instead of simply providing teenagers with sex education (promoting the view of the body as a machine without emotion), we should also educate them about love, attaching as much importance to emotions as to hormones.

Men and women are different; only when we accept these differences can we really love each other. The goal is not to understand each other completely (is it even possible?), but rather to simply love each other and be happy. Two musicians who play well together might not understand why they produce such great music together; that's part of the magic and the mystery of life. We must learn to value the "right chemistry" without knowing anything about that particular chemistry. Men and women can achieve together a higher level of love and pleasure than any drug will ever give them. We should make this our goal as the winner of the war of the sexes.

3. Why are the homeless homeless in a nation of homes? There were no homeless people in Russia under the Communist regime, but millions lived in forced labor camps. There were no homeless in Germany in the late 1930s, but there were concentration camps. There were no homeless in Sweden, but most of the achievers were leaving the country, and the socialist regime was bankrupt.

It is precisely because we have more chances to own our homes in America that we have homeless. Owning a home ranks near the top of most Americans' priorities, to the point where it is considered a God-given right. A home is part of your identity; it's where you get your bills, tax notices, and junk mail. A monthly mortgage payment is proof of your trustworthiness—the larger the payment, the more trustworthy you are.

It is because of the opportunities to succeed in America that by comparison, a lot of people feel poor. We have to remember, though, that we have the "richest poor" in the world. The most overweight poor people are in America; obviously our poor can at least eat, even too much.

We have to accept failure, as part of the American mind. Americans currently believe that if you have opportunities, you are responsible for your own fate. We view the homeless as individuals without identities. Ask any middle-class New Yorker if he knows the name of even one of the hundreds of derelicts he happens to pass in a single day, and the chances are good that he won't. We turn our eyes in the opposite direction, because nothing scares an American more than the possibility of definite failure.

Our adolescent view refuses to see situations with no hope. That's why we refuse to see death in a realistic manner and our "funeral homes" look like motels. It's also why we don't keep our dead in their homes. We really have no culture of death. For the Egyptians 4,000 years ago, the meaning of life came from the meaning of death. In America, we are adolescents who are invulnerable; although we know better, we like to think that we will never die, that technology will soon give us new bodies, and that with money we can buy everything, including eternity.

This desire to escape from unpleasant realities also drives our perceptions of mental illness. In a nation where therapy is more popular than sex as an indoor sport, we harbor a true aversion to any sort of mental illness that is more serious than garden-variety neuroses.

Many, perhaps most, of the homeless people wandering the streets of America's largest cities are mentally ill—the product of an ill-conceived social policy of "deinstitutionalization" that was supposed to have been accompanied by community support and appropriate drug therapy, but was not. Those who are not genuinely mentally ill are often drug or alcohol addicts.

The homeless crisis is a medical emergency on a par with AIDS, and should be approached as such by public officials. Contrary to the best arguments of some that homeless people are simply asserting their "lifestyle" rights, no competent person "chooses" to sleep on the sidewalk in urine-soaked clothing in hot and cold weather.

The first challenge is to separate the medically incompetent from those who are simply poor and living in sub-standard conditions, or who have no home at all. Most big cities own land and hundreds of abandoned buildings. If we could enroll the homeless in a "build or renovate your own home" project run by volunteers, in which they could learn carpentry, plumbing, electrical work, and painting, we could form the nucleus of a "re-build America" program. Materials could be donated by corporations, with appropriate tax credits, and land and buildings could be supplied by the cities. The entire project could be done with no extra spending required from the government.

The "working homeless" could accomplish something that they could be proud of—a home and an identity. They would gain confidence, self-esteem, respect, and knowledge. Giving them money or shelter that they do not earn simply reinforces a cycle of dependency. This is why more than 30 years of trying to help the poor by giving them assistance has simply increased the poverty level of the inner city poor and kept them out of the American mainstream.

The mentally competent homeless have to be looked upon as temporary homeless people, immigrants to the American experience. Given the same chances that are available to all new immigrants, many would make it.

4. Why and how do cultures get out of balance? When one force gets out of balance (Germany 1939, Russia 1917 and 1991, France 1789, America 1969), other forces try to compensate; this is the systematic aspect of culture. However, if this reinforcement pushes in the same direction, it can produce self-destructive actions that will assure the end of a culture (Nero burning Rome, Napoleon trying to occupy Moscow in winter, Nazi Germany destroying the Jews and their valuable contribution to German culture). From the fall of the Roman Empire to the end of the Soviet Union, the same historical pattern repeats itself. This pattern can be explained as an attempt to change the CNA (time, space, and energy) that results in the subsequent death of a culture. In other words, a misuse of energy results in the self-destruction of a culture.

The extreme bureaucracy in the Soviet Union resulted in potatoes rotting in the countryside while people starved in the cities. It is not that there was no food; rather, the government did not let the food reach the population. This crisis was thus the product of the Soviet culture (its CNA), not of a genuine famine. This is a prime example of what happens when a society is closed to new ways of thinking.

As seen earlier, American culture receives new immigrant energy all the time. This is not a problem, but rather a solution, as long as we don't let one fanatic group dominate the others, and as long as we respect the original fabric of America. The danger in America might come from groups that are losing ground with the American mainstream, the dividers for whom the American dream has yet to come true. Although millions of African Americans have made enormous strides and live solidly middle class lives, there is still a large and seemingly intractable underclass of minorities that threatens to self-destruct in a climate of violence and drugs. One solution is to reinforce the idea of unity with new immigrants, and to treat the minority underclass as new immigrants with no past, rather than as perpetual victims.

Another risk could come from the American force of caring and generosity. We might try to blame and to tax the rich, giving to and protecting the poor. In doing so, however, we would destroy the American drive for individual achievement and responsibility. The result might be a Sweden or a Russia, with no incentive for self-achievement, no entrepreneurship, and no reward for innovation or risk-taking.

Still another hazard in America is the force that says that the rights of the individual are paramount, even to the detriment of society. We already spend millions of dollars on criminals who wait 15 years or more before their final appeals are exhausted. We are a nation where criminals are more protected than victims, where suing your neighbor is a national sport, and where the rights of the individual are often ranked above the needs of society. Instead of adhering to the Musketeers motto, "All for one, and one for all," our society is rapidly moving toward, "All against one, and one against all," or, "Me against everyone."

In Japan it is considered immoral to sue your neighbor. You want to be modest, non-confrontational, and in search of harmony (family harmony, community harmony, personal harmony). The same positive force exists in America, seen in local communities taking over their destiny and trying to fix their problems, but an opposite force represents a danger: individuals against individuals, and not caring how many people lose, as long as individually, we win.

Our legal system is so complicated that most people feel that it's getting out of hand. The purpose of our judicial system is not justice anymore, but politics. If the results of a first trial do not satisfy the government, the media, or a special interest group, someone might be tried again for the same crime. Isn't this unconstitutional? When a convicted criminal can appeal for more than a decade, and still get taxpayers' money for his support, something is wrong.

The solution? Getting back to basics and simplifying everything. If you sue someone and lose, you pay all of the expenses. If you win, the other guy pays. Better yet, let the losing attorney pay!

Rewards should be limited, and frivolous lawsuits should be punished. Tort lawyers should be highly taxed. Gains from lawsuits should also be highly taxed, much like an inheritance. We should make it more attractive to work hard and to produce than to pretend to be a victim and try to cash in on the legal system. Lawsuits don't produce anything.

5. Could America fall like the Soviet Union? We are foolish to think that this country couldn't fall. If our adolescent forces become dominant, the potent mix of drugs, crime, lawyers, teenage pregnancy, and single-issue group rights activists could lead to the fragmentation of our union into small, medieval-style city states, racist ghettos, and multinational corporations with no single national loyalty, perhaps even with their own professional armies. Most of our large cities could be devastated, and capitalism could flee the U.S. to find refuge in highly protected enclaves. America could become a frontier—the Wild West all over again.

Several other scenarios might also result from the American mindset. There is the civil war scenario, due to growing tensions between blacks and whites, rich and poor, and males and females. There is the radical liberal scenario in which America could become a communist country without the label, with several groups permanently on welfare, a hyper-atrophied bureaucracy and red tape, as well as taxing and spending extremes.

Still another scenario might come from the extreme right. The McCarthyism, Russ Limbaugh, Pat Robertson side of the American mind. This "America first," "America: love it or leave it," attitude is the same force that created prohibition and the red-baiting phobias.

This last scenario is the most probable, because it fits the American mindset. When too much weight is put on one side of an axis, a culture reacts by putting as much weight on the other side.

The liberal lawyers and equality radicals of 1960's America went too far. Today, we are still paying the price for their liberal philosophies. It's clear that it is not enough to have generous ideas. One must understand how the cultural mind works: sooner or later the core culture will reappear and repeat itself, or a society will disappear.

America will fall only if we fail to achieve a balance. Several forces in action in the American mind make me believe that a fall will not happen.

America is a young culture. As Oscar Wilde puts it, "The youth of America is their oldest tradition. It has been going on now for 300 years." Our liberal immigration policies provide a permanent influx of new blood, new hopes, and new dreams. These immigrants are people who want to make it—the Asian minority makes up 3 percent of America's population, and 30 percent of its MBAs.

We are very flexible and mobile. The media credits a lot of importance to layoffs, but such structural changes have come at regular intervals since the beginning of the Industrial Revolution, always accompanied by a widespread perception of intractable unemployment. Old factories with old "routine" jobs will move to places where workers are paid less. But jobs with high added value, such as service activities, will do well in the U.S. The service sector is one aspect of the American economy that is highly profitable and that creates a surplus, rather than a deficit. If old jobs are disappearing, new and different jobs will be created. These types of changes simply mean that American culture is adapting itself to a new economy.

Americans thrive on chaos and at pulling together when there is a perception of danger. America as a culture has a strong survival instinct. It is a nation of survivors. Marx said that the proletariat had nothing to lose but its chains. Likewise, Americans have nothing to lose but their dreams. As long as American dreams have a future, the nation will not fall.

Because many American principles are universal, they speak to all the cultures of the world. America is a culture created by all the survivors of the world. If this nation were to change, or lose its CNA, these survivors would have to transfer their hopes and dreams to another place or create another culture. Because we are in permanent adolescence, though, we have more future than past, more dreams than reality, and more hopes than resentments. We are constantly re-creating ourselves. The Soviet Union fell because its people had no hopes, no dreams, and no future left. America can, and must, avoid that fate.

6. Why is loneliness an American disease? Americans don't want to be rich, famous, powerful, or successful, although they constantly strive to achieve these things. They really want to be loved; armed with this insight, we can go beyond superficial explanations or interpretations of American behavior. Why did we go after Saddam Hussain? Oil, money, power? No, it was to be loved, or to show to ourselves, the world, and God that we are good, lovable people.

These are the basic forces of the "lonesome cowboy" structure. At the end of the movie, the hero always rides off into the sunset alone. Even if the girl standing there waving, and is nice looking and loving (and she always is), the call of the wild is always stronger. The hero has dispatched the bad guys and saved her father's ranch but as he is stiff, he is not worthy of her love. He must prove himself again in a new time and place. The cliché is always the same, even the music. The girl stays there, also alone, hoping that someday he will return.

Our culture then layers on the idea of the "impossible dream." The adolescent American mind thus believes that Miss Perfect and Mr. Right exist, and that one day they will appear in our lives. We believe that this person will fulfill all our needs, transform our lives, and make everything perfect. Americans keep believing it;

even after several divorces, they keep getting married. The U.S. has both the highest divorce rate and the largest number of people who disapprove of divorce.

This is a classic cultural neurosis. When the self that you experience is close to your ideal self, you are okay, but when the gap between the two is too large, you are in trouble. America is in trouble. We have the highest percentage of single parents in the world, and the lowest percentage of people who are unmarried and living together. The cultural script is clear; we have no concept of emotion and sexual fun, but rather we have unrealistic expectations. We get married, it doesn't work, and we try again and again, until we finally give up and live and die alone. The best-selling books, after those about diets and about how to become rich, are those on how to live alone.

Other cultures are different. The Japanese, for example, are almost the opposite of Americans. They have one of the lowest divorce rates, the lowest percentage of children born out of wedlock, the lowest percentage of single-parent families, and the lowest rate of teenage pregnancy.

At the same time, the Japanese mind does not relate to marriage and relationships like the American mind does. In family matters, Japan is the most conservative of the major industrial nations. Divorce is rare, and single mothers still anomalous. Marriage remains an expectation of adult life. It is seen as a patriotic duty, important to the nation's moral and economic well-being. The Japanese believe that Western marriage is such a precarious proposition because it rests on the transitory states of passion and love. Because American love is an adolescent kind with high unrealistic expectations, it ends in loneliness. Japanese love, on the other hand, is a stable and pragmatic. Indeed, the Japanese language does not contain the word *love,* merely "like a lot" (dai suki desu).

Loneliness is the direct result of the American mindset. We have no culture of how to enjoy, respect, or please one another. Our parents didn't imprint us with the required mental highways, and our adolescent culture reinforces the separation between sex, love, pregnancy and family. These elements of our lives are moving away from one another, so we see the "other" as an enemy.

What's the solution? Look at how men and women relate in other cultures. American women have told me that when they arrive in Italy, they suddenly feel like women again. In Italy, flirtation is a fun game; it's never really serious, and everyone knows that. The same behavior exhibited by an Italian man in Italy is okay, but by an American man, it's not acceptable. Why? Because women know that each culture is different, and that American men are more violent than Italians.

American mothers must start teaching their children by example in the way they relate to men; to their sons, they need to emphasize love and sensuousness, as well as how to relate to women. American fathers need to teach male sensuousness and emotions to their daughters in the same way. If we love our children, there is no more beautiful gift than teaching them how to have a life full of pleasure and love—that is, how to transform their lives into masterpieces of joy. The stark alternative a life of loneliness.

7. Can America retain economic dominance? The American mind is programmed to be number one. And the fact is, we are still the world's most dominant political, military, and economic force. Success is partly perception. The code is this: if we're good, we should be the winners, and we are good so we are the winners. For Americans, money is the proof of this success, and we have more of it than anyone. There is also a moral dimension in regaining economic dominance in fields where our industries are challenged, a type of moral mission to prove to the world that our principles are universal. Americans don't have an ideology; we are an ideology.

What elements of the American mindset will lead more and more to economic dominance? The first positive element is that we are never sure; we don't have a plan or an ideology. The Russians had plans and an ideology that was supposed to run their bureaucracy like a church. They had strong unity, but did not allow any diversity.

Another one of America's strengths is that we are not intellectual. We may not read, but we believe in action and we believe in ourselves. We learn from our mistakes, and we have a divine mission: to make this planet better for our children. Our culture reinforces these messages: "Get back to basics," "the bottom line," "keep it simple, stupid." We know that our principles are good because we are number one, which means that the American mind cannot allow another nation or culture to dominate it economically, because that would indicate that our principles are wrong.

The real economic challenge comes from our former enemies, the Japanese and the Germans. Although we won militarily against them, it often seems like they are taking their revenge on us economically. Although we are still more powerful and more successful than Japan or Germany, we get depressed when Hondas are the best-selling cars in America, or because Japan has a large trade surplus. The fact is, America will always dominate Japan economically. Why? Japan has limited space. That's why, historically, they have been imperialist invaders. Today, that invasion is only economic. They don't expect to dominate in lifestyle, only in technology. No one wants to become like the Japanese socially. At the opposite pole, Americans have an open-space policy and an open-space mind. Thus, we have room for expansion.

Unlike Japan, where the only way to be Japanese is to be born one, Americans are a nation of immigrants. America exports its culture and lifestyle around the world. It is the American mindset that makes the major difference. The Japanese mind is too slow to react, too stuck in the past, too sure of its divine superiority, too racist, and too closed. They don't have our crime rate, but they don't have our number of Nobel Prizes either.

The Germans' greatest strength, and also their greatest weakness, is their fondness for "standards." Max Weber once said that happiness was an ideal bureaucracy. The solution is the right rules, the right laws, and the perfect system. This is all very nice when talking about products or soldiers in the Army, but rejecting other people's standards and cultures in favor of your own makes it very difficult to create a unified Europe. Today, Germany cannot invade Europe militarily, and it cannot economically dominate the world without the rest of Europe. Due to their inability to accept other cultures, combined with this necessary dependence on the cooperation of its neighbors, Germany will most likely never be able to seriously compete with the United States, economically. In a world where the rules keep changing and systems keep falling, we need the American spirit, ingenuity, and bias for action. Germans simply don't have this flexibility.

Although we tend to take it for granted, our primary economic partner is Canada. Although we have many concerns about Canada, we have no serious problems with that country. We even have a tendency to think of Canadians as our brothers and sisters (when in fact, we have very different cultures and mindsets). Mexico is also already a part of America. California, New Mexico, Arizona, and Texas have long histories of influence and interdependence with Mexico, and many cities in California bear Spanish names (San Diego, Santa Barbara, San Francisco, Los Angeles).

That North America is an economic market is obvious. Canada, the U.S., and Mexico have a far better chance to accomplish economic unity with a profitable outcome for everyone than do 15 ancestral enemies in Western Europe, dominated by the Germans.

The real strength of the American economy, though, is the American mind. Americans are ordinary people who can do extraordinary things. The collapse of the Soviet Union, the very difficult, and by no means certain, birth of European unity, and the impossibility of opening the Japanese mind to change leaves us as the certain winner in the race for economic dominance.

SECRET 6:
THE MORE GLOBAL, THE MORE LOCAL: Quality is the passport to global markets, but the code for quality differs from culture to culture, market to market, person to person.

You need to know what quality means in each culture or market, and to achieve quality you need to have clarity of purpose.

CHAPTER 18

CLARITY OF PURPOSE

In any campaign, clarity of purpose makes the difference.

Clarity of purpose is what always makes a difference, in times of peace even more than in times of war. Born in France during wartime, I kept my sense of purpose for more than 50 years concerning the American goal for peace in Europe. Now a proud American, I feel even more strongly about that mission.

Only America can fulfill this task. Are we ready to lead the world in this area again? It's very clear that we are not. But my understanding of the way the American mind functions and my experience of our different codes tells me that we are never ready. We weren't ready in December 1941 when the Japanese attacked Pearl Harbor, but we still won the war.

Once again, America doesn't understand what is going on or what the new rules of the game are, after the disappearance of its "favorite enemy." This nation will win again, though, as it develops stronger world leadership. Because we don't think this is impossible, we will do it—if we take a bold step toward a new vision, mission, and clarity of purpose.

The first step toward world leadership is accepting that cultures have an unconscious and understanding how our collective mind functions. This can also have a very important impact on your personal life, because this collective mind is a crucial element of your own personality. How you as an individual react and function, successfully or not, in the areas of money, sex, and fame is due largely to how well you are in sync with American archetypes and codes.

The collective American mind is powerful. It can destroy you, or it can make a winner out of you. By learning to put your energy in the right direction—in line with codes—you will learn faster from your mistakes, and you will ultimately succeed.

This new science of archetypes can help you decode other cultures, as well. Accepting that other cultures also have a unique unconscious is crucial for business. At an age when *diversity* is a key word, it is fundamental to understand and accept the fabulous richness and variety of cultures, within America first, and then throughout the world. By succeeding in becoming one people, with a plurality of ethnicity, races and cultures, we might prove that we are the last, best hope for mankind. No other nation, no other culture, and no other group of people as diverse as we are has ever accomplished as much as we have. We have an obligation to the world; only Americans can make the paradigm shift required to create a new global world.

What Has to Be Done

When Freud came to America at the beginning of the 20th century, he made a famous statement: "They don't realize that I am bringing them the devil." The time of individual psychoanalysis, though, is over. We aren't "bringing the devil" anymore, but with the possibility of decoding cultures, we do hope to bring in a new era of understanding and partnership among cultures, and to create a better world for our children. People around the world are pressing their governments to put money and energy into finding a cure for our common enemies. It is just as important to find a cure for cultural madness; otherwise, the children we would have saved from disease will die in drive-by shootings or tribal rivalries. If I only needed one example of this phenomenon, the systematic destruction of Sarajevo and the total incompetence of the Europeans to deal with it could be enough. Unfortunately, however, there are so many more examples: Ireland, India, Georgia,

Macedonia, Tibet, the Kurdes, Algeria, the resurgence of religious fanaticism, the incredible fascist wave in Germany, France, and Italy, not to mention the formidable comeback of the Chinese culture, with more than 2,000 years of history and 1.4 billion people.

The Cultural Madness Renaissance

It is well known in Europe that in wartime, the number of people suffering from neuroses diminishes. Why? Because people are more concerned by the outside, physical war than by their inner war. Things are clear. You know which side you are on and who your enemies are, your identity is no longer in question, you must obey orders, you have the common goal of winning the war, and you know what your top priority is: staying alive. But when a physical war ends, people re-experience the same emptiness that they had before. They are left alone with their old demons, as if they were "full" of the war and are now in a postpartum depression.

The Cold War is over, and we are in this type of post-war madness. Not forced to take sides between two big "parents" anymore, the "children" can now go back to their ancestral search for identity, play their old games, chase their favorite enemies, and defreeze all of their mummified hatreds. The world is becoming a Jurassic Park of repressed cultural shadows.

We might want to treat all cultures equally, when in fact, it is more respectful to accept their fundamental differences. If we acknowledge that children have different needs than adults, and that people living in the country have different needs than people living in cities, why can't we accept that Americans might have different needs than French or Italians?

Every Culture Has an Unconscious

This is the new point of view—it is a new science whose purpose is to explain the opaque nature of contemporary society. What we see happening in the world today looks like history turning a new cycle. We see the sad spectacle of Nazi flags fluttering in South Florida as Israeli Foreign Minister Shimon Peres came to speak, Zhirinovsky winning 22 percent of the votes in parliamentary elections in Russia while declaring that he wants to "protect the downtrodden and keep both Germany and Russia ethnically pure," and German Manfred Brunner winning an approval rating of 20 percent in a national poll by pledging to form "an authentic party of the right that does not fear to end history's taboos." Add to this the tribal killings in South Africa, with some tribes joining forces with whites supremacists, and the resurgence of religious fanaticism in Algeria, where the generals who fought for freedom against France do not respect the outcome of free elections that give the religious party the majority.

All of these facts are extravagant because there are no grounds for them in traditional explanation. These collective behaviors, independent of individual history, must be derived from another source. I see a basic distinction between a personal and universal unconscious on one hand, and a collective, cultural unconscious on the other. The latter has no basis in personal experience, and is instead a cultural, historical, and geographical answer to biological needs for survival that have been imprinted and internalized by a group of people, mainly outside of their awareness.

Every Culture Has a Shadow and Persona

Every cultural unconscious has a shadow that keeps reappearing under certain conditions, usually provoking the same results. I don't believe that history repeats itself, but I do believe that the unconscious forces that pre-organize the way Americans, Germans, or French function do not change. The Poles, Russians, and Dutch have no doubts that there is a German shadow; the Chinese, Koreans, and Filipinos have no doubts that there is a Japanese shadow. But are we aware of the American, Mexican, and Canadian shadows?

If history does not repeat itself, some manifestations of the dark sides of cultures can recreate the same horrible consequences, even if this occurs under different forms. We can prevent this from happening by decoding cultures. The emergence into conscious awareness of these cultural forces sets the fundamental task for the therapeutical process of cultural archetypology. Individuals must learn to distinguish what is ego from what is not ego—that is, to distinguish the conscious ego from the archetypal content of the American, French, German, or Japanese collective unconscious.

Every culture has a collective persona. Part of it is conscious, part unconscious. Even if some aspects of this persona are well known by cultural analysts and researchers, most of it remains out of awareness of its members. The forces of the collective persona structure individual behavior, even when individuals think that they are free to choose and are in control. They don't realize that their choices are restricted by their collective unconscious. The average American woman does not feel comfortable without a bikini top on a crowded beach. The average French woman does. Even if each of us is different, we do have things in common with the other members of our tribe: our mental highways and logic of emotion.

A Cultural Archetypology of Everyday Life

For 25 years, I have studied cultural forces worldwide for major corporations whose main purpose was to sell products or services. In doing so, I have developed a process that allows us to see cultural archetypes. Using archetypology to uncover the forces behind shampoo in Japan, toilet paper in the U.S., money in Canada, cheese in France, and quality in Spain, I came up with a unique methodology for decoding cultures. I found that knowing archetypes and decoding cultural forces in action behind the scenes could increase sales of toilet paper or improve measurable quality of products. In doing so, I also developed a sense of mission.

Just as it is important to find a cure for AIDS, it is also vital to find a cure to collective cultural madness. Not only can we bring to consciousness the shadows of cultures, but we can also bring more freedom into our own lives, helping individuals to become aware of the collective forces pulling the strings. If you are an American, you might want to know what to do about violence. If you're German, you might want to know how to keep Hitler's ideals dead. If you are French, you might want to know how to prevent bloody revolutions that kill thousands of innocent people and restore kings the country was supposed to be rid of. If you're

Russian, you might want to know why potatoes, under the Soviets, never managed to find their way to starving cities.

By decoding the unconscious forces of our cultural personalities, we can free ourselves from bondage and ignorance. As a culture, a nation, or an individual, we can pioneer a new global world where cultures have rights, just as individuals do.

Chapter 19

The Archetype of Quality

Mistakes help us become better people.

Today, quality is part of the code of American business. Japanese business also has a code of quality, but the American code is different than the Japanese code. We have the answers to our problems right here in our own culture, so copying the Japanese is a big mistake. Of course, we can adapt their ideas and learn from them, just as they can learn from us.

Continuous improvement is not for Americans; It's too boring. The Japanese may go to the same job every morning and try to do it a little better each day. But not Americans. Americans love to destroy things, and thus the United States is the only culture that has used the atomic bomb twice. The American perception is that there is no creation without destruction.

By contrast, Europeans have a hard time being creative because they have difficulty with the idea of destruction. Take Paris, for example. Who would want to destroy all of those gorgeous old buildings to create a new Paris? Of course, nothing in the old Paris works; plumbing is faulty, and there is almost no air conditioning.

An American's first imprint of quality is when something does not work. Therefore, the first association with the word "quality" is a negative one. When your boss says, "I want to talk to you about quality," you think, "What did I do wrong?" Americans assume that things are supposed to work. That is their definition of quality.

When we want to motivate our employees about quality, we give them a manual and tell them to "read it carefully," or in other words, to "do it right the first time." The employee smiles in agreement because he doesn't want to lose his job. But as soon as you are gone, the same manual that you spent so much time and money to design gets tossed in the bottom drawer.

There's a cliché about Americans having a bias for action. It's true that Americans are gung-ho, but there is wisdom behind this attitude. We learn by doing. Let's look at the following scenario: For 20 years, I have been trying to learn Japanese. I have a sensi, a master who tries to teach me. When I go to class, I dress in special clothes. I prepare my ink, brush, and paper. The sensi asks, "Are you ready?"

"I'm ready."

"Close your eyes." I close them.

"Wait."

"Okay, I'm waiting. But what am I waiting for?"

"For the perfect picture. When you have the perfect picture inside, you can go."

"How long do I have to wait?"

"Five or six years. But once you have the perfect picture inside, you'll do it right."

Can you imagine American workers waiting five years for the perfect picture? It's never going to happen, nor would this approach ever work. Americans simply don't learn this way. They are in a permanent quest for identity, with no titles and no old families. Unconsciously, they have a need to destroy the past in order to create something new.

Why Total Quality Control Failed

We can't use a Japanese mental highway to achieve quality in America, because we don't have the same logic of emotion. The Japanese have a different mental highway. Their religious and cultural backgrounds concerning quality, continuous improvement, and perfection contrast dramatically with the American orientation. In the Japanese culture, perfection is attainable. Their first imprints with perfection are positive. By achieving perfection in Japan, you become a national treasure, a master, a mentor, a teacher, a god who is not tied to time and place. This is why the Japanese will wait until they get "a perfect picture inside." They are slow to start, but they get excited when they get close to perfection. A highway is already in place, we just don't use it anymore. There is no "highway maintenance program" in the American mind to support this approach. We must explore the American mental highways concerning quality, taking into account our past imprinting and experiences of quality.

Let's examine why "Total Quality Control" is an inherently negative concept for Americans. The words "Total Quality Control" are guaranteed to elicit revulsion. Why?

• ***Total.*** We relate this word to totalitarianism, dictatorship, and bureaucracy. In many ways, the word "total" means extreme power, and this is perceived as dangerous, pretentious, and negative in America.

• ***Quality.*** Americans associate "quality" with something that doesn't work, since their first imprinting experience of the concept of "quality" is usually negative. When something works it is not necessarily of good quality, but if it doesn't work, then it is definitely of poor quality. The word *quality*, then, is either neutral or negative, and the archetypal translation is a turn-off and is threatening.

• ***Control.*** We don't want control. We, the people, have the power. "Control," like "quality," turns out to have extremely negative connotations, because Americans don't want to be controlled. There is a long history in this country of fighting against a central government with too much control over states, enterprises, or individuals. In many ways, the first immigrants came to this country to avoid excessive control.

And we wonder why Americans can't get excited about TQC! We have disregarded the cultural codes.

Improvement/Recovery Archetype

Continuous improvement is completely boring to Americans. We need to set impossible goals and create impossible dreams. We must be challenged. In America, we don't want to become the best of what we are—i.e., the best cab driver. Rather, we want to become president of the cab company.

The "comeback" mentality is also typically American. We fail and bounce back. In Japan, if you don't do it right the first time, you traditionally kill yourself. There is no comeback.

When Americans finally achieve a major goal, they have no more motivation. Remember the 1980 U.S. Olympic hockey team beating the Russians and winning the gold metal? Cincinnati Reds fans will never forget the 1990 World Series—nor will Oakland. We must learn to understand these mental highways of our American corporate culture, and use them to develop new approaches to achieving quality.

As seen earlier, Rocky Balboa is a good example of America's approach to success. He is also a fitting model of the way Americans achieve quality. Rocky is the quintessential underdog, who must fight the champion against whom he has absolutely no chance of winning. But Rocky is the gutsy American: he's got a big heart, lots of nerve, and little brain. Initially, he loses. But he picks himself up and goes at it again, and again, and again. In other words, he perseveres; this is the American spirit. Rocky illustrates the opposite of "doing it right the first time," and this is how Americans achieve quality—through sheer perseverance.

Two Archetypal Discoveries

In two important studies—one on quality for AT&T and one on improvement for the American Quality Foundation—I provided an understanding of how American cultural forces impact quality and improvement.

AT&T had a problem, and had failed badly at their first attempt to solve it. The company needed to teach new concepts of quality to 50,000 managers who would then transmit them to their full workforce. They had already spent over $2,000,000 attempting to understand the Japanese concept of quality, and had designed and instituted a training program based on what they had learned in Japan. They found that it was inexplicably unattractive to their American employees. Therefore, they realized that they needed to understand better the American concept of quality, rather than superimpose the Japanese perspective.

My study revealed that the phrase "total quality control" appealed to Japanese workers, but was deadly for Americans. AT&T eventually redesigned their quality control program around an American archetype of quality and had outstanding success

When I began working with AT&T, they had spent millions of dollars developing a program to teach managers trendy business principles, such as, "Do it right the first time," "total quality control," and "zero defects." None of the managers was interested, so they asked us what they were doing wrong. We redesigned the program, giving managers tasks to do, and we videotaped them failing at these tasks. The people who came in talking about "doing it right the first time" and "zero defects" failed again and again, but then learned from their mistakes. My challenge was to discover the unconscious archetype that was crucial in getting Americans motivated to produce quality products and services.

"Zero-defects," in America, means perfection. For the Japanese, perfection is attainable because they believe that they are the chosen race, and superior to other people. Many believe that they are directly related to God through their Emperor. For a "divine race," achieving perfection sounds reasonable. Americans, however, do not view themselves in this way; they see themselves as the most human people in the world. For them, only God can accomplish perfection. My studies showed that the unconscious American translation of the word "perfection" is "death." When we say to American employees, "We want you to attain perfection," they understand that this is desirable, but they don't actually want to achieve it.

Americans believe that by failing at the beginning, they can triumph over their mistakes and succeed "the American way." It is a basic part of the American culture to do things this way. As Winston Churchill observed, "You can expect Americans to do it right—after they have tried everything else."

Understanding the American logic of emotion behind quality was crucial to understanding why AT&T workers didn't like the concept of "total quality control." These three words represent the most negative combination possible to the American unconscious, so we can understand why this goal was so poorly received by AT&T managers who didn't want to be in charge of such a negative mission. What did AT&T do differently once it understood the archetype? It stopped copying the Japanese and started seeking quality the American way—through trial and error. Americans are not as interested in the end product as they are in the journey, or the process of trying, failing, trying again, and transforming and improving themselves through the process. So, the training program I devised to teach quality started with a planned failure.

Whereas the Japanese would give managers a rule book to study, so that they could perform tasks properly the first time, AT&T developed a process in which initial failure was built in, so that the managers could learn through trial and error to create quality that they would then view as a personal accomplishment.

For the American businessperson trying to enhance quality at work, the lessons of the acceptance and management of error in order to achieve higher quality are invaluable. Look at the number of American start-up businesses that don't succeed, due to the widespread feeling that anyone can take a chance because failure is culturally acceptable in American society. You always get a second chance in America, and there's always an opportunity for a comeback. Indeed, "comeback" and "underdog" are two strong American archetypes. AT&T was so impressed by my study, that they made their proprietary information available to anyone who asked for it and set up the Quality Foundation to spread the information.

Another study, conducted for the American Quality Foundation, dealt with personal improvement. Results of this study showed that discomfort was the number one motivator necessary for an American to improve. Unconsciously, Americans seek discomfort to push themselves toward success. Succeeding, or arriving at an endpoint of an aspiration, and having nowhere else to go leaves nothing more to reach for, and so Americans unconsciously seek dissatisfaction. The implications of this archetype of discomfort are broad in regard to the way Americans live their lives, work at their jobs, play, and maintain their relationships.

In addition, Americans improve by first de-constructing—that is, by taking apart what exists, and then starting all over. The image of an entire block of apartment buildings being imploded is eerily American. We prefer to start from scratch instead of trying to improve something bit by bit. The success of re-engineering comes from this passion for deconstruction.

As with all of these studies, there are potentially more important implications than the specific marketing information. The way educators design teaching programs, from grade school to advanced degrees to corporate training, should be subjected to reexamination based on the results of this quality archetype research which shows how Americans learn. The design of books and manuals and the place that competition has in a learning environment also require reassessment in the face of this information.

Quality in Different Cultures

We have seen already that in the American mind, the code for cheese is "dead," the code for food is "fuel," and the code for timber is "killer." These examples have explained how to encode and decode cultures. Then this decoding process must be applied to improvement.

Virtually every quality initiative launched in the U.S. during the last 20 years was modeled after the Japanese experience—or at least the American interpretation of the Japanese experience. You name it, we did it: quality circles, Taguchi, JIT, hoshen planning. After spending billions of dollars copying the Japanese, the last thing American executives wanted to hear was that their houses has been built on reclaimed ideas. In the end, though, in spite of all their rationale, Americans are not Japanese, their processes are not ours, and what motivates Japanese workers does not motivate American workers. I don't care how many Japanese eat at McDonald's or wear Levis; the two cultures could not be more different if they came from different planets.

The Japanese have more than a dozen words for quality, each with a precise meaning. Americans have only one word that is vague, elusive, and practically meaningless. If Americans are to reclaim economic leadership of the world, we must do it with American models based on American codes, described in American terms, and respective of the American logic of emotion.

American code for quality: It works. In America, quality is the password for many different elements of our lives, from having time to enjoy our children to buying products that we don't have to bring back the next day. Owning or producing a perfect product is not important to us; we're happy if it does what it's supposed to do. In other cultures, the key dimensions of quality, or their codes, are dramatically different.

German code for quality: Standard. In Germany, the dominant element of quality is an obsession with standards. Max Weber, a German sociologist, insisted that the ideal situation for happiness was when the ideal state and the ideal bureaucracy ran everything, and when our lives were simply following rules and respecting standards. Thus, we can understand why German children read Lego instructions so carefully.

Japanese code for quality: Perfection. In the Japanese mind, perfection is an attainable goal, and the only one that deserves attention. If a Japanese person achieves perfection, he will be respected immensely, for he is almost divine, and the Japanese "soul" is proud of him. His ancestors from past centuries are proud of him, and his descendants in the next several centuries will also praise him. Because of what he has done, he now transcends time and space. Not only is perfection perceived as possible in the Japanese culture, but it receives the highest rewards, and is afforded an almost religious fervor.

French code for quality: Luxury. The French have a completely different attitude toward quality. In France, quality is a class statement. Even the Socialist and communist government of Mitterand, elected in 1981, realized that France excelled in the areas of champagne, foie gras, perfumes, and haute couture. So he created the Commité Colbert, whose function was to promote quality, the same way that Louis XIV asked his minister (Colbert) to do this in the 17th century. The whole idea was, "beauty for the sake of beauty."

The other dimension that is fundamental to understanding the French code for quality is that luxury is useless, and that's why the French can't live without it. If you buy a scarf because you are afraid to catch a cold, that is not luxury or quality—that's necessity. But if you buy a scarf, especially a very expensive one by a famous designer, to put around your shoulders as an ornament, this is quality. Why? Because you don't need it there. By wearing it, you make a classy statement and demonstrate that you know what quality and luxury are.

How Do We Reward Adolescents?

The American culture is a young, adolescent one. One fascinating result of our quality research was a completely new way of looking at rewards and recognition for members of such a culture. Most of the time, we reward people without understanding the logic of emotion behind the quality archetype. Acknowledgment of something we accomplished six months ago is useless; it looks backward to what is already regarded as "history." All of the certificates of attendance that we hang behind our backs in our offices are "tombstones." The past is dead; they are only proof that you might have been good some time ago. They don't tell you how good you are today. Rather than rewards looking toward the past, we need rewards that look toward the future.

In other words, we need to reward people in "animal time," not six months or a year later. Consequently, we can easily evaluate any reward system simply by determining whether this system functions in animal time, or not. MBNA (credit cards) has created a system of feedback in animal time. Their employees can see every day if they have accomplished their goals. At the end of the day, they look at a big sign showing the results of the day, and cheer if they have achieved their goal.

New potential identity. This is the most important part of a reward system. If you accept that Americans are in permanent search of new identities, providing these new potential identities is obviously crucial. This new potential identity should not be too remote, though, existing in an ideal future. On the contrary, it should be real and in the present.

New tools. Rather than money or tombstones, new tools are ideal rewards. They are something concrete and practical that will be useful in helping us achieve our next potential identity. These could be bicycles or computers, but they must be related to a new potential identity. If I need to be in better shape for my new potential identity, I will use the bicycle every morning, instead of a car, to get to the train station. If I need to be computer literate, I will start my initiation program right away. The new tool must fit into the basic elements of the American recipe, i.e., animal time, bias for action, mistakes and frustration.

Many quality programs just don't get it. They create cognitive dissonance, something that occurs when our intellectual understanding of a concept is at odds with our emotional response: "It makes sense to do this, but my heart's not in it." Many of the slogans of the quality revolution fail to motivate Americans because they contradict the stronger cultural forces of the quality archetype. They fail to tap into the emotional energy needed to fuel an improvement process.

Because my archetypal findings concerning quality have profound implications for how we view and manage quality and the improvement process, the American Quality Foundation decided to validate these archetypal findings. They enlisted The Wirthlin Group, specialists in strategic marketing and communications, to validate the archetypes and to assess the impact of applying them. Using its own methodology, The Wirthlin Group confirmed almost all of the key points of the archetypal research, including the fact that mistakes help us become better people.

Nothing Is Perfect

When AT&T's Network Systems invited me to apply the archetype discovery process to study the human side of quality, here's what we learned:

Quality has a strong connotation. For most Americans, quality is a negative word because they first learn about it when something goes wrong or when expectations are not met, and so their first imprint of quality is a negative one.

Americans' expectations of quality are not high. While the Japanese equate quality with perfection, the Germans associate quality with standards, and the French believe quality means luxury, Americans equate quality with "it works."

Americans accept imperfection. Americans believe that it is human to be imperfect. In fact, an error or imperfection represents an opportunity for improvement.

Americans value nurturing and caring. When a person tries something and fails, it provides others the chance to show that they care. It also gives the person who failed the energy to try again. When a product or service fails, the customer expects the problem to be fixed. The fixing process allows the customer to experience the caring and concern shown by the company, leaving the customer with positive feelings.

The process (effort) is more important than the product (outcome). Becoming the best as something—a hobby, job, or athletic event—motivates Americans. Producing the best products or services does not. Thus, quality must be make personal.

Americans view change positively only if they are in control of the change. Change that they control promises improvement or new opportunities. But is they don't control the change, they will view it with suspicion or negatively and they might resist it.

Americans prefer breakthroughs rather than incremental improvements. For most Americans, improving a little bit every day for the next 10 years is boring. Breakthroughs, on the other hand, are exciting and progressive.

A challenge or a crisis excites Americans. The bigger the challenge, the better it is. Challenge and crisis motivate Americans to achieve breakthroughs.

Americans equate perfection with a dead end. Once a situation is perfect, there are no new challenges or future possibilities. Thus, the concept of "zero defects," which has the goal of perfection, carries a negative connotation in the American culture. The focus on improving processes is wrong. Consider the phrases commonly associated with process improvement: doing it right the first time, statistical process control, Pareto analysis, histograms, control charts, just-in-time manufacturing, and on-time delivery. There is no consideration for the people who are involved in those processes

Americans have a bias for action. Americans' first response to a challenge or crisis is to act rather than plan. For example, people usually read instructions only when all else fails. American women, when running into problems with vacuum cleaners called their neighbors instead of reading the instruction manual. The same phenomenon occurs with computers. Instead of reading the manuals, people usually start working on the computers right away; if there is a problem, they call someone or maybe read the instructions. In relating this to the business world, companies shouldn't expect employees to scour quality and training manuals and make detailed plans before they attack a problem. Similarly, companies shouldn't expect their customers to read instruction manuals before using their products or services.

American don't do things right the first time. Americans learn from trial and error- in other words, by making mistakes, experiencing failure, and learning from those mistakes. Thus, when companies urge employees to do it right the first time, they are asking them to omit a step in their learning process. Doing something right the first time goes against Americans' human nature. Even Winston Churchill saw this when he said that you can expect Americans to do it right after they have tried everything else before. That is an insight into this American archetype.

Not doing things right the first time and making mistakes inevitably makes Americans feel frustrated, disappointed, angry, depressed, or even guilty. These feelings, although negative, represent energy that can be transformed into positive action. Americans require a certain amount of frustration, anxiety, discomfort or dissatisfaction to get started on the improvement process. If Americans are comfortable, there is not impetus to change. A crisis, such as the possibility that a company will fold, creates anxiety and, hence, impetus to act. A vision or dream, such as wanting to win a contract, also causes action due to the dissatisfaction encountered by comparing the dream or vision to reality.

Companies have to accept that employees will make mistakes. It is absurd for management to say "I don't want you to make mistakes" or "I want you to do it right the first time." People can't do that. They become desperate in this situation because they do not have a way to learn. In their quest for quality improvement, some U.S. companies saw that Japanese were doing well, so they copied the Japanese improvement processes. But these companies are discovering that American and Japanese ways are different. Although Americans seldom read instructions and make mistakes, they learn very fast from their mistakes. When you know how to tap into the right logic of emotion—the right cultural archetype—you wake up the sleeping giant.

Companies need to reconsider their improvement processes, taking into account the purposes of an improvement process. Once again, the purpose of a process is not just to improve the object, but also to improve the person. The person should be able to learn and grow. People want to make a difference, to become a better person and to create a better world. People are biological. So, processes cannot be cold, abstract or mechanistic. This emphasis leads to bureaucracy, the most dangerous virus on earth. Bureaucracy means that nobody knows why things are the way they are. Nobody can argue and reject the rules or processes anymore. Bureaucracies are usually ruled by incompetent people who are in power because they stick to rules and processes. Bureaucracy is slow to react and after a while, adaption isn't even possible. In a rapidly changing world, adaption is vital. By exaggerating the need for perfect processes and doing it right the first time, U.S. companies are becoming more inflexible and bureaucratic. Their processes are becoming obsolete because those processes can't adapt to the situations that are changing around them. And people are becoming frustrated because these processes are very limiting. Companies need to realize that they have best processes possible at this point and that employees' ability to create and adapt is better than any process.

Companies should always tap into employees' creativity and innovation. For creativity and innovation to occur, three groups need to exist: 1) logicians to define the problem to be solved; 2) poets to come up with "crazy" ideas; and 3) technicians to sort through the ideas to determine whether they are possible at this time. For those ideas that are possible, the technicians say, "If we have these materials and if we did this, it would be possible." This the "if" statement becomes the new problem, which goes back to the logicians to define. This process forms a triangle. It represents the next generation of precesses, because it is less mechanistic and bureaucratic and more biological in nature. It is characterized by continual creation, innovation, and adaptation. Just as human beings constantly change to their surroundings, so must processes.

Companies should emulate the brain's ability to be creative, innovative, adaptive, and flexible. The brain has unlimited potential. It constantly receives information from the body, adapting itself to this input, re-creating itself all of the time. Since people are constantly re-creating themselves to adapt to the changing world, but the processes in which they work are not, frustration results. Companies need to take advantage of this frustration and turn the negative feeling into a positive energy to bring their processes into the new biological dimension.

Rediscovering the Logic of life

In an effort to get more high-quality products and services out the door, companies have focused on the details, analyzing every element in their processes, products, and people to tweak performance. But many companies have lost sight of the vision, the final goal. To understand the final goal, companies need to take a global point of view. When you see Earth from space, you suddenly realize that every person, company, culture, country, and continent is part of the grand system of life. We need to understand how changing one element influences the others, and how to take care of it to preserve life. Thus, the final goal is to *preserve, expand, and protect life.* This is the power of life, the key element of the ultimate quality relationship.

Companies can go from having a static vision to a dynamic one. With a static vision, a company strives to have simple, closed systems. These systems have linear causes and effects and are subject to balancing forces, so they are stable, solid, and rigid. As a result, the behavior of these systems is easy to predict, reproduce, and reverse. These systems can be compared to a crystal, a solid substance that is rigid and bound by its geometric planes.

With a dynamic vision, a company strives to have complex, open systems. These open systems have a circular causality and are in a constant state of flux, so they are fluid but dynamically stable. They have stationary states, but there is continuous change and growth. As a result, the behavior of these systems is unpredictable, impossible to reproduce, and impossible to reverse. These dynamic systems can be compared to a cell, a life form that is always growing and reacting to its environment

In addition to adopting a dynamic vision, companies also need to adopt a whole-systems approach. Currently, most companies only use an analytical approach—wherein a system is isolated into parts or elements, and each element is then analyzed to see how it interacts with the others, usually modifying one element at a time. It is a very disciplined approach to learning about a system's details. But these strengths become weaknesses when this approach is used to analyze complex, dynamic systems. Thus, a life-systems approach is needed to study such systems.

In the life-systems approach, a more global view is taken. The system is broken into groups of elements. These groups are then modified. A theory is then developed to explain the groups' effects on the system. Since a dynamic system is in a constant state of flux, it is impossible to reconstruct the situation. Thus the validation of results doesn't come from repeating the process but rather from comparing the theory with reality. The resulting models aren't nearly as detailed as those developed using the analytical approach; however, they are useful in real life. The detailed models produced from the analytical approach are hard to implement. The life-systems approach is very efficient for complex, dynamic systems. It provides a multi-disciplined approach to learning about a system's goals.

With a dynamic vision and a life-systems approach, companies are better equipped to survive in the 21st century. Instead of creating processes and products, companies will be creating life.

From the first cultural imprint, which engraves the logic of emotion, to the constant reinforcement, which creates the mental highways, we become cultural beings. But the only way we can become multi-cultural beings is through a *series of relationships*. Although we are in relationships, we do not have a culture of relationships, and this is the relationship challenge. In schools, we are taught facts, how to work with figures, and how to use computers. We are taught how to be analytical. We are never taught about the art of the relationship. This is why many of us are "relationship illiterate."

Relationship literacy must now be promoted. Both adults and children need to be educated in the art of the relationship. Perhaps this is a modest opening to a new science of relationships. Only when we integrate the symbolic, systemic, and synergistic dimensions in a symbiotic system will we have the foundation for a quality relationship culture.

Our global ecosystem is fragile, and so we should concentrate on preserving it rather than fighting each other for it. From space, our differences are insignificant. What is obvious is the solidarity of the human race. We are temporary passengers on spaceship Earth. Together, we can create a better world for our children, a world where they can live meaningful lives full of quality relationships.

SECRET 7:

THE THIRD WORLD WAR IS UNDERWAY—AND IT IS CULTURAL: *Cultural awareness is the key to success and to personal and collective freedom.*

The future is dead. This is the time of the return of archetypes. How will your organization position itself in this multi-cultural mess? What is your strategy? You need a vision for globalization. In the absence of leadership, globophobia spreads and protectionism prevails. When leaders don't understand cultural archetypes, we see failed marketing campaigns, miscommunication, strikes, and wars.

Chapter 20

The End of the Future as We Know It

We have watched the death of our last future. There is no room for tomorrows.

With the new millennium, the future—as we used to know it—is dead. We have watched the death of our last future. The time is *now*. There is no room for tomorrow.

The future is gone. No more future—only the present—"now time." I want everything *now*, and I don't want to wait. The magic numbers are "24" and "7." All day, everyday. All the time, everywhere, from the Internet to cell phones. Never has the present been so full and so busy and the future so . . . empty. What took over? Technology! That's it. No more past, no more future, just technology. Young people listen to Techno music, and the stock market makes new millionaires everyday (Technology gain). Everywhere we see the power of new technology, which emphasizes the present, the "now." We are watching the apotheoses of the "now culture."

My question is, "Where is the soul?" Remember "the Soul and the Machine?" This was a pact with the devil (the Faustian archetype again). Are we expecting technology to save us? Now, to be saved, do we have to give up our souls?

Archetypes in Action

Archetypes in action can help decode what is happening and give us some archetypal insights.

1. Technology is the cortex, and will go global. America will lead the way because technology fits so well the American archetype—adolescent time is now.

2. But the soul is emotional, limbic, local. We can predict a return of the archetypes as a way to balance the danger represented by globalization and technology.

The millennium apocalypse did not occur. We now have to deal with a present that has no future. We are the future. But can we live only within technology?

The return of the archetypes will be a re-discovery of local, meaningful, unconscious structures. Technology will be used to make these structures available to everyone, everywhere, and now.

If we succeed in having all the cultures of the world know one another and respect one another, then the "machine" will have a soul—again.

How Crisis Brings Back Archetypes

This is the time of the return of archetypes. I mean a *Big Return*. Remember: the more things change, the more they remain the same. We love to see new billionaires lose billions of dollars. We love to see that what goes up always comes down—from rags to riches and back to rags again. Our time is like the time when some religions opposed people flying in airplanes, because we were not supposed to get too close to God. We live in a time of uncertainty, and such times always bring back old archetypes. We feel safe with them. We know them like old friends. We know their good side and their bad side.

In Europe at the beginning of the 20th century, people used to say, "We need a good war" to put clocks back at the right time, to go back to simple truths and values like life and death. In time of war, we have certainty. We know the enemy. He even wears a different uniform so we can identify him. And we have a simple set of goals: To survive, to win, to defeat the enemy. But today we don't really have an enemy—everything looks fine. And yet, this situation is terrible! This is the time for the return of collective neurosis. In times of war, we don't have neurosis. There is no time to doubt, no time to question ourselves, no time to wonder what to do. We are reptilians all the time—either alive or dead, heroes or traitors. There is no ambiguity. But today we are uncertain. Is Clinton good or bad? Is the Internet bubble dead or still alive? What about values, families, hard work? Europeans are having an identity crisis; American unions are afraid of globalization; and the rest of the world is afraid of Americanization. Cuban Americans demonstrate on behalf of Elian Gonzales. In Miami, Cubans are chanting "War, War." They are asking for the return of the old enemy, the old archetype. We can expect more of these demonstrations: back to basics in America, anti-imperialism, Anti-Americanism, and globalization. Writing in the *New York Times*, Joseph Kahn defines *globophobia* as "an international force that has singled out global integration as the primary cause of environmental and social problems."

How your company deals with this "international force" will make the difference between success and failure in your globalization effort. The WTO demonstration in Seattle was just the beginning. I predict that globalization will be the new common enemy. This is an emotional issue that has no rational explanation. We have an emotional force in action here, and no leader to balance it.

"We have an enormous job to do to convince opponents, many of whom I think are wrong, that they can live with globalization," declared Tony Blair, the British Prime Minister, at the World Economic Forum meeting in Davos, Switzerland.

Obviously this statement *is* the problem. People need more than just to know that "they can live with globalization." They want to know *why* they have to live this way. How will this change their lives? They need a leader with a vision. The need hope. Today no one fits the leader archetype, certainly not Tony Blair, Bill Clinton, or Al Gore. So, be careful. Globophobia might become the next crusade with strong anti-American feelings.

How will your company position itself in this mess? What is your strategy? Every company needs a vision for globalization, not just numbers and a rational explanation. This is why we need to discover the globalization archetype and break the code of the logic of emotion behind it. You want to know why people react this way before they call you "MON-SATAN" (Monsanto) or destroy your workplace (McDonalds).

Today globalization is seen less as spreading prosperity around the world and more as:

- Growing inequality between rich and poor
- Failure of law and ethics to control science and technology
- Environmental pollution and waste
- Rapid spread of financial instability
- Destruction of *my* local culture and tradition
- Americanization (i.e., superficialization of the planet)

Unless people worldwide are involved in a positive way and unless we know their logic of emotion and their archetype, globalization will not work. We need a new leader with a vision to show us the way to the promised land, to connect us with hope. And we don't have him or her. We need leaders who understand cultural archetypes. Globalization is in trouble, thanks mostly to the absence of American leadership.

I do not believe that politicians will play the leadership role. They are too busy trying to get attention, and some don't even have a foreign policy. So corporate chiefs will have to take the lead. We need an alliance of global business to win against what President Ernesto Zedillo calls "a peculiar alliance of forces from the extreme left, the extreme right, environmentalist groups, trade unions of developed countries, and some self-appointed representatives of civil society." And what do they want? "To save the people of developing countries from development."

Clearly, the absence of leadership is creating such confusion that globophobia is spreading. It is time for action. We need to show the world that free trade and economic growth—not protectionism—feed the world and take children to school. If we don't act now, we might slow down globalization for many years. But if we act now, we will create a better crusade for life and growth, movement and expansion—not restraint, protectionism and death! This can only be done by understanding and decoding archetypes.

This is why we are now working with some Fortune 100 organizations—to break the code of successful globalization.

Let's break the codes of *global* and *globalization* and understand the logic of emotion behind them. Why the Battle of Seattle? What does it mean for us? What is a global product, brand, communication, PR campaign, strategy, team leader, and organization? We need a breakthrough in understanding the global archetype.

What happens when leaders do not understand cultural archetypes? Failed marketing campaigns, miscommunication, strikes, and wars.

In 1989, Americans believed that the Cold War was over. A new world order was coming. We thought we were friends with the Russians and could start investing in the former Soviet Union. And then we had the Chechen War.

I predicted the resurgence of Russian Archetypes—not a switch to American capitalism and democracy. This is exactly what happened—the Russian chaos, with a return of culture wars after three generations of repression. Because they did not believe my prediction, Estee Lauder lost 60 percent of their investment in Russia. Now we have the old Russian Archetype (300 years old) in action against the Chechens. Putin is trying again to get rid of the Chechen Archetype, just as Stalin tried by deporting 450,000 Chechens. It's another instance of the Warrior Archetype. But if Stalin, the Czar, did not succeed, then Putin will have a difficult time. And if we try to tell him something, he will threaten us with his nuclear arsenal. Here again is the Russian archetype in action.

Archetypal leaders are the only ones who can avoid a new world war. These enlightened leaders need to lead the world against our *common* enemies.

Seven Common Enemies

Seven new common enemies are changing and reshaping the world, politically and economically.

1. The next global epidemic or virus.
2. The return of Fascism in Europe.

3. The proliferation and widespread use of nuclear warheads by dictators.
4. The comeback of religious wars and fanaticism.
5. The out-of-control biological research.
6. The new Internet terrorists.

7. Bureaucracy. I define *bureaucracy* as "extreme power given to extreme idiots." Dictatorship is extreme power given to evil intelligence. The result are people who stop thinking and taking initiative, procedures and processes that slow down everything, and even kill people. More people died in America last year because of medical mistakes and out-of-control procedures than died during the whole Vietnam War. Many people believe that the Swissair plane crash occurred because the pilot was following German Swiss procedures, which are even worse than the German ones. In Europe, Germany and France are the most bureaucratic cultures. In Asia, Japan is the worst, as evidenced in the slow reaction of the bureaucracy to the last earthquake.

The new economy requires quick, fast, and free reactions. Bureaucracy is slow and expensive. Brussels is a good example of European bureaucrats in action. I call them the *Eurorats*. What is their mission, their goal? To expand, to reproduce themselves. To get more money, more power, more people, more buildings. How can they do that? Because we let them do that. How can we stop them? By making them accountable, by judging them on performance measures and results. Simplify everything. Apply the same principles that we apply in business to bureaucrats. Ask: Do we, the customers, need what you are doing? If yes, can you do it faster, cheaper, with fewer people and with more efficiency and higher customer satisfaction?

If the new economy means *fast* and *free*, the slow and expensive bureaucrats are out. Like in Europe, no more borders, no more customs, no more custom officers. It's free; it's faster. If this is the future, bureaucrats need a mutation; they need creativity, intelligence, innovation, and a high faculty for adaptation. If they can't mutate, they might disappear or kill the system.

The real danger is the concentration of power in one person or entity. We see that old dragons never die when we watch the resurgence of Fascism in Europe.

After Kosovo and the Albanian genocide, now Mr. Putin is perpetuating a new Chechen genocide, repeating what Stalin had done when he sent 450,000 Chechens to Siberia where half of them died. We also have the Far Right party making up half of the government in Austria.

The danger is real. France alone has about 15 percent communists in the government since Mitterrand took power in 1981, and about 15 percent Far Right voters who follow Jean Marie Le Pen. So, about 30 percent of the French belong to an extreme political party. Although Germany recently gave the right to foreigners born in Germany to apply to become German, the German Neo-Nazis still burn to death Turkish immigrants who have lived in Germany for several generations.

Globalization is perceived as the danger, and the Fascist archetype as the solution. Unfortunately, we know what that mix leads to. Looking at Kosovo and Grozny gives us a glance of what could happen again.

Archetypes are like unconscious dragons. They never die. They go into hiding for a while waiting for the right moment to come back.

On this side of the Atlantic, we have the American "sleeping giant" Archetype. We don't even have a foreign policy. Henry Kissinger, who is Jewish and German, may be the only American who fully understands the need for an American foreign policy. Europe needs strong American leadership. The world needs a strong American president. Let's hope that George W. Bush will learn history and geography, and Al Gore will stop putting oil on the anti-global fire, giving ammunition to all the anti-American demonstrators of the world. We need an Archetypal leader with a vision—one who understands the power of the archetypes, or history may repeat itself. The new global leaders of business and government need a deep understanding of cultural archetypes.

If we hope to prevent the return of old ghosts, we need a new division of power. We need to separate culture from economy, military, and politics. Today no one will argue that church and state have to be separated. And, we all agree that military power has to be controlled by democratically elected leaders. But when we approach cultures, we encounter a vacuum. Nobody is in charge of culture. When Mitterrand won the elections in 1981 in France with 51 percent of the 25 million voters in a France of 55 million inhabitants, he claimed he *was* France, and he used the socialist/communist rose (the flower) as his new symbol. This claim was ridiculous in light of the fact that he had less than one-fourth of the French behind him. Politicians cannot be icons of culture. They will always try to slant the culture in their favor, to own the soul of the people. But they cannot. They can only try to destroy by force a soul they cannot own.

To stop this disastrous tendency, we have to reinforce a complete separation of power. We have to take seven steps:

1. Acknowledge that cultures have power. They have economical power (See Max Weber—*The Protestant Ethic and the Origin of Capitalism*). They have military power (See the Chechen warrior archetype). They have political power (see the Clinton "Comeback Kid" archetype). This power comes from the fact that cultures shape the collective unconscious through archetypal codes.

2. Realize that cultures existed before nations. The concept of nations was invented by Bonaparte, before he became Napoleon. Cultures should be separate from nations. The Kurd culture is not owned by the Turks or by the Iraqis or by the Iranians. So we should be very careful not to speak about the "Kurd nation" but of the Kurd "culture." I personally do not care about the French *nation*. But I care deeply about the French *culture*.

3. Identify and promote cultural leaders who embody the culture, away from political and economical concerns, such as Henry David Thoreau, Walt Whitman, and Charles Schultz.

4. Put somebody in charge of promoting, developing, enhancing and protecting a culture. (Malraux was Ministre de Culture under de Gaulle).

5. Promote the united cultures of the world. Major American companies—like Boeing, P&G, Coke, GM, Ford, and Kellogs—need to get together to show the world that their goal is not to destroy, swallow, and melt all the cultures of the world into an American pot of cola, hot dogs and blue jeans, but to respect the other cultures as equal cultural partners.

6. Teach our children to value their own culture, to respect other cultures, and to see the beauty and value of other cultures.

7. Promote the rights of cultures. Cultures should have rights. This is why in Paris on January 1, 2000, we made the official *Declaration of the Rights of Cultures*.

These seven steps of this new separation of power are deeply needed if we want more peace and fewer cultural wars like the Chechen, Kosovo, Africa, and Timor wars.

These are the tools we offer to the leaders of tomorrow—the seven secrets of how to succeed in going global and the seven steps of the new division of power.

I have accumulated an incredible bank of data, all the codes of culture that I have studied for 30 years. Biologists have decoded the human DNA. I intend to decode the human CNA. CNA is for a culture what DNA is for an organism. Using these codes, I help companies sell cosmetics, cars, food, beverages, services, and high technology, and I have a proven success record. But now I would like to find leaders who want to use these codes to promote the right of cultures. I need a new Moses.

The Moses Archetype

We need "follow me" leaders. We need people at the top who understand the leader archetype. I often meet CEOs and presidents who are good facilitators, managers, and bean counters. But when confronted with a new situation, unknown terrain or crisis, they are lost. I also meet some who are archetypal leaders. They are inspired connectors and "follow me" leaders. Let's explore these qualities of the archetypal leaders.

Inspired. These leaders have a vision; they have seen the promised land. They go to the mountain and speak with God.

From Lee Iacocca to Martin Luther King, they had a dream. They were inspired before they ever tried to inspire others. I once met John Chambers (Cisco), and he is definitely an inspired leader. But Horst Schutze (Ritz Carlton), Bob Lutz and Bob Eaton (Chrysler) are inspired leaders too. Bean counters want to bring value to shareholders. They only speak numbers (cortex). This is never where the vision and dreams are. As a consequence, shareholders lose value.

Connectors. When your employees are asked to do something, they have to see how this request is connected with the big picture, the vision, the crusade. To put a man on the moon for the first time and bring him back home—that is a big picture. To increase shareholder value by 10 percent each year is not. Employees will make sacrifices to put a man on the moon because it's exciting; but they won't make sacrifices for the shareholders because it's dumb. So, they fight against management (the spring 2000 Boeing strike) to get more money. When people are in love, they don't argue about money. When they get divorced, that's all they do. The connector-leader keeps people in love with the vision, the dream.

Follow me. Once you have the vision, then you connect everything people do with this vision. Then the next thing to do is to get on your horse, put on your hat with the white panache (a white feather used by Henry IV, telling his troops to follow him on the battlefield), and then go. Leaders lead. It is so simple, and yet it is forgotten so often. GM desperately needs a "Follow Me" leader, but neither Richard Wagoner nor Jack Smith are of this kind. (Under Jack Smith, GM's market share dropped from 35 to 29 percent.)

If you can have all three—be an "inspired, follow me connector"—and a good showman (or woman) and a good communicator, then the shareholder value will follow.

By using the Seven Secrets and the Seven Steps, by promoting the Rights of Cultures, and by using the appropriate cultural codes, we can make this planet a better place for our children.

The Rights of Cultures

The following declaration was presented and signed on January 1, 2000, in Paris on the rue de Rivoli in front of the Salle Du Jeu de Paume (Place de la Concorde). This is where the French revolution had its beginning in 1789 and its subsequent impact on the Rights of Man.

My guests included Eric Margolis, an American; Dana Baines from Canada, Jessie Verjans from Belgium; Emmanuelle from Spain; Rene Olivier, a researcher at the Institute Pasteur from France; and my friend Nelly's family, her two daughters, and her husband Felix who is a great cello player from Armenia. Nelly is a piano player, as well as her two daughters. For me they all symbolize the permanent Diaspora of Cultures in need of Rights. Lorenzo, my oldest son and Sophie, ma Sagasse, were also there. At midnight Nelly and I symbolically signed the following declaration:

DECLARATION OF THE RIGHTS OF CULTURES

01.01.2000, Paris, France

1. All the cultures of world have rights similar to the Rights of Man.
2. Their first right is the right to exist.
3. The cultures of the world represent a universal patrimony. They belong to all the inhabitants of this planet. They are their creations.
4. We declare that it is a crime against humanity to deprive a member of a given culture of access to his culture or of any other culture of the world.
5. It is also a crime against humanity to repress or destroy (even partially) a culture.
6. The Rights of Cultures are limited by the respect of all other cultures in the same way that the Rights of Man are limited by the respect of the same rights for the other inhabitants of this planet (men and women).
7. Every culture has the right to have all the different elements of the culture respected, including (but not limited to) its beliefs, customs, religions, philosophies, language, education systems, art in its different forms (music, poetry, dance, cooking, folklore, and clothing).

8. All the human beings of this planet have the inalienable rights to access all the other cultures of this planet.
9. Cultures are not right or wrong, good or bad; they are different. This diversity is what constitutes the richness of the cultural patrimony of the human species.
10. The cultures of the world can only live, grow and flourish in a system of complete separation of powers (i.e. the political, military, religious, legal, and executive branches must be separated from the culture power.) No culture is the exclusive property of a nation or a political, economical, mediatical or military power.
11. As a consequence, the national representatives cannot present themselves as the exclusive representants of a given culture.
12. The political power is temporary. The cultural reality is timeless.
13. Each culture has the right to communicate its constitutive elements, its principles and beliefs, to the rest of the world but does not have the right to impose them.
14. The representants of a given culture have the duty to respect the laws of the citizens of the country which have been decided democratically and to respect the Rights of Man.
15. As long as these cultures respect the democratic laws of the citizens and the Rights of Man, their rights to exist cannot be infringed.
16. The mission of the Declaration of the Rights of Cultures is to give the fundamental basis and reference to allow the cultures of the world to know each other.
17. Cultures are alive. They grow and change and keep recreating themselves. It is a crime against them to want to freeze them or to want to stop them from transforming themselves.
18. We solemnly declare that all the cultures of the world have the right to a representation similar to the right of nations, which expresses itself in the United Nations organization. This representation of cultures will be done in an organization named the United Cultures, and this organization will slowly replace the United Nations.
19. We solemnly declare that no globalization of the world is peacefully possible without a deep respect for the Rights of Cultures.

For many years now I have been asking the question, "Why are the cultures of the world at war?" The answer is that they are afraid they will disappear as cultures, not because they want political independence. That's why the world needs a new declaration of the same magnitude as the declaration of the Rights of Man.

I had planned the signing of the declaration of the Rights of Cultures for the symbolic date of 1 January 2000. It was supposed to happen in a castle in Normandy, but nature stopped me from going to Normandy. That new year's day, a terrible storm destroyed 40 percent of Versailles trees and made travel hazardous throughout most of France. The best alternate place I could find for the signing was in front of the Salle Du Jeu De Paume at the Hotel Intercontinental where the allied forces had their headquarters after the liberation of Paris in 1945. Now you can understand why I believe nothing happens by chance, random, or accident. Since all my guests had to leave before dawn, the signing happened at midnight, when the Eiffel Tower next to us became like a space shuttle taking off in the middle of a storm of light and flames to fly toward a new millennium. So many archetype symbols and forces converged in this historic moment. Of course, champagne was "De Rigueur," and we all felt a new era had begun.

You, too, can start a new era in your organization by respecting the rights of cultures and by applying the seven secrets of marketing in this multi-cultural world.

Glossary of Archetype Terms

Archetypal: The quality of a structure that best expresses the forces of the archetype.

Archetype: A pre-existing structure or pattern that enables human beings to meet biological needs and understand the human condition. It is imprinted at an early age when, as children, we discover and experience the external world. There are two kinds of archetypes: the Jungian Universal Archetype, which we call schema (schemata, plural), and the Cultural Archetype. In this book, the term "archetype" refers to the latter.

Universal archetypes: Universal archetypes are related to the biological structures or schemata that preorganize human life. A universal archetype (i.e., "mother") is imprinted in humans wherever the species exists. These psychic and behavioral forms are present in all members of the species, but develop uniquely in each individual. Together, the universal archetypes make up the collective unconscious.

Cultural archetypes: Cultural archetypes are those structures that are shared by a single culture. They are the cultural grammar that gives meaning and significance to any element of a given culture at a given time. Every element of a culture has an archetype. Cultural archetypes are inherited, but are not genetically transmitted. They preorganize our perception of the world and the way we react to it. They differ from one culture to another, but are common to all members of a culture or subculture.

Archetype manager: The person who leads the archetypal study process. He/she is the center of communication for all the members of the core team and the archetype team.

Archetype Studies/Discoveries: The approach developed by Dr. G. C. Rapaille to decode the cultural mind.

Archetype Studies Process: A proprietary procedure for discovering cultural archetypes. The entire process involves the participation of an archetype manager, a core team, an archetype team or steering committee, and three archetypologists from different cultures; it consists of 10 imprinting groups and three "recap" sessions. The heart of the process, the imprinting group, is a three-hour procedure that accesses a level of information never obtained otherwise. The process begins with one hour of discussion (similar to a focus group). The second hour uses free association to reveal the first level of unconsciousness (latent structures); then, the "once upon a time" stories begin to provide the logic of emotion. The third hour makes use of the alpha mental state to get unusual new revelations.

Archetypal team: Ideally, the archetypal team is composed of all the people who will be implementing the results of the study; these team members should be involved from the beginning (the meeting in which the issued are defined). Each member should have the opportunity to attend one of the imprinting sessions. Members of the archetypal team should be present at all "recap" sessions.

Archetypologist: An expert in the structural analysis of cultures. The cultural archetypologist has done his/her own cultural analysis, i.e., he/she is aware of the cultural forces that pre-organized his/her world vision, system of beliefs, etc. An archetypologist is familiar with several languages and several cultures. To avoid cultural biases, archetypologist always work in multi-cultural teams.

Axis: The connection linking two forces (polarities) of an archetype. An axis depicts the way two forces are organized. They might be opposite, complimentary, figure/ground, etc. This relationship or function is revealed only when the axis is analyzed. The axis is permanent and constant. A culture maintains a balance between forces as people's behavior moves along the axis.

Biology: Biology gives us the priorities for survival: breathing is more important than drinking, which is more important than eating, etc.

Certified archetypologist: An archetypologist who has received the proper training provided by Archetype Discoveries, Inc. To keep his/her certification, the archetypologist needs to prove that he/she is up to date on new developments in methodologies and has successfully passed the appropriate tests every year.

Chronology: The chronology of imprinting refers to the order in which elements of a culture are presented to an individual and are imprinted. In the American mind, for example, the aroma of coffee is imprinted before its taste, and is associated with home.

Cliché: A frequently repeated statement containing information that is well-known and commonly accepted within a culture.

CNA: Cultural Nucleic Archetype, the core or center of a culture. The three basic elements of the CNA are time, space, and energy.

Code: A code is a simple, synthetic way of understanding the order and the meaning of an archetype. The code is the structure of the forces that organize a culture (the way we think and function); it is a system of signals by which a convention is transmitted. The cultural codes that are the subject of this book are unconscious. Bringing codes into awareness and decoding them can illuminate the American psyche and help explain why we are the way we are.

Cognitive structure: The schema that an organism has available at any given time with which to interact with the physical environment. Cognitive structures result from biological maturation.

Cultural cognitive structure: An archetype (or mental highway) that an individual has available at any given time with which to interact with the environment. Cultural cognitive structures result from cultural maturation.

Collective Unconscious: (See Unconscious)

Core team: A group of four to six persons who attend all 10 imprinting sessions and all recap meetings. Immediately after each imprinting session, they analyze the "once upon a time" stories and imprinting stories. The core team functions as a sounding board to test the cultural resistance and acceptance of the archetype discovered. The group has to "try" several archetypes before it finds the one that "fits." The core team is also useful in working with the archetypologist to make the findings acceptable to the larger group (the archetype team). Lastly, the core team designs the action plan for implementing the archetype.

Critical Period: The period in an organism's life during which an important development occurs. If the development does not occur during that time, it may never occur.

Crystallization: The process by which a cultural archetype assumes permanence and definition. Crystallization of archetypes enables culture to be transmitted from one generation to the next. Language is the first step in crystallization: the imprint receives a name. Whenever that word or label is used, the imprint becomes deeper, even when the original experience has faded from consciousness. Cultural archetypes gradually become crystallized into norms and rules, and finally into laws.

Cultural anthropology: The part of anthropology dedicated to understanding the impact of culture on human beings.

Cultural Cognitive Structure: (See Cognitive Structure)

Cultural Shadow: Just as C.G. Jung spoke of the shadow as the hidden side of a personality (Dr. Jekyll and Mr. Hyde), the cultural shadow is the dark or hidden side of a culture. We have to understand this dark side and help the members of the culture become aware of the shadow and control it. For example in America the John Wayne figure represents the archetype of Americans as morally good, strong and incorruptible. The cultural shadow is always present in such figures as Jimmy Swaggert or Charles Monson.

Culture: The whole body of socially transmitted behaviors, beliefs, and feelings that ensure a specific population will survive and endure. A culture provides the pre-existing structures or common patterns (archetypes) that enable a group of people to meet their biological needs and understand the human condition. The structures that evolve and are transmitted in one culture will be distinct from those in any other.

Epistemology: The study of knowledge. The science of science.

Field Theory: The belief that the environment consists of interdependent events. In psychology, field theory means that behavior and/or cognitive processes are function of many variables that exist simultaneously, and a change in any one of them effects all the others.

Forces: Forces—drives, attractions, repulsions—are the way a culture deals with its biological needs and assures its own survival. Forces are culturally specific, even if some forces are the same in several cultures. Forces are the strong magnetic attractions that create an archetype's dualistic character. Every cultural archetype is composed of two forces, pulling in opposite directions. For example, if there is a force pulling toward diversity, it will be opposed by a force pulling toward uniformity. It is this energy to attract and repel that causes movement (life) in a culture.

Forces vs. Content: The organization of the elements versus the elements themselves: the grammar versus the vocabulary; the kinship system versus the individual members of the group.

Gestalt: (plural: gestalten) A German word meaning "pattern" or "configuration." A movement in psychology initiated in 1912 by Wertheimer (1880-1943) and co-founded by Kurt Koffka (1886-1941) and Wolfgang Kohler (1887-1967).

Gestalt Analysis: The analysis of the elements of a list of words or the words of a text to discover the latent structure and/or an isomorphism. The principles of gestalt analysis are proximity, similarity, continuity, and inclusiveness.

Grammar: The rules of syntax and morphology that govern language. We speak of a cultural grammar, which has the same function that grammar has for language—it is the way the elements of a culture are organized in order to make sense.

Hero/Heroine: An extraordinary human being, revered because he/she risked everything to find out the meaning of life and returned to share it with us. The hero/heroine is the protagonist in a myth.

Icon: Stereotypical image that captures the emotions associated with a stereotype character or situation, e.g., an anti-war hippie putting flowers in a gun barrel; pioneers drawing their covered wagons into a circle.

Imprint: The permanent impression made on our unconscious by the initial experience of an archetype and its accompanying emotion. This learning process cannot occur in the absence of emotion, which provides the energy for imprinting (emotion causes the brain to release neurotransmitters, which establish the learning connection—the neural highway). From the imprinting moment, the imprint will be repeatedly reinforced, and it will strongly condition our thought processes and our emotions. There are both biological and cultural imprints; the latter vary from culture to culture and reside in the cultural collective unconscious.

Imprinting: The rapid formation of an attachment between a human being and an environmental " object." This object could be a thing, a person, a concept—or any element of the world. Imprinting was originally described by Konrad Lorenz in 1952. He found, for example, that a newly hatched duckling would from an attachment to any kind of moving object and follow it as its mother, provided that the object was presented at just the right moment in the duckling's life. Lorenz also found that imprinting occurs only during a critical period, which we call a window in time, after which it is difficult, if not impossible, to imprint. Emotion is the energy necessary to imprint the neural pathways (mental highways). The sooner an imprint occurs, the stronger it is, and the longer it will last. An imprint related to survival and engraved at a very early age will last forever if regularly maintained and reinforced.

Imprinting Group Sessions: The Imprinting Group comprises the participants in an imprinting session, a carefully designed process that lasts three hours and takes people back to the imprinting moment for the subject being explored.

Imprinting Moment: The moment in time at which an archetype is imprinted in our unconscious. The imprinting moment occurs during the window of time when such imprinting can and does occur, which may vary from one culture to another. The deepest and most important imprints occur early in life, during the time when children learn language.

Insight: What is experienced when a latent structure becomes conscious, when we become aware of the cultural forces that are shaping our lives.

Instinct: The inborn capacity to perform a complex behavioral task, sometimes called species—specific organizations of behavior that are inborn. Universal archetypes are culture-specific organizations of behavior that are acquired (learned) and transmitted by parents or substitutes.

Isomorphism: Similarity of form, structure, patterns, grammar. The study of "the space between the notes," the relationship between the different elements (words, nouns, etc.) of a text.

Labeling Moment: The moment when a very specific word (or group of words) is associated with the imprinting moment, and that structure is imprinted. (Imprinting can also occur without a word or label being associated with object of the imprinting moment.) The "label" is the name on the door that leads to the mental highway and logic of emotion.

Latent Structure: The unconscious dimension of the archetype's code. Although unexpressed or unknown, it exists as part of the whole, and once we become aware of it, it completes our understanding of reality. The latent structure is what the archetype process seeks to discover.

Logic of Emotion: The internal order that cultural forces respect. This logic is related to the way (the order) in which the emotion was initially imprinted in our unconscious. Understanding the imprinting structure, the chronology, and the forces (quaternities) gives us the logic—the ordering of priorities.

Law of Pragnanz: The overriding principle in gestalt psychology, which states that all mental events tend toward completeness, simplicity, and significance.

Magnetic Field: An image that describes the dynamic dimension of the forces that shape a cultural archetype. The magnetic field is always present, even if it is empty, and it is not dependent on the structure, but the content gets its meaning only because of the way the structure organizes it.

Maintenance: The unconscious activity of using mental highways without our being aware of doing so. Our mental highways are maintained and reinforced all the time in dreams, free associations, jokes, language, movies, songs, cliches, and stereotypes, maxims, mottoes, etc.

Mental Highways: The mental connections that have been imprinted, reinforced, and maintained and represent the collective software that people use to understand the world. When we are born we have billions of potential connections in the neuronal network of our brains, but we have no telephone numbers. Learning through imprints creates the telephone numbers and establishes the connections. Mental highways are the telephone lines or numbers that are available in a given culture and are the most frequently used by the members of the culture. The cars that use the highways are called cliches, stereotypes, icons, heroes, etc.

Mission: A very specific goal, which has deadline (e.g., President Kennedy's goal of putting a man on the moon "before this decade is out"). Once the mission has been achieved, we need another mission.

Myth: A story or tale of a hero/heroine. The script of this story is known by everyone in the culture. The myth always relates the exploits of a her/heroine who does something extraordinary and brings back some meaning or wisdom from the journey. Myths often deal with the power of a supreme agency. There are universal myths that concern life, death, and resurrection, but eery culture produces its own version of these myths. Identifying our couture's myths and heroes can help break the code of the American mind.

National Character: The stereotype of a nationality, based on popular wisdom, e.g., Scots are tight-fisted; Chinese are inscrutable.

Opinion: What people say about something (a topic, a person, and idea). An opinion is highly changeable and has a short life. The fact the people say that they are going to vote for a given candidate does not mean that they will do so. People are usually not aware of why they have the opinions they express.

Paradigm: A point of view, shared by a substantial number of scientists, that provides a general framework for empirical research. A paradigm is usually more than just one theory and corresponds closely to a school of thought or "ism." The archetypal point of view represents a paradigm, as it gives us a new way to look at the world—it adds a new dimension that was previously "out of awareness."

Principles: Values, code of ethics, honor. Some examples of principles: work hard; never give up; never kill an unarmed enemy; protect the widows, the poor, the orphans, etc.

Principle of Closure: The tendency to complete incomplete experiences, thereby making them more meaningful (incomplete gestalt). But a complete gestalt is more difficult to change, even if it is perceived as negative.

Purpose: What we are trying to accomplish. Why do we want to put a man on the moon, or to find the Holy Grail? The real purpose for the Pope who launched the first crusade was perhaps to unify the European knights and get rid of the powerful Muslims who were threatening power.

The Pyramid of Unconscious: This diagram represents the divisions of the conscious and unconscious mind. The broad base of the pyramid is occupied by biology, which preorganizes human life according to common structures or schemata, which are permanent and unchanging.

The next level is occupied by culture, which provides the pre-existing structures or patterns that enable us to meet our biological needs. Archetypes reside at this level of the unconscious; together they form the collective unconscious described by Jung. Cultures last for centuries and change almost imperceptibly.

The next level of the pyramid represents the person, the individual unconscious. As we assimilate language and archetypal structures, and the emotions associated with them, our personality gives these different weights and values. Part of these experiences will slip from memory but linger in our individual unconscious. Each individual unconscious is unique, and it is accessible only through psychoanalysis. The individual unconscious lasts the length of a person's life.

The part of the pyramid above this level represents the emergence of the superego and the beginning of consciousness, which comprises behavior (how we act, what we do) and opinion (what we think, what we say). Both are sustained and shaped by the unconscious forces that underlie them. Behavior can change readily (how we act is subject to continuous revision), but opinion, which has the shortest life of all, can change whenever new information is provided.

Quaternity: From quatro, *quatre*, meaning "four." North, South East, and West are quaternity. Quaternities were used by Jung to describe universal archetypes. A quaternity is made up of four forces, creating a dynamic cultural field of tensions that organizes anything that happens in a given culture, at a given point in time. A quaternity is one of the forms used to describe a cultural archetype.

Repetition: Reinforcing an archetype by repeating it. Once a "mental highway" has been imprinted, the organism will have a tendency to reinforce it by repetition. This behavior can be observed among little children, who find pleasure in repeating a song, dance, gesture, or game, whereas adults get bored very quickly with such reiteration.

Rite and Ritual: These refer to an unconscious code that is embodied in a system of behavior. This codified system condenses the hero's journey into a form that ordinary people can take some power from. Rituals are the way people establish a relationship with spiritual or divine powers or with the secular substitutes for those powers (e.g., ideals). The ritual is repeated, and retains its sacred dimensions, even when it no longer has links to its origins. How members of a culture greet one another, which hand they use if they shake hands, etc., is based in some long-forgotten ritual. Unlike a custom, a ritual refers directly to latent forces and to a certain sacredness or inviolability. Everyday, mundane routines can be described as rituals, and these take on added importance in cultures where religious rituals are less prominent. Although ritual may refer to a body of rites or ceremonies, ritual and rite are often used interchangeably.

Rights of Cultures: Just as people have individual rights and collective responsibilities (duties) cultures should also have rights and duties. In addition to the rights of man (human rights, *les droits de l'homme*), we think it is time to recognize the rights of cultures.

Schema: (plural: schemata) A universal archetype (Jung), a basic biological structure for survival. A schema is the potential to act certain ways in order to survive. For example, the "grasping schema" refers to the general ability to grasp things; it is the cognitive structure that makes all acts of grasping possible. A schema can also be though of as an element in an organism's cognitive structure.

Script: The personal, individual life structure. Every script is unique. For the most part we are not aware of our individual scripts, which is why we keep repeating them. For example, a person bounces from one job to another, always blaming the boss, the company, the environment, and never examines his/her own script for the real reasons of the dissatisfaction. The purpose of psychoanalysis is to make people aware of their script, to free them from repeating it indefinitely.

Stereotype: A person or thing that is considered to typify a well-known and predictable pattern of behavior, as in, "professors are absent-minded." A stereotype is not factual, but it nonetheless rings true with people because they recognize a grain of truth in it.

Structural Analysis: Structural analysis, one of the archetypologist's tools, considers a culture as a structure or system, a harmonious and coherent whole, in which every piece is inextricably joined to all others and cannot be understood by itself. Structural analysis is essentially functional, for it studies how every element of a culture functions within the whole structure.

An important phenomenon in the field of cultural structural analysis is the existence of stable and unstable cultural systems. As in the world of animals or plants, certain cultural systems are stable—they are successful and vital for the survival of the species because they are as harmonious as possible; others, which are less harmonious, are unstable. No completely incongruous cultural system is known to exist.

Although structural analysts frequently speak of "the German mind," or any other culture, every culture has at least three systems: the predominant one; the one that is outgrown; and the new one that is developing. If a system were perfectly harmonious and coherent, it would never change; but all cultures grow and decline, and change sooner or later from one system to another.

Structuralism: The belief that by studying one element of a culture's structure we can come to understand part of or the whole structure. Structuralism, as I use it, should be understood as hewing closer to Levi Strauss's point of view and practice that to that of Edward Bradford Tichener. Structuralism is in opposition to functionalism: Tichener excluded from consideration value and use, as well as interested and personal attitudes of common sense and technology. Borrowing tools from linguistics, psycholinguistics, and anthropology, I do not exclude anything. For me, any element of a culture reveals that culture, because of its interaction with the rest of the culture.

Structure: The organization of the elements, which is independent of them. For example, the melody is independent of the notes; the triangle is independent of the three elements that shape it (they could be three fruits, three stones, three pencils). The structure information is what is transmitted when two people, one male and one female, have a child. The child is predictably a human being (instead of a bird or fish) because the parents have transmitted the structure information, i.e., human being. The content information (blue eyes, brown hair, etc.) may vary, which is what makes every human being unique.

Symbol: An expression or manifestation of the logic of emotion, which it synthesizes and concentrates. It is charges with emotion and meaning. Symbols are imprinted at an early age, and from that point on, the symbolic meaning is inseparable from the word or object or concept it represents. Symbols connect all the people who share the same imprints.

Synchronic Cultural Archetypology: The study of the cultural forces, axes and quaternities, as well as the logic of emotion and various codes of a given culture, at a given moment in time. Taxonomy: ration. The collective cultural unconscious is where all the shared imprints of a culture—the cultural archetypes—reside. The cultural collective unconscious is what all members of a culture have available to them to function and survive in their culture. The archetypal structures can explain behavior once they are brought into awareness. The discovery of archetypes is in effect the psychoanalysis of a culture's unconscious.

Vision: The "impossible dreams" of culture, which includes the pursuit of happiness, equal opportunity, etc.

"Wow!...Oh, I knew that!": This is what happens when someone becomes aware of an archetype. The "Wow!" registers surprise, astonishment. Then, after a short pause, the "Oh, I knew that!" means that the archetype was already present in the unconscious.

Appendix

Seven People Who Have Influenced Me

The following seven individuals played a major role in my own intellectual development. Without them, I might not have become an "archetypologist." Two, Freud and Jung, are world renowned; others are known only to a relatively small group of anthropologists, sociologists, and analysts. Because of their formative influence, I have highlighted their relevant contributions.

1: Alexis De Tocqueville.

The ancestor of them all was a 26-year-old French aristocrat who came to America in 1831 to study penal conditions here and wrote about America so perceptively that his *Democracy in America* remains a relevant, luminous classic over 170 years later. As Daniel Boorstin wrote, "de Tocqueville has the ring of prophecy."

I find him an extraordinary precursor for another reason: His methods, analysis, and powers of deduction are extraordinarily in advance of his time. Nowhere in de Tocqueville's work is there any reference to "archetypes," "imprints," or any of the glib sociological jargon that makes so much social analysis literature unreadable today. But take the following passage:

> To understand a man, we must watch the infant in his mother's arms; we must see the first images which the external world casts upon the mirror of his mind, the first occurrences that he witnesses; we must hear the first words that awaken the sleeping powers of thought, and stand by his earliest efforts if we could understand the prejudices, habits, and passions that will rule his life. The entire man is to be seen in the cradle of the child. The growth of nations presents something analogous to this: they all bear some marks of their origins. If we were able to go back to the elements of states and to examine the oldest monuments of their history, I doubt not that we should discover in them the primal cause of the prejudices, habits, passions, and all that constitutes what is called the national character.

Democracy in America abounds in such prophetic anticipation of imprints and archetypes, whether de Tocqueville is toying with the science of linguistics: "The tie of language is, perhaps, the strongest and the most durable that can unite mankind," or simply stating basic truths that later sociologists only "discovered" a century later: "The happy and powerful do not go into exile, and there are no surer guarantees of equality among men than poverty and misfortune."

De Tocqueville was perhaps the first contemporary historian of his day who also functioned as social anthropologist, sociologist and cultural analyst as well as historian. He was among the first to realize the importance of bringing together these different strands of knowledge into a coherent whole. He intuitively anticipated Einstein's *Theory of Relativity*: he was probably the first "relativist" ever. He was one of the first to draw from different sciences to explain the true nature of America in 1831.

This is why his observations, deductions, and comments are so illuminating—they remain extraordinarily pertinent today. Here are few examples:

On the press: "The influence of the liberty of the press in America does not affect political opinions alone, but extends to all opinions of men and modifies customs as well as laws"

On equality and class relations: "There exists in the human heart a depraved taste for equality, which impels the weak to attempt to lower the powerful to their own level and reduces men to prefer equality in slavery to inequality in freedom."

On money: "Nearly all Americans have to take a profession ... In America most of the rich men were formerly poor."

On conformity and uniform patterns: "I do not believe there is a country in the world where, in proportion to its population, there are so few ignorant and at the same time so few learned individuals."

On the distrust of intellectuals: "There is no class in America, in which the taste for intellectual pleasures is transmitted by heredity, fortune and leisure. Accordingly, there is an equal want of the desire and the power of application of these subjects."

On the "can do" approach to problems: "The citizen of the United States is taught from infancy to rely upon his own exertions in order to resist the evils and the difficulties of life; he looks upon the social authority with an eye of mistrust and anxiety, and he claims its assistance only when he is unable to do without it."

On the nature of political leadership: "In the United States, I was surprised to find so much distinguished talent among the citizens and so little among the heads of government. At the present day the ablest men in the United States are rarely placed at the head of affairs."

No one reading de Tocqueville today can fail to be amazed by the current relevance of almost all his generalizations about America, culled from acute observation, an insatiable curiosity and the fact that he looked at America in a quite unprecedented way.

There is another reason why I regard de Tocqueville as both a precursor and role-model: he came from a long line of French aristocrats and was profoundly disillusioned by the current state of affairs in his own country, wracked first by the French revolution of 1789, then by Napoleon's insatiable ambition to dominate the whole of Europe, leading to disaster, economic ruin and the restoration of the modified, mocked, "bourgeois" Louis-Philippe monarchy—a lame-duck regime which de Tocqueville knew would not last. The culture he came from was completely unlike the American culture he set out to study—and he did so by seeing himself as a "professional stranger," someone from another planet.

His observations were so acute, and his conclusions so original, precisely because he understood that it was not merely the Atlantic Ocean that separated the American and French cultures: he realized very quickly that although some aspects of the American way of life—aspects that were completely familiar to them and which they took for granted—came as a huge shock to him, Americans were equally baffled by some of de Tocqueville's own instinctive reactions, arising out of his own French culture, which he took for granted. It was largely thanks to de Tocqueville that I would start using the "professional stranger" approach, in group sessions with students, and, later clients—not just to shock, but because this enabled me, and those I was working with, to start looking a at problems in a completely different way.

But my greatest debt to de Tocqueville lies in the very evidence he left behind—in those monumental two volumes on the nature of American culture, as he was the first to perceive it in 1831. Almost everything he wrote holds true, and has been tested by time. Using a classic literary style which may seem to us elaborate, but was current then, throughout *Democracy in America* de Tocqueville is writing about American imprints and cultural archetypes.

When I am asked: do cultural archetypes really exist? my reply is: read de Tocqueville and see for yourself. And when I am asked, If archetypes exist, how durable are they? My answer is: "If some of the American cultural archetypes de Tocqueville described 170 years ago are still going strong today, we can assume they have a long life."

2: Sigmund Freud (1856-1939)

Freud introduced so much into our daily vocabulary. We talk about Freudian lapses and Oedipus complexes without being aware that we owe these very concepts to a Viennese professor. I mention Freud here because of his impact on me, even though Freud would almost certainly have rejected the notion of "cultural archetypes." I well recall the moment he first left his mark on me. I was struck by his compelling analogy of the individual unconscious: two people are in a room, trying to communicate with each other. Suddenly there is an incredible noise on the other side of the door, and all chances of a meaningful conversation cease. The noise is incredible, not necessarily threatening but ongoing and all-pervasive, rendering all communication impossible. The noise is not recognizable—the people in the room have no idea whether it is made by a human, an animal, machine, or natural calamity. There is no sense of danger, but there is this incredible presence on the other side of the door. To find out more, and put a stop to it, the only thing to do is open the door and ask: What's the problem?

The noise, according to Freud, is our unconscious, "opening the door." Freud is saying that when the unconscious becomes that disturbing it is impossible for a human being to function.

To me, this was a far more compelling illustration than Freud's explanation of what actually lay on the other side of the door. For Freud, the unconscious was something shameful and frightening: everything sexual that we dare not refer to consciously, all our taboos and unmentionable, socially unacceptable thoughts and desires end up there.

As a student, I underwent Freudian analysis myself, but I never accepted this view: was the unconscious no more than this "basement of the soul," this grim, murky repository of the unspeakable? His doctrine seemed both too dogmatic and too restrictive, especially in the light of my field experiences among the Indians in Nicaragua and Brazil. I was, however, compelled to recognize that Freudian psychoanalysis was certainly effective: my own case was a dramatic illustration. As a very young man, I was burdened with an inexplicable, visible affliction: though I was already doing some lecturing and public speaking, such activity was agonizingly painful. Before I was due to speak, I would blush, tremble, break out into a cold sweat and, sometimes, find it impossible to express myself at all. This condition vanished after my analysis—yet another example of the mysterious power of the unconsciousness.

Another element in the body of Freud's work remains the bedrock of most practicing psychoanalysts: his theories on the interpretation of dreams. In Freud's view, no one dreams at random; the content of the dream consists of two elements. The first is based on real-life elements in the dreamer's life over the past few days. So if you dream about a large shaggy dog, it is likely that you saw or heard about one in real life shortly before you dreamt about it. But the dog does not really matter: what happens to the dog, in your dream. is really "you." In other words, the pattern is what matters: the dog itself may be irrelevant.

To me, the power and originality of Freud's approach to some of the problems he dealt with were far more important than his theories. But after his death, increasingly dogmatic, intolerant followers began treating every scrap of his writings with biblical reverence. Freudian doctrine became a "revealed truth," a religion even mild critics attacked at their peril. Such questioning of Freudian orthodoxy has, of course, become routine: his "Oedipus complex" theories have been challenged by anthropologists who showed that in some tribes the notion of the "father" was unknown (the role assumed instead by the mother's brother); and the fact that his findings were based on a small, narrow class of patients, overwhelmingly middleclass and female, in the city of Vienna, have been the subject of countless critical books and endless debate.

But for me, Freud remains a "guru," if only for his momentous discovery of the importance of the individual unconscious and his early work on the interpretation of dreams, even though I cannot help asking myself whether, in different surroundings, Freud's teachings might not have taken a completely different course.

3: Carl Gustav Jung (1875-1961)

Early in life, as a brilliant clinical practitioner in Zurich, Jung became famous for devising word-association tests. He would rattle off a list of specially chosen words at his patients, demanding an instant, unthinking response. They had to utter the first thing that immediately came to mind. It was a simple, effective way at delving into someone's unconscious, and is still used today, though now mostly as a party game.

Jung is often associated with the concept of "archetype," but what does the word "archetype" mean? Jung himself provided the answer, in an early essay that underlined his break with Freud—and requires a brief , historical overview of their chequered relationship.

At first Freud and Jung were quite close. When they began working together, Freud regarded Jung not just as the most gifted of pupils (almost an adopted son) but as a very special asset: from the outset, Freud's psychoanalytical theories had come under bitter, and often antisemitic, attack, and Jung, who came from a long line of Swiss protestant theologians, provided Freud with badly needed credibility. As Freud wrote, in 1908: "It is only his arrival on the scene that has removed the danger of psychoanalysis becoming a Jewish national affair."

But to Freud's chagrin, the two very soon went their very different ways. Jung's interests soon focused on things Freud regarded as irrelevant: on recurring myths and patterns in religions and literature of all kinds, old and new, Western and Eastern, including fairy-tales, the folklore of "primitive cultures" as observed by leading anthropologists. Above all, Jung and Freud parted company because Jung, early on in his clinical experience, came to believe that Freud's insistence on the all-importance of the individual unconscious, and his conviction that it contained all our repressed, socially unacceptable emotional fears and longings, were wrong.

Jung believed that the "collective unconscious" was just as important as the "individual unconscious." Moreover, in Jung's view, there was nothing somber or shameful about it. On the contrary. The hypothesis of a "collective unconscious" was not an easy concept to grasp. It belonged "to the class of ideas that people at first find strange but soon come to possess and use as familiar conceptions." As he wrote in a now-famous article, "I have chosen the term 'collective unconscious' because this part of the unconscious is not individual but universal; it has contents and modes of behavior that are more or less the same everywhere and in all individuals—the contents of the 'collective unconscious' are known as archetypes."

For Freud, it was a given that since each individual's unconscious was uniquely distinct, all people are infinitely different. Jung passionately wanted to prove that all people were, at heart, psychologically similar. He tried to prove this through the study of "universal archetypes," though even Jung, for all the intensity of his convictions, was aware, in the 1930s, that it would meet considerable resistance—not least from those who argued that since he was dealing with the unconscious, how could he refer to what was, by very definition, "unknowable?" Jung's early answer: "The archetype is essentially an unconscious content that is altered by becoming conscious and by being perceived, and it takes its color from the individual unconscious in which it happens to appear."

Years later, he wrote: "No archetype can be reduced to a simple formula. It is a vessel we can never empty and never fill. It has a potential existence only, and when it takes shape in matter it is no longer what it was. It persists throughout the ages and requires interpreting ever anew. The archetypes change their shape continually."

An "archetypal content," he added, expressed itself "first and foremost in metaphors."

The obsessive question at the back of Jung's mind was: "What are the archetypal features of human nature?"

Jung asserts that all the essential psychic characteristics that distinguish us as human beings are determined by genetics and are with us from birth. These typically human attributes Jung called archetypes. He regarded archetypes as basic to all the usual phenomena of human life. While he shared Freud's view that personal experience was of critical significance for the development of each individual, for Jung the essential role of personal experience was to develop what was already there—to activate what is latent or dormant in the very substance of the personality, to develop what is encoded in the genetic makeup of the individual, in a manner similar to that by which a photographer, through the addition of chemicals and the use of skill, brings out the image impregnated in a photographic plate.

Jung drew up a list of "universal archetypes" which, he claimed, were common to all humankind: The "Mother," the "Father," the "Hetaira" or "Love Goddess," the "Amazon," the "Medium," the "Wise Man," what he called the "Trickster" (perhaps more accurately rendered as the "court jester" or "fool" in the Shakespearian sense of the term)," the "Son," and the "Hero," to name the essential ones. He believed that some archetypes were not confined to humans, for even some birds and beasts, he argued, could be said to have fathers and mothers.

Jung owed his discovery, in part, to his voracious reading habits and limitless intellectual curiosity: everything was grist to his mill, but especially all that could not be explained rationally—and this included not only myths and religions, but also tantric philosophy, yoga, and even tarot cards. He did, however, also draw extensively on his own clinical experience, discovering, for instance, that not only did many of his patients have similar dreams, but that these very same dream patterns occurred, according to anthropologists, among Kenyan tribes and in other "primitive" communities.

The same could be said of constantly recurring patterns in different religions, myths, folk-tales, pictorial art—even psychoanalysis itself. "Water," he wrote, "is the common symbol of the unconscious." His Swiss patients dreamed of familiar Swiss lakes, but in African and Asian tribes water could be the "valley spirit," in China water became the "water dragon" embracing both yin and yang, the ever-recurring opposites in Taoist philosophy. Recurring "universal archetypes, " he claimed, could be found in the most unexpected places. He cited the case of one of his patients, a relatively uneducated, profoundly disturbed man, whom, he found one day standing at the window, wagging his head and blinking into the sun. "He told me to do the same, for then I would see something very interesting. When I asked him what he saw, he was astonished that I could see nothing, and said: 'Surely you see the sun's penis—when I move my head to and fro, it moves too, and that is where the wind comes from.'"

At the time, Jung dismissed it all as part of the patient's schizophrenia. It was only many years later that he happened to discover that a "Mithraic ritual" unearthed by a philologist in a Greek manuscript over 2,000 years old, contained exactly the same explanation of the origin of the wind, and that the relevant passage began with: "You will see hanging down from the disc of the sun something that looks like a tube." There were other surprising, discoveries. He found, for example, that deeply embedded in most myths and religions, there was a recurring notion involving space, or rather, "extremes" or "opposites." As an example, "spirit' always seems to come from above, while from below comes everything that is sordid and worthless."

In fact all archetypes, he came to believe, "have a positive and negative aspect." In time, he would parley this into his theory of "axis" and "quaternities" ties"—by which he meant a form of metaphysical "compass-points," a vertical and horizontal "grid" by which archetypes could be measured and evaluated. As a student and aspiring psychoanalyst, I included Jung on my curriculum although I was never an expert, still less an orthodox "Jungian." But it was impossible not to be intrigued by Jung's thesis that, regardless of racial, ethnic, national, linguistic or intellectual differences, differing environments and levels of cultural sophistication—in other words regardless of whether those under scrutiny were Eskimos, New Yorkers or New Guinea aboriginals—certain common patterns could be discerned in all of them, in all of us.

What was more fascinating still was his even bolder conviction that we were all genetically programmed, practically from the origins of the human species, to harbor in our unconscious a certain number of universal archetypes.

What I discovered, when I started undergoing Jungian analysis as a budding psychoanalyst was exhilaration: it was so different from the joyless, passive Freudian process.

The unconscious, I realized, need not just be Freud's grim, scary "basement of the soul." There was no need to be afraid of it. On the contrary, it was full of possibilities, a treasure trove replete with all the myths of humanity and the accumulated wisdom of centuries; in other words, exposure to it could be, and indeed should be, a joyful, enriching experience.

There was something else: in Jungian analysis, you don't lie down on a sofa; you're face to face with the analyst. The process is far more in the nature of a dialogue: you are trying to understand what part of your unconscious is you and what part of it derives from the archetypal "collective unconscious," how the two relate, and how to establish some kind of communication between the different levels of your own unconscious. It was far more stimulating, intellectually, than the routine Freudian, stream-of consciousness psychoanalytical process.

Jung's work influenced me in several ways. First of all, I was fascinated by the very duality of the man: on the one hand, he was the somewhat "square," Protestant descendant who looked like a banker and came from a long line of theologians, very Swiss, very formal, very conscientious towards his patients, leading a blameless, somewhat austere life. But within this strict moralist lurked a bold, somewhat crazy adventurer, someone playing with fire, willing to experiment with ideas, hidden forces, inexplicable phenomena that others shied away from—like extra-sensory perception and Zen Buddhism. In later life, his mysticism increased, and he showed increasing—even obsessive—interest in those phenomena that defied all rational and conventional psychoanalytical explanations: alchemy, extra-sensory perceptions, levitation claims by mystics. In his last years, he even became interested in UFOs.

Whereas others were content to isolate problems under scrutiny and deal with them in a coldly scientific, clinical way, he was constantly looking for universal meanings and patterns, and this in turn compelled him to look beyond the conventional body of knowledge of medicine and psychoanalysis. It was this lifelong interest in other cultures that I was drawn to.

What I also liked was a trait most uncommon among original thinkers who end up heading schools of thought. He never said: You must believe in me and no-one else, to become a true Jungian you have to discard everything that does not fit in with my own theories, there is no room for the slightest dissent. Unlike Freud, he had no sycophantic courtiers around him, always on the lookout for Freudian heresies. On the contrary, he was something of a loner, constantly expanding, amending and altering his own body of work. His definitions of archetypes kept changing.

From my own, very limited experience, I also realized that for all the incongruity of many of Jung's theories, there was a great deal of truth in his assumption that dreams were not only the emanation of the individual unconscious, but could also be shown to contain the proof of the existence of universal archetypes. I, too, began spotting recurring dream patterns in patients of different origins and language.

I began asking myself whether these common dream patterns, which Jung ascribed to all the inhabitants of the planet, might not be common to the people of the same culture, for in my own clinical experience—dealing in Switzerland with children brought up in its three different languages, Italian, French, and German—I began finding evidence of this. Their dreams differed, but recurring patterns occurred within the same language. Toward the end of his life, Jung said as much: He implied that his "universal" archetypes might not be so universal after all. They might, he wrote, "differ from one culture to another." My own interest, soon growing into an obsessive quest for cultural archetypes, was simply taking what I had learned a little further.

Both Freud and Jung had discovered a fascinating aspect of reality—Freud the "Individual Unconscious" and Jung the "Collective Unconscious." But both seemed restrictive in their approach. What intrigued me was the promise "universal archetypes" held for something else, although I had no clear notion of what this might be. Soon, however, I started believing that Cultural archetypes might be the missing link to even greater awareness, providing an even greater understanding of reality than these two giants had enabled us to perceive.

4: Bruno Bettelheim (1903-1990)

For three years, Bruno Bettelheim was a guest lecturer at seminars I ran in France shortly after beginning my clinical practice. He fascinated me for several reasons: he was an authority in the field of autistic children, which also became my chosen field, but he was also a Nazi concentration camp survivor, and this implied an extraordinary mental and physical resilience against almost impossible odds; above all, his methods, in the treatment of autism, appeared to point the way to possible, highly original solutions to this terrible, still misunderstood affliction.

Bettelheim's controversial but highly original approach to autism—and mentally or emotionally disturbed children in general—undoubtedly stemmed from his personal experiences in Dachau and Buchenwald in 1938-39. At the time of his arrest (for being both a Jew and a vocal anti-Nazi) he was already well known in psychoanalytical circles, as one of Freud's most promising pupils and practitioners. What was most remarkable, in Bettelheim, was his recognition of the limits of conventional analysis: as he wrote, many years later, of his concentration camp days, "What struck me most was the realization that those persons who, according to psychoanalytic theory as I understood it then, should have stood up best under the rigor of the camp experience, were often very poor examples of human behavior under extreme stress."

He also admitted that "the impact of the concentration camp did for me, within a few weeks, what years of a useful and quite successful term as head of the University of Chicago's Orthogenic School for disturbed children analysis had not done." I found this recognition of the limits of "classical" psychoanalysis refreshing, and the tough lessons he learned from his ordeal well worth studying.

In 1938-39 Dachau and Auschwitz had not yet become systematic extermination camps, but the conditions Bettelheim described were just as appalling as they later became in the 40s—the main difference being that killings by SS guards took place at random, as part of the routine terror, and extermination chambers had not yet been institutionalized. Starved, physically and mentally broken, set to work 18 hours a day in brutalizing conditions, Bettelheim believed he owed his survival to his decision, shortly after his arrival in Dachau, to study his fellow-inmates, to try to understand what was going on psychologically as "an example of a spontaneous defense against the impact of an extreme situation. Although at first I was only dimly aware of this, it was meant to protect me from a disintegration of personality I dreaded."

Himself half-dead after an appalling journey resulting in the deaths of several fellow-inmates through starvation and repeated beatings, he realized that his chances of surviving the first three months in Dachau were slim. His reaction was: "how can I protect myself from becoming as the others are?" In time, his concentration camp experience helped him a great deal in his later work with children, for, as he put it, "Inmates were depersonalized, and this meant being treated like helpless children. Like children, prisoners lived in the immediate present. They lost their feeling for the sequence of time, they became unable to plan for the future or to give up tiny immediate satisfactions to gain greater ones in the near future. They were unable to establish durable relationships. Friendships developed as quickly as they broke up. Prisoners would fight one another tooth and nail and declare they would never look at one another or speak to one another, only to become fast friends within minutes. They were boastful. Like children, they felt not at all set back or ashamed when it became known that they had lied about their prowess."

Also like children, the camp inmates were in the situation of "knowing only what those in authority allowed them to know." Even the rules concerning trips to the toilets (prisoners had to ask special permission during working hours, and report back after visiting the latrine trenches) was a form of "education in cleanliness" that recalled the earliest days of childhood.

In Dachau and Buchenwald, many prisoners regressed fast into childhood: "Non-political middle-class prisoners, as a group, fared worst: what upset them most was being treated like ordinary criminals. Their self-esteem had rested on a status and respect that came from their positions, their jobs, being heads of families. Then all of a sudden everything that had made them feel good was knocked out from under them."

Bettelheim noted that the political prisoners were better armed, that the "common criminals" in the camps were protected to some extent by their ability to lord over the "respectable" inmates—and that the Jehovah's Witnesses fared best of all: their convictions helped them from regressing into childhood, or into complete fatalism. The "fatalists" simply "gave up all action as pointless because all feeling was merely painful or dangerous, they inhibited it all. Eventually this extended backward to blocking off the stimulation itself."

Bettelheim's concentration camp experience also helped him understand amnesia and other disorders among prisoners, including emotional ones: "Anything that had to do with the present hardships was so distressing that one wished to repress it, to forget it. Only what was unrelated to the present suffering was emotionally neutral and could hence be remembered." Bettelheim became, after his release from Dachau and his escape to America, one of the world's leading experts on autistic children, as head of the University of Chicago's Orthogenic School for disturbed children. His interests, though very diversified, were mainly clinical—unlike my own—but my debt to him is considerable.

It was not simply that he related concentration camp violence to the world of the emotionally disturbed child, and drew a parallel between the totalitarianism that bred places like Dachau and Buchenwald and the totalitarian violence to which children were submitted, usually unconsciously. Bettelheim's brutal analysis of concentration camp behavior provided me with badly needed evidence: In extreme situations, not just concentration camp "inmates" but individuals of differing social, cultural and ethnic categories reverted to childhood. What Bettelheim proved was that in extreme crisis, people reverted to basic survival principles—they went back to their archetypes.

As Bettelheim explained, "It is not so much the actual power of the parent that makes him seem omnipotent to the child. In the beginning, the infant feels free to be a non-conformist, to take candy out the jar or money out of his mother's purse. The parent may inhibit these things, but the child will still try to do it surreptitiously. But one day the child suddenly wakes up to find that the parents, without being present, have created a painful conflict in his mind—the conflict between his own desires and their past prohibitions. And at this point, the parent begins to seem godlike, all-powerful, to be feared as potentially inimical."

This power for creating unmanageable inner conflicts in the child must be compared with the power of the total state to create similar conflicts in the minds of its subjects. The child, like the nonconformist, originally resented the power that controlled him. But any power that is strong also exerts tremendous appeal. After all, nothing succeeds like success. And successful power over the child has such great appeal that it becomes internalized as his standards and values."

As he was to point out, from his coldly dispassionate study of fellow-inmates in both Dachau and Buchenwald, "nearly all the non-Jewish prisoners (in Dachau and Buchenwald) believed in the superiority of the German race."

Bettelheim, in the tradition of Freud, Jung and many other analysts, stressed the biological importance of a child's first years—and their impact on the rest of his life. What happened, he wrote, was that "the parent seems omnipotent because he has the power to withhold the substance of life—food. Under Hitler, the State had exactly the same power. Living in such a society, all citizens were as dependent as children for the substance of life."

The small child, Bettelheim wrote, "fears his parents displeasure, lest they withhold what he needs for his very existence; for the infant, this is symbolized by food. That fear is much more basic than his later fear of losing the love and respect of his parents. The S.S. reactivated this same basic fear by starving prisoners "to such a degree that they lived in continuous anxiety about what food, and how much, they would get. The results were very similar to those one can observe in the infant who is afraid his parents will stop feeding him."

Conversely, Bettelheim added, "it is difficult to deeply terrorize a people that is well fed and well housed." He also showed me that some of my intuitive convictions—the importance of emotion as a lightning rod, without which there could be no imprinting—were also backed by his own personal experience, and his emphasis on the biological importance of the first few years of a child's life confirmed my belief that the most important imprints were those that occurred in those early years.

I was also influenced by the theories that underlay his work with autistic children. These children, he claimed, under stresses, had become fatalists—like the "Moslems" in concentration camps, they had simply "given up," and no longer reacted to anything. To bring about a change for the better, it was essential to bring about a change in their behavioral patterns. No matter how small the change, or how apparently insignificant, anything new in their behavior—a new way of handling a pencil, of tracing an apparently meaningless line on a piece of paper, any new gesture or even the minutest change of expression—might trigger a change for the better.

Bettelheim was convinced that even the most "hopelessly" passive, apparently mentally handicapped, or violent autistic children (for such a condition often included moments of intense, unprovoked, frightening violence) had their own, private "language"—their code. An autistic child did not speak the language of other children but, in his own tormented way, he spoke; Bettelheim was convinced that autistic children, whether through their catatonic behavior, compulsive repetition of certain self-destructive gestures or acts, or outbreaks of violence, are trying to tell us something. If only we could enter into the autistic child's private world and "break the code," we would then understand their language.

This prompted Bettelheim to reflect that for very disturbed persons the impact of conventional psychoanalysis was not sufficiently strong to promote the necessary personality changes: "The impact of psychoanalysis itself, or of a life organized on its basis, had to be in effect all the time, not just one hour a day," leading him to believe that what autistic children needed most "was to live in a human environment that was not yet existent, and which had therefore to be specially designed for the purpose."

There was much, in Bettelhein's theories, that remains controversial: for instance, he believed that the mother's attitude towards her child was a key element—that the child's utter dependence on its mother was such that autism could occur if she failed to meet her baby's craving for love and security. But at the same time in *Love Is Not Enough*, he insisted that a mother's intelligence was just as important as love—perhaps even more so. He attributed a large number of cases to emotionally disturbed parents and homes, but was unable to explain why, in so many cases involving neurotic mothers, emotionally deprived children, and broken homes, autism failed to occur.

Despite these loopholes, I was impressed by Bettelheim's theory that autistic children had chosen a kind of "inner death" to stay "biologically" alive. He never referred directly either to "archetypes" or imprints but provided me with precious support in workshops, endorsing my "logic of emotion" theory. He wrote: "What reinforces self-esteem and true independence is not fixed and unchanging, but depends on the vagaries of the environment. Each environment requires different mechanisms for safeguarding autonomy, those that are germane to success in living according to our values in a particular environment." If, for "environment," we substitute the word "culture," here was a clear indication that we were thinking along the same lines.

5: Konrad Lorenz

Farmers had been aware of it for generations: when recently hatched birds like ducklings or goslings are hand-reared, they strongly prefer the company of their human keeper to that of their own species. If the tiny fledgling birds' "natural" mothers are not around, they will develop an equally strong attachment to whatever animal they encounter—a hen or sheep—and such dependency lasts until the birds become adult.

Konrad Lorenz, the Nobel prize-winning animal behaviorist, studied this phenomenon under laboratory conditions. He called it "imprinting." It was irreversible, but only if the "foster-parent" intervened within the first 24 hours of the bird being hatched. There were other, less dramatic examples of imprinting in other animals (jackdaws, wasps, even ants) but this was by far the most spectacular: Lorenz, a born showman, illustrated this by striding into lecture-rooms followed by several ducklings or goslings he had "imprinted"—visual proof that invariably delighted his students and ensured considerable media attention.

Needless to say, I found Lorenz's work on imprinting fascinating. My concern, however, was with humans. And Lorenz was extremely wary about drawing conclusions about human behavior. As a scientist, he felt this could only remain an unverifiable conjecture. He said as much to one of his admirers, Richard I. Evans, who asked him what the possible human implications were. Lorenz's answer: "That is a big leap. I think this is an unverifiable statement, but if you regard the work of a very old and almost forgotten psychiatrist, Krafft-Ebing, on fetichisms, you get the impression that some of his patients' behaviors were analogous to imprinting. You can't validate such observations, of course."

The closest he ever got to relating animal imprinting with human behavior was in his somewhat pessimistic overview of young people and their tendency to systematically reject and attack their elders. In the early 1970s, when such conflict between generations was at its height, he said: "I think the closest you get to human imprinting is that critical phase when the adolescent gets skeptical about the parental culture and casts around for new causes to embrace. He attaches himself to some ideal cause, but his ideal cause leads him to disappointment. Such frustration affects this young person to the extent that he never again attaches himself to another ideal with the same emotional strength which he exhibited towards his first love."

I felt intuitively that imprinting must relate in some way to the human species, but at the time Lorenz was right: This was scientifically unverifiable.

There was another field where I valued Lorenz as a guru: his brief comments on a form of imprinting that was prevalent among newly born babies, and was related to my own treatment of autistic children. As Lorenz pointed out, highlighting the work of another, less-well known scientist, Rend Spitz, "If an infant is deprived of a personal bond with the mother, which is established a few months after birth, the child will resent strangers. If, in an orphanage, where nurses serve as mother figures, this bond is broken in the course of the routine change of duty, the child will try to form a new bond with the second nurse. Then the second mother figure is rotated, and the infant tries to establish the bond a third time. When it loses its third mother figure, the child withdraws and loses the faculty to form further social contacts. This is certainly on the precultural level, and may result in the development of autistic children.

Spitz's contribution to the treatment of such children was to insist that they not be looked after by a variety of nurses chosen simply by the vagaries of work rosters, but that each child be assigned a "permanent" surrogate mother-figure. In all cases where this practice was followed, the "withdrawal symptoms" were attenuated, and in some cases they disappeared completely.

Lorenz pointed out that geese could be similarly deprived of foster-parents, and this resulted in identical "social isolation:" if two "autistic" geese were put in a pen together, "they sit in opposite corners, back-to-back, ignoring each other."

What intrigued me about Lorenz's "imprinting" experiments was that he was convinced that the imprinting in animals like ducklings and geese was genetically programmed, that the answer lay in biology.

At this stage, I was intuitively convinced that imprinting must occur in humans as well as in the animal world, but was also aware that until this could be scientifically proved, few people would take me seriously. Such proof, however, was soon forthcoming. An internationally known British psychiatrist, Dr. John Bowlby, concluded that "attachment behavior in infants, though slower, is of a piece with that seen in mammals." The way attachment behavior (in infants) develops, he wrote, "can be included legitimately under the heading of imprinting."

Although Lorenz's theories triggered new interest and research into the role of neuro-processors and the different functions of the brain, the breakthrough came from Henri Laborit who was not only a biologist, sociologist, and expert on modern psychoanalytic and sociological theory but also a prominent neuro-surgeon. He was able to prove scientifically what I had only perceived intuitively.

6: Henri Laborit

Surprisingly, in America at least, Henri Laborit is still known only to a small circle of specialists. In an age of increasingly narrow specialization, he is an anachronism: a renowned neuro-surgeon (and head of research of a major department at the Hospital Boucicault in Paris) who has applied his scientific knowledge—including his impressive array of laboratory tests on the workings of the nervous system—to problems that go far beyond the conventional range of scientific problems.

His breadth of intellect and exceptional knowledge not only of biology but of anthropology, sociology, and psychology are on a scale with the earlier "giants." Laborit's experiments have made scientific history, but what sets him apart from most of his peers is his ability to apply his scientific and intellectual curiosity to fundamental questions: What is memory? Is our nervous system an infinitely complex amalgam of energetic impulses? If so, how do these impulses relate to what we commonly refer to as "imagination" and "creativity?" To what extent are they genetically inherited, "programmed," and related to the biological need of survival? How do biological patterns, or "structures," relate to the environment? Are they related to the evolution of the universe? His prodigious curiosity focuses on questions whose answers will continue to elude us. Such questions include: How and why do human beings use their brain as they do? How do biology, anthropology, and what we know of the evolution of the universe affect our knowledge of the human condition? How do human beings relate not only to biology, but to the evolution of the cosmos as a whole?

Until recently, the scientific community prided itself on its oddly "unemotional" concern with scientifically provable facts, relating cause and effect. "Emotion" could not be scientifically evaluated and was not supposed to impinge on rational thought; therefore, it was ignored. Like mechanical engineers, scientists were expected to break everything down into separate elements, the better to analyze them.

This rigor was certainly responsible, in the 19th and early 20th century, for many major scientific discoveries. But it left untouched those areas—the Unconscious was one of them—that could not be directly "tested" under laboratory conditions in the way that microbes could be observed, viruses cultivated, or atoms artificially created.

Using high-tech brain scanners, cell "staining," computers, and animal experiments, a new breed of scientists, Laborit among them, have since mapped "the highways and traffic patterns of the emotional brain." In a series of laboratory tests, for instance, Laborit was able to relate the transmission of "emotions" to different areas of the "biological" brain. He showed how drugs used to paralyze neuro-transmitters could "block" long-term memory in the brain; above all, Laborit was instrumental in redrawing our own mental map—altering the way we perceive memory.

Based on our accumulated intellectual and literary inheritance, from Plato to Descartes and all the way to Proust's "madeleine, " instilled in our minds is the notion of memory as a series of "stored" images, a series of self-contained, finite, box-like entities labeled "childhood," "mother," "sex" and so on. Thanks in part to Laborit, memory is now perceived as something completely different. As he and others have shown, using scientific tests, we do not "store" images, feelings, and emotions. The past does not exist, at any rate in this convenient "attic" form. We don't "store it away" or "reactivate" it, as novelists as different as Balzac and James Joyce would have us believe. What are stored are processes, an infinite number of connections between different neurones.

At the risk of over-simplification, my analogy of memory is that within each of us there is the equivalent of a series of "telephone exchanges," operating simultaneously. These exchanges have infinitely complex, infinitely numerous potential connections. By pushing the right button, we are able to "make a connection," activate a series of sequences, involving taste, smell, love, hate, nostalgia, whatever: these activated "circuits" can be our evocation of an incident in our past, something that happened once, brought to consciousness, thanks to the existence of the complex circuitry within the human body.'

We all experience the irritating quest for the name of an author or title of a book or film. The name is on the tip of our tongues. We may even "see" the person in our mind's eye, without being able to record his or her name. Almost invariably, without any conscious "thought," the elusive title or name pops up: the circuitry has been triggered; the connection has been made. We begin losing our memory when these connections become faulty. Laborit stressed that such connections do not last—they have to be maintained. Memory, he wrote, is like a muscle. If not exercised, it atrophies.

Laborit proved that emotion was transmitted to the brain through the nervous system. He and other scientists were able to identify those parts of the brain that responded to different kinds of emotion. Laboratory experiments and tests on accidentally brain-damaged humans have shown, for instance, that the "limbic" or "visceral" part of the brain deals with basic, instinctive phenomena, that emotions are transmitted to the amygdalian part of the brain, and that one of the functions of that part of the brain known as the "cortex" is to act as a constant rational monitor of our emotions, organizing, evaluating, and relating them in their proper perspective. We also know that in humans the "limbic" brain is practically all that babies use for the first 18 months of their lives, that the amygdalian functions develop later, the cortex later still.

This, too, was the subject of experiments the Swiss biologist Jean Piaget conducted on his own three children to determine the different stages of growth in a child's emotional and intellectual life. Both Laborit, Piaget, and the French analyst Jacques Lacan, who highlighted the importance of language (his pet theory being that each individual unconscious harbored its own private language, and until this language was understood no analytical breakthrough could take place) were among those whose findings enabled me to "break the code" to understand the logic of different cultures—a crucial step in my own exploration of cultural archetypes.

7: Ruth Benedict (1887-1948)

I regard Ruth Benedict, the pioneering, innovative social anthropologist and Columbia University professor, as a pioneer who dealt with cultural archetypes without being consciously aware of the fact. In her early work, *Patterns of Culture*, written as a philosophical commentary on her earlier fieldwork, she wrote: "No man ever looks at the world with pristine eyes. He sees it edited by a definite set of customs and institutions and ways of thinking. The life-history of the individual is first and foremost an accommodation to the patterns and standards traditionally handed down in his community. From the moment of his birth the customs into which he is born shape his experience and behavior. By the time he can talk, he is the little creature of his culture, and by the time he is grown and able to take part in its activities, its habits are his habits, its beliefs his beliefs, its impossibilities his impossibilities. Every child that is born into his group will share them with him, and no child born into one on the opposite side of the globe can ever achieve the thousandth part."

Benedict was writing at a time when Hitlerism was starting to cast its shadow over the world, and one of her concerns, in *Patterns of Culture*, was with the growth of racial and ethnic prejudice (reflected in her later *Race: Science and Politics)* and ways of preventing the spread of racist dogma. But her main fascination was with the transmission and perpetuation of patterns of culture. She wrote: "An Oriental child adopted by an occidental family learns English, shows toward its foster parents the attitudes current among the children he plays with, and grows up to the same professions that they elect. He learns the entire set of the cultural traits of the adopted society, and the set of his real parents' group plays no part. Man is not committed in detail by his biological constitution to any particular variety of behavior. Culture is not a biologically transmitted complex."

What bound men and women together, Benedict insisted, was their culture—the ideas and the standards they had in common. "If instead of selecting a symbol like common blood heredity and making a slogan of it, the nation turned its attention rather to the culture that unites its people, emphasizing its major merits and recognizing the different values that may develop in a different culture, it would substitute realistic thinking for a kind of symbolism which is dangerous because it is misleading."

In many ways, Benedict was a precursor of the so-called "structuralists," epitomized later by France's Claude Levi-Strauss, an anthropologist-philosopher somewhat mistrusted in America because of his intellectual arrogance and haughtily asserted theories even in the face of practical anthropological fieldwork that failed to bear them out. Levi-Strauss, a brilliant literary stylist who for all his iconoclastic writings, delighted in his election to the elite "Academie Francaise," with all its attendant intronization rituals (newly elected members wear elaborate court uniforms including ceremonial swords) was, by his own account, far less interested in people than in structures common to different cultures and societies, whether "primitive" or "advanced," beginning his first major work, *Tristes Tropiques*, an account of his one and only field trip, with the words: "I hate all voyages and explorers"—an unexpected admission for an anthropologist to make.

Benedict, had she lived, would almost certainly have been attracted to Levi-Strauss' "structuralist" theories, for she was drawn to the work of the gestalt (configuration) psychologists who "have shown . . . that it is not enough to divide perceptions into objective fragments. The subjective framework, the forms provided by past experience, are crucial and cannot be omitted." And she was to become world-famous for applying these same gestalt theories to an analysis of the Japanese character, at the close of World War II, at the request of the U.S. State Department, which became an immediate post-war bestseller, *The Crysanthemum and the Sword*.

In 1945, Roosevelt's Cabinet was obsessed with the problem of a defeated, crushed, humiliated Japan. Long before the Hiroshima and Nagasaki bombs that actually ended the war, it was clear that Japan had lost its gamble and would be militarily occupied. Should Emperor Hirohito be made to abdicate and stand trial for war crimes? Should the Imperial System be allowed to remain in place? What would be the reaction of the Japanese to military occupation? Would there be kamikaze acts of violence against the occupiers? With unusual acumen, the U.S. State Department commissioned an anthropologist, Ruth Benedict, to answer these and other related questions. Her findings proved highly accurate, and this was all the more surprise in that Benedict was not a Japanese specialist, had never been to Japan in her life, and with the war still going on had to base her research on those Japanese she was able to debrief in America.

Even more surprising, in retrospect, was that the State Department, despite the contrary advice of other specialists, followed Benedict's recommendations. The Emperor was neither compelled to resign nor brought to justice, and the local Japanese administrative structures were allowed to continue to function without overmuch American interference: the only major breach with the past, apart, of course, from the introduction of democratic principles in the Japanese constitution, was the breaking-up of the "deibatsu," the huge Japanese conglomerates that had, in many respects, ruled Japan. Their disappearance only reinforced their theory of the permanence of archetypes, for new "deibatsu" quickly came into being—and these immensely powerful conglomerates quickly regained the importance of the old ones. Today, they virtually control Japan.

Benedict's *Crysanthemum and the Sword* was epoch-making not only because, for the first time in history, an anthropologist was being asked to apply her skills to forecasting the future rather than record the present, but because of the way she set about her task. She studied Japanese films, literature, and legends as well as the pattern of the Japanese language itself—applying the lesson she had earlier referred to in *Patterns of Culture*, paying particular attention to "the subjective framework, the forms provided by past experience"—in other words, the gestalt. To understand Japan, she wrote, "we had to understand Japanese habits of thought and emotion and the patterns into which these habits fell. As a cultural anthropologist, I started from the premise that the most isolated bits of behavior have some systematic relationship to each other. I took seriously the way hundreds of details fall into overall patterns."

The Crysanthemum and the Sword was, and remains, a brilliant piece of detective work: using her skills as a trained anthropologist, what Benedict actually achieved was an evocation, through stream-of-consciousness interviews with Japanese residents in America through her studies of literary, religious, and historical myths, movie plots, family reminiscences, of the Japanese archetype—and hypothetical Japanese archetypal reactions in the event of defeat and American occupation. Her predictions turned out to be almost 100 percent accurate.

Part of the originality of her study was that it broke with current conventions—the view of the Japanese as predatory, inexplicably cruel, irrational monsters—and showed how Japanese and American cultural archetypes differed so strikingly that the collision course between them had been practically inevitable. The American "live and let live" philosophy, she wrote, was in complete contrast with the Japanese view that it was Japan's inherent right to rid Asia of anarchy and establish a hierarchy where everyone "knew their proper place," for "inequality has been for centuries the rule of their life at just those points where it is most predictable and most accepted. Behavior that recognizes hierarchy is as natural (to the Japanese) as breathing."

But for me there were two lessons in *The Crysanthemum and the Sword* that I regarded as even more crucial, and would be of enormous importance to me as a future archetypologist. First, she proved that the baffling "opposites" in the Japanese character (rudeness versus politeness, violence versus aestheticism, a passion for things Western versus extreme conservatism and xenophobia, etc) were not contradictions at all but part of a whole—an "axis" whose extreme opposites were, in fact, two sides of the same coin, and that the Japanese character could not be understood without taking these two, cohabiting extremes into consideration. As Benedict put it, "I began to see how the Japanese saw certain violent swings of behavior as integral parts of a system consistent with itself."

The second lesson had to do with language: Benedict was one of the first to realize the importance of going behind commonly used words to illustrate what lay behind them. Japanese word usage and grammatical patterns vary enormously according to whether the person addressed is a woman, a social superior, or a social inferior. Even common responses like "thank you" do not have the same meaning they do in English, but reflect Japanese unease at repayment of favors or kindnesses even of the most trivial. She showed that language was crucial to the understanding of any cultural pattern.

About the Author

Dr. G. Clotaire Rapaille is an internationally known expert in archetype studies and creativity, and has written more than 10 books on these topics.

Dr. Rapaille's technique for market research has grown out of his work in the areas of psychiatry, psychology, and cultural anthropology. His unique approach to marketing combines a psychiatrist's depth of analysis with a businessman's attention to practical concerns. One of his books, *Creative Communication,* has become the standard reference for the French advertising industry. He is a sought-after lecturer on creativity and communication, and has appeared on French national television as the host of two weekly talk shows.

His world travel, term in the diplomatic corps, and extensive marketing research on product archetypes for international corporations have given him a fresh perspective on American business and society. He is fluent in English, French, and Spanish.

He received a Masters of Political Science, a Masters of Psychology, and a Doctorate of Medical Anthropology from the Université de Paris, Sorbonne.

Dr. Rapaille has taught at the Sorbonne, Paris, France; St. Ignace, Antwerp, Belgium; Esade, Barcelona, Spain; INSEAD/CEDP, Fountainebleau, France; Thomas Jefferson College, Michigan State University, Michigan, USA; CPSI, New York State University, Buffalo, NY, USA; Geneva University, Switzerland; University of California Los Angeles (UCLA), Los Angeles, California, USA;

HEC/ISA (Business School), Paris; and Jouy, Josas, France; Medical School UNAN, Managua, Nicaragua.

Psychologist, psychoanalyst, cultural analyst, educator, and marketing expert, G. Clotaire Rapaille brings interrelated careers to the challenge of cultural decoding. As founder and president of Archetype Discoveries Worldwide, and with offices in major world centers, his international reputation in creativity and archetype discoveries is unparalleled. Out of 25 years of custom-designed and applied research on cultural archetypes worldwide comes the conceptual and informational background for this book.

His current work includes a consulting practice serving Fortune 100 and international businesses, a lecture tour in the U.S. and Europe, and writing projects. In the press, here and abroad, Dr. Rapaille has received such accolades as "Marketing Guru," "The New Pope of Communication," and "The French Marshall McLuhan."

ABOUT ARCHETYPE DISCOVERIES

Archetype Discoveries, founded in 1974 in France, has its international headquarters in Boca Raton, Florida, with additional offices in New York and France, and affiliates in Mexico City, Sydney, Tokyo, Paris, Vancouver, Cleveland, Dallas, New York, Seattle, and Toronto.

Approximately 150 archetypal discoveries have been successfully conducted in Asia (Japan, Taiwan), Europe (Belgium, England, France, Germany, Holland, Italy, Norway, Spain and Switzerland), North America (Canada, Mexico and the United States), South America (Argentina, Brazil, Venezuela), and Australia.

Archetype Discoveries has recently developed a program that will allow an organization to explore its archetype(s) in a foreign market without leaving the United States. The study groups will be made up of 10 recent U.S. immigrants from the country being studied. Archetype Studies is now conducting a test of Russian Archetypes (TSAR) and has plans to study Japanese archetypes (SHOGUN), Chinese archetypes (MING), Mexican archetypes (MAYA), and South American archetypes (INCA).

The archetypologists who make up the firm represent 15 different countries and speak a total of 18 languages.

Archetype Discoveries Worldwide has been successfully guiding its clients' interests in marketing, advertising, research and development, and personnel since 1974. Its reputation earned as the premiere firm in breaking the codes of cultural archetypes has come as a direct result of its commitment to customer satisfaction in implementing this unique process.

OTHER BOOKS OF INTEREST

FROM EXECUTIVE EXCELLENCE • 1-800-304-9782 • WWW.EEP.COM

PETER BENDOR-SAMUEL

Turning Lead into Gold

For the first time, the principles of outsourcing are explained in Turning Lead into Gold. In this book, Peter Bendor-Samuel uses the analogy of medieval alchemists turning lead into gold to instruct readers on how to turn profit-inhibiting processes into sources of value and profit.

Hardcover book **$21.95**

LARRY DAVIS

Pioneering Organizations

In this book, Davis identifies the factors that must exist to develop and sustain pioneering organizations—organizations that achieve extraordinary performance, through a total commitment to excellence and progress.

Hardcover book **$21.95**

CHIP BELL

Customer Love

Customers who love you will go out of their way to take care of you. They don't just come back; they don't simply recommend you; they insist their friends do business with you. Learn how loyalty comes from partnering, not from "wowing" the customer

Hardcover book. **$19.95**

ROBERT J. SPITZER

The Spirit of Leadership

This book probes deeply into all the major roots of organizational spirit. It explores themes such as ethics, credibility, wisdom, fair conduct, charisma, self-examination, contemplation, commitment, and purpose.

Hardcover book **$24.95**

WILLIAM ONCKEN III

Monkey Business

Many managers find themselves running out of time while their employees are running out of work. This book is written to help hopelessly overwhelmed managers get those monkeys off their backs and return them in to the hands of those they hire. Explores the value of assigning, delegating, and controlling.

Hardcover book **$16.95**

WARREN BENNIS

Old Dogs, New Tricks

In today's dog-eat-dog world of competition and ongoing change, people in every position—especially the "old dogs"—must learn to work as teams rather than as "lone wolves." They must learn the "new tricks" of collaboration and innovation.

Hardcover book **$24.95**